Flashpoints

Dr Dvir Abramovich is Director of the Program in Jewish Culture and Society at the University of Melbourne and the Israel Kipen Senior Lecturer in Hebrew and Jewish Studies. He is also chairman of the B'nai B'rith Anti-Defamation Commission. Regarded as one of the country's leading commentators on Israeli society and politics, Dr Abramovich has been interviewed on radio and TV, and has contributed numerous opinion pieces to local and international publications. He was President of the Australian Association of Jewish Studies and editor of the *Australian Journal of Jewish Studies* for eight years. Dr Abramovich is the author and editor of three books.

To my wife Miri, and my children Lori and Ethan, for their love, support and encouragement and for giving me the time to write

Flashpoints

Israel, Anti-Semitism and the Holocaust

Dvir Abramovich

HYBRID
PUBLISHERS

Published by Hybrid Publishers

Melbourne Victoria Australia

©2014

First published 2014

National Library of Australia Cataloguing-in-Publication data:
Abramovich, Dvir, author.
Flashpoints: Israel, anti-semitism and the Holocaust /
Dvir Abramovich.
9781925000900 (paperback)
Newspapers – Sections, columns, etc.
Holocaust, Jewish (1939-1945)
Antisemitism.
Israel.

940.5318

Cover design: Art on Order
Cover photo of Jerusalem: Copyright: <a href='http://www.123rf.com/
profile_silverjohn'>silverjohn / 123RF Stock Photo</a>

Contents

Introduction

I love writing and have an opinion on just about everything. Throughout, it has been a great adventure, and lots of fun, to jump into the fray and to comment on life and politics as they happen, in real time.

It's not easy to put your viewpoints and thoughts in print. In fact, it's hard work and risky. And it's a little like a mixed martial arts contest. You have to come out swinging quickly and land a lot of punches before your lose the fight. Or in my case, lose my audience who may turn away, or put the newspaper down, or move on to another website. The point is that you have to get to the heart of the matter without wasting too much time if you want to catch the drive-by readers who are scanning the paper and who may pause for a second to glance at your article and may, just may, be tempted to read on.

But it's rewarding. I stopped counting the number of times people have walked up to me and said they liked what I wrote, or didn't, and then went on to tell me why I'm wrong and why they are offended by my judgment. And that's without mentioning the letters to the editor or the comments left on the sites where my pieces have been featured. I cherish the feedback because success for me means that I managed to get the reader's attention, that I managed to start an argument or a conversation, and that I managed to take them along with me on a trek of exploration and reflection.

Scattered throughout these pages are personal observations, meditations, commentaries and expositions about a huge array of topics, events and people. They are mostly centered on three key themes: Israel, anti-Semitism and the Holocaust, though I cast my net widely to take on and evaluate a variety of other explosive issues and personalities.

I write as I see things. That's always been my approach. Throughout, the pieces dissect the forces at play and the competing narratives on any given question. They challenge the prevailing wisdom and offer a counterpoint to the simplistic, bumper sticker way of thinking. Often the critique is brutally harsh and blunt. But, I would argue, my essays are always fair, well researched and contain breadth and depth based on careful and close analysis. Oh, and they are illustrated and backed up with ample evidence.

In various ways, I try to reach out to a broad array of people from all walks of life. In all of this, my underlying goal is to compel the reader to think about the critical and urgent world issues in a different way to what they may have heard on the radio or seen on the evening news. Sure, I try and ruffle some feathers, but my ultimate aim is to shine a light on hidden dimensions and to point out angles and nuggets of knowledge or details they may have missed.

In short, I state my case, I back it up with plenty of facts and information, and I leave it in the trustworthy hands of my audience to make up their own mind.

And don't bother trying to work out whether I am left, right, centre, or whatever label you want to tag me with. If you try, you'll be left dazed and confused because I don't fit neatly into any category. Those who have followed my writings know that they can count on me to never look the other way when a subject that I am passionate about comes to light. Whether it is Mel Gibson's anti-Semitic rants, or the Gaza Flotilla, or John Safran's silly Holocaust antics, or the BDS, or Oliver Stone, or Yitzhak Rabin's legacy, or Holocaust trivialisation, or the Arab-Israeli conflict, or the United Nations' anti-Israel bias, or President Obama's policy towards Israel, or Family Guy, Michael Jackson or Triple J. I tackle the controversies honestly, and do my darnedest to hold people, groups and institutions to account, as well as to expose the inconsistencies, hypocrisies, idiocies, hatred, exploitation and double-standards.

Yes at times, my no-holds-barred style is confrontational but rest assured it's never personal. I always engage with the issue. And I don't pretend to get things right all the time. Looking back at the collection of insights penned over more than a decade, I was struck by how several of my predictions and hopes for the future were misplaced or flawed. To give but one example. Back in 2005 I backed the disengagement from Gaza. I believed it was the right call by the late Ariel Sharon and wrote that this bold step might actually lead Hamas to give up on its genocidal aims against Israel. As you know, that never happened. On the other hand, despite some occasional blunders, I often hit the mark. As early as 2003 I warned about the threat of a nuclear Iran; I rightly foresaw the demise of the Road Map to Peace; I correctly assessed the increasing importance of the Security Barrier in preventing terrorist attacks; and I accurately foreshadowed the creeping normalisation and mainstreaming of anti-Semitism and anti-Zionism.

As must be clear by now, I feel very lucky to have been on this journey of writing and am very grateful to those who have been along with me on this incredible ride. That over the years so many of you have been interested in what I have had to say, and have now bought this book, is my greatest reward.

ISRAEL

Toppling Saddam Hussein was the right call

March 28, 2003

The truth is never allowed to be simple. I am all too often surprised when I hear critics say that everyone who supports the war against Iraq is a gung-ho hawk. Anyone who has studied history and international relations can say with a clear conscience that confronting tyranny is in humanity's interest.

Given the horror of weapons of mass destruction, what's wrong with making the world a safer place by going after terrorists and the states harbouring and supplying them? What's wrong with protecting the citizens of the world and ensuring the security of generations to come? Surely, such a duty is vested in every single leader and person.

Does anyone really believe that the UN inspectors could have discovered Saddam's undeclared arsenal or contained his unquenchable appetite for sinister military expansion? Does anyone doubt that the moment Iraq became a nuclear power it would not seek to carry out its ideological commitment to destroy Israel or make political gains by shaking its nuclear fist. It's impossible to ignore this scenario.

A balanced review of the situation reveals that, by all accounts, Saddam has proven to be a despot controlling an evil regime capable of heinous crimes. He has invaded neighbouring countries, gassed his own people and let al-Qaeda operatives roam Baghdad. Rabbi Berel Wein has argued that Saddam's brutal terror and cruelty is unparalleled, even in the neighbourhood of the Middle East.[1] In the 1991 Gulf War, Iraq fired a volley of 39 scud missiles on Israel. Since then, Saddam has provided patronage to Arafat and has fanned the flames of Palestinian violence by offering financial assistance to the tune of $US25,000 to the families of suicide bombers.[2]

It's a shame that most have forgotten the Kurds and the Iran-Iraq war that left 675,000 dead and injured another million. It's also a shame that the world has forgotten that, if not for Israel's controversial bombing of Iraq's Osirak nuclear plant in 1981, the stakes now would be much higher for all involved.

Oddly, attention has been deflected from the reality that Saddam

Hussein has refused to abide by the international will for twelve years and has sought to build a tremendous arsenal of nuclear, chemical and biological weapons. Clearly, allowing Saddam to supply weapons of mass destruction to terrorists would have been felt far beyond the region.

Holocaust survivors Elie Wiesel and Simon Wiesenthal have argued that appeasing dictators does not lead to peace, pointing out that if Europe's great nations had intervened against Hitler instead of placating his aggressive ambitions in Munich, then perhaps six million Jews might not have died and the world would have been spared the unspeakable horrors of World War II. It is common wisdom that Iraq hid its WMD where inspectors would never have found them and would not have hesitated in using them or blackmailing the world with them as North Korea is trying to do.

The naysayers who predicted the US-led attack on Afghanistan's Taliban regime would unleash more instability and conflict have been proven wrong. A cataclysmic event like a coalition victory could have a positive ripple effect. To be sure, success in Iraq could deliver a major blow to all radical movements and improve Israel's position in its war against Palestinian fundamentalists. Likewise, it may send a clear message about spreading democracy in oppressive states and yield a renewed push for peace that breaks the deadlock of the second *Intifada*.

In a February 26 speech, Bush said that after a regime change in Iraq he would attempt to revive the Israeli-Palestinian peace process. In fact, last week he committed his administration to a 'Road Map' – as drafted by the US, UN, European Union and Russia – for the Middle East.[3]

There is some precedent. It was the 1991 Madrid Conference, brokered after the first Gulf War, that eventually led to Oslo and brought peace with Jordan and nearly with Syria. An installation of a western-oriented successor to Saddam would strengthen the position of other moderate Arab countries and may discourage administrations such as Syria from supporting Islamic militants. No doubt, a democratic rule in Iraq would reduce the military and financial lifeline of Hamas and Islamic Jihad. Likewise, Israeli Prime Minister Ariel Sharon believes that removing Hussein would generate new momentum in the peace process. In the aftermath, the region will be presented with an American president, armed with increased leverage, who could credibly say to all parties that in the same way that he has shown that he is serious about fighting terror, they must show they are serious about peace with Israel. You reap what you sow.

While a majority of Israelis are in favour of the war, recent polls have indicated that Israelis, living with a crisis-of-the-day lifestyle that has claimed over 700 Israeli lives over the last two years, are more concerned with the sluggish economy, Palestinian attacks and national politics. They know that Syria, Hezbollah and Iran may pose a bigger threat after the disappearance of Saddam Hussein.

Road traps on the Road Map to peace
June 20, 2003

Likkud member and Israeli Parliamentarian Uzi Landau called it 'sugar coated cyanide',[4] while others deemed it a road trap for Israel. And yet, when President Bush released the so-called Road Map to Peace[5] in May, I crossed my fingers. When Prime Minister Ariel Sharon and Palestinian Prime Minister Mahmoud Abbas accepted the plan, I was filled with a sense of potential optimism that here at last is a mechanism that could address the hopelessness and despair in the region. After all, this was the first time an Israeli government voted for a plan that explicitly called for the creation of an independent Palestinian state on the West Bank and Gaza by 2005 and the removal of Jewish settlements outposts erected since March 2002. Further, any way out of the hug of death and nerve-rending war footing which Israel has found itself in, that looked out for Israel's long-term security interest and that really hammered out a just and lasting solution had to be given a chance. That was the reality on the wall.

No one has illusions. Like many others, I was sceptical that a comprehensive settlement that has long eluded Israel at a tremendous cost of life could be realised through this plan. But I knew, as the American Jewish Committee knew when it adopted a policy statement in its annual meeting, that any attempt to bring the peace process back on track should be supported. As Sharon told his cabinet, 'I don't like the Road Map either, but it's a lesser evil'.[6] And as Yossi Alpher, Israeli Security analyst observed, 'We're not looking a warm and fuzzy peace for a generation or two at least'.[7] Certainly, by no stretch of the imagination, was this about enemies learning to love each other in a few months. In essence, the Road Map was really a starting point for negotiations, an effort to jumpstart the stalled process rather than an all-encompassing, finished blue print for peace. It did nothing to remove any of the perennial stumbling blocks such as the sediment of decades of hatred. Instead of showing a final destination, it merely offered a way to get there.

To be sure, the steps in the US-backed publication are obvious and in the past this path led nowhere except to more violence and bloodshed. Now, only two weeks after the initiative was approved by Israel and the Palestinians, and after a fresh spate of terrorist attacks in Israel in which 17 Israeli civilians were killed, it seems the Road Map will join a long list of failed initiatives such as the Mitchell Report, the George Tenet Understanding and other accords. Robert Satloff, from the Washington Institute for Near East policy, who has stated that the Road Map is quite impractical because it presumes that an enormous amount of work can be done in very short, brief periods,[8] must be saying, 'I told you so'. So too the settlers, who argued that this was a Road Map to hell. And so too, the conservative wing of Bush's own party, who have already called this strategy 'dead on arrival' and who have sparked debate in Washington over whether or not Secretary of State Colin Powell has the full support of the cabinet.

From the outset, the 2000 word proposal was plagued with a truckload of problems. It is hardly a surprise that Israel has added 14 riders, demanding, for example, that the Palestinian Right of Return is not included in any future negotiations and that only the United States oversees the completion of the Road Map and not the other members of the quartet. Likewise, Secretary of State Powell's assertion that there are no US plans to change the Road Map since it is a good document betrayed an odd rigidity in the administration's thinking that could be a deal-breaker. Even more troubling, and the particular element that set it apart from the Oslo Accords, is that the Road Map was put together by parties other than Israel and the Palestinians – these two had no role to play in the creation of the Road Map as with Oslo. So, it was inevitable that either party will have significant amendments and changes it wants to make. Then there is the problem of credibility – let's not forget that the co-sponsors of the plan can hardly be called loyal and traditional allies of Israel.

Other obstacles are evident. The ambitious, three-phased plan does not address thorny, final status issues such as sovereignty over Jerusalem, final borders, access to water, and the Palestinian demand for a right of return. Also, it unwisely calls for a parallel process rather than a performance-related plan that is based on actual performance instead of mere declarations and adherence to arbitrary deadlines – a requirement that, given the depth and complexity of security impediments on the ground, is warranted. Alongside these difficulties, there are also signs that Arafat intends to reassert his control over security affairs – earlier in May he issued a presidential decree for the establishment of national security, a move in violation of the Road Map. Consider also that the Arab states have not shown to Israel and its people that they are prepared to back the Road Map, that they are prepared to recognise Israel and support the emergence of a peaceful and democratic Palestine, and that they are prepared to live in peace with Israel.

The fact there are still people out there hopeful the Road Map can succeed is mainly due to the commitment shown by President Bush to the Middle East process. He has certainly talked to talk. However, if the last two weeks are any indication, the steely resolve and courage to steer the Road Map across the tough terrain and emotional land mines required by the president have gone AWOL. First, although he set an end to terrorism as a condition for starting the process, he launched the Road Map in Jordan while spates of attacks were wreaking havoc in Israel. Secondly, when Israel responded after three Israeli soldiers were murdered, Bush harshly criticised Israel for jeopardising the peace process and for threatening its own security. Incredibly, following those murders, Powell expressed the fervent hope that terrorism would not get in the way of the peace process. In truth, Bush cannot ask Israel that it relax and ignore the ongoing slaughter of its people while he works to broker a peace deal. Equally, Bush should remember that a majority of 87 US senators out of 100 and more than half of the House of Representatives have signed letters stating that Israel should make no sacrifice at all until after the Palestinian Authority prove it is capable of cracking down on the violence. The blood-soaked events of the last week are a telling marker that a wait and see approach is not the way. The Palestinian government must understand the concept of cause and effect and it must understand that Israelis cannot continue to die without response.

Above all, the Road Map's greatest prospective downfall is Palestinian failure to crack down effectively on militant groups who have swiftly rejected the Road Map out of hand and have vowed further acts of murder. In fact, in the last two weeks three primary Palestinian terrorist groups, Hamas, Islamic Jihad and the al-Aqsa Brigade, banded together to attack and kill Israeli soldiers. These terrorists are armed to the teeth and are ready for more homicidal missions. Let there be no confusion. The Road Map is clear: Abu Mazen's government must take away their illegal weapons, establish control over various other groups and dismantle their terrorist capabilities. Obviously enough, no one anticipates a 100 per cent success, but what is needed is a 100 per cent effort, which is clearly absent.

Those familiar with the Middle East know that often people act out your worst nightmares rather than your best hopes. The ominous early days of the Road Map provide little hope for its long-term implementation and sustainability. I hope to God I'm wrong.

The case for Israel's fence of life

October 10, 2003

As I write this column, they're saying on the radio that at least 19 people are dead, among them a baby girl and three children in a homicidal bombing at a crowded Haifa beach restaurant.[9] This news and the images I have just viewed still have the power to shock me.

How many slayings of innocent Israelis does it take for rationality to kick in? Are 873 Israelis over three years, which includes 105 children under the age of eighteen a sufficient number?

The terrorists always find a way to slip into Israel, as did the 29-year-old Jenin woman who blew herself up in Haifa a few hours ago. She entered through an area where the security fence is yet to be erected.

It's sad that those who criticise the security fence, usually as a knee jerk reaction, don't pause to reflect on this simple question: why does Israel need such a buffer?

International law recognises that every country has the right to defend itself against those wishing to destroy it. Putting up a fence to keep out murderers falls in every way within that right. The fence is a natural and understandable response to the hundreds of ghastly strikes that have emanated from the West Bank.

Further, the fence is a peaceful means to do so and can always be moved or changed when in the future new borders are determined. Ehud Olmert expressed the right sentiment when he observed, 'A dead victim of terror cannot be brought back to life. The dead are gone forever. Fences are reversible; death is not.'[10]

Often overlooked is the fact the fence was conceived in the ashes of relentless bombings and that it has broad support across the political spectrum (latest surveys show about 70 per cent approval), driving home the message that Israelis have had enough of this intolerable situation. It's hard to deny the evident need Israel has for a security barrier. Terrorism and rejections are the root cause for the fence. As President Bush noted in July, Hamas could make the barrier 'irrelevant' if it folded its terrorist tent.

Still, the US administration, including the President and Secretary Powell, has voiced its concern over the security fence. National

Security Advisor Condoleeza Rice stated that the construction is not consistent with the US view of the Middle East.[11] Neither is the wantonly carnage of Israelis, Ms Rice. It's surprising that Bush, who has said Israel has every right to protect its citizens and who should know the history of the Middle East, expects Israel to trust the Palestinian Authority for its safety rather than a security fence. Surely Israel cannot afford to wait for the Palestinians to stop the terror or for substantive change in the attitude of the Palestinian Authority even if that means Washington may penalise Israel through its loan guarantees.

Besides the theatrics, what right does the United States have to dictate to Israelis what they can and cannot do, given that that the scale of bloodshed of the last 1000 days is, comparatively speaking, comparable to 14 September 2011 attacks? Israelis elected Ariel Sharon as their Prime Minister to act in their best interests, not Bush. Weighing up the question of whether he should make the President happy or protect his constituency, I think the moral calculus for Sharon is crystal clear.

Also, imagine how many Israelis would be alive today if the fence was put up five years ago. And how many attacks could have been averted. All too often, the personal stories of Israel's victims of terror take a back seat to the big picture debates. Sympathies are rarely reserved for civilians killed or mutilated by those against whose crimes this barrier is being established. For now, as journalist Hope Keller puts it, 'This grim roulette ("Will my kids' bus explode?", "What if we pick the restaurant that gets blown up tonight?") appears to be Israel's future.'[12]

Ask yourselves: what other option does a democracy have (short of a full-scale war) to protect its citizens from future attacks? The fence will certainly stop truck bombs, sniper attacks on Israeli motorists and infiltrators heading toward the coffee shops and buses within the heartland. Admittedly, the fence will not alter the heinous ideology of killing Jews and will not be foolproof – but at least the freedom to carry out such actions will be limited.

We know that not a single bomber has penetrated the wall in Gaza, there since 1994, although they are trying day by day. The Israeli government has already agreed to a two-state solution. This is not the issue. The issue is how to allow Israelis to live a life free from the gruesome, murderous strategies of the terrorists. Nothing so far has indicated that Israel has serious partners with whom to negotiate a peace. So far, the Palestinian leadership has clearly shown that it has no intention to of dismantling terrorist organisations, in defiance of the first requirement of the 'Road Map'.

In the absence of credible leaders, why should the Israeli government stop building an effective and legitimate barrier that will save lives? And make no mistake, saving lives and ensuring the safety of its populace is the most morally compelling reason that any government has. In fact, it is its primary obligation.

This week's slaughter should strengthen the resolve of the government and the Israeli people to continue with the fence. Can you blame them?

Power people as important as peace treaties

April 16, 2004

As violence spirals out of control, I sometimes find it hard to fight despair and even harder to ever see a time when Palestinians, Arabs and Israeli Jews will be allies. Yet, over the last few years, various groups have been doing exactly that, and their ongoing initiatives are proving that the past doesn't have to be a guide to the future.

It has been observed that, 'In peace-building it is not enough to draft diplomatic agreements between leaders; a reconciliation process needs to happen among the peoples in conflict.' This is widely known as 'track-two' diplomacy. And indeed, as the situation deteriorates, the benefits of compromise and peace need to be inculcated amongst those who have only known conflict, guns firing and bombs exploding. True, previous disappointments have produced many cynics and doubters, who view any endeavour though the monocle of distrust. Yet, any misgivings and finger-pointing must take a backseat to the possibility of resolution, denying madness another victory. The inarguable truth is that the average Israeli and Palestinian wants to live in dignity, wants to enjoy and cultivate the beauty of his land and wants to educate and raise his children in safety.

In his new collection of essays, *Death as a way of Life: From Oslo to the Geneva agreement*,[13] Israeli novelist David Grossman manages, despite the pessimism that encircles his daily living, to see through the darkness into the humanity of Israel's arch-nemesis. Admirably, Grossman refuses to submit to the grip of hopelessness enmeshing many, noting that each side must jettison the natural proclivity to assign blame and to work hand in hand to defeat the extremists on both sides who have pushed the two peoples sliding into an abyss.

Did you know that in 2002 Michael Sabah, the Latin patriarch of Jerusalem, Rabbi Melchior, Israel's then deputy Foreign Minister and Sheikh Talal Sidr, a then minister from the Palestinian Authority, were awarded the Coventry International Prize for Peace and Reconciliation for their pioneering efforts in drafting the Alexandria Initiative, signed by the Israelis and Palestinians to advance common religious grounds and dialogue between the three faiths?[14]

13

Have you heard about the *Pathways to Reconciliation* project, a pilot program that sends about 80 educators, Jewish Israeli, Arab-Israeli and Palestinian to Antalya, Turkey, to participate in a conference entitled 'Continuing Dialogue in Times of Crisis'? Much of the program's power comes from the tremendous change in the mindset of the participants it engenders. The two camps talked for hours; they wrote questions and comments on cards that were anchored to the wall for everyone to read; they took part in various tasks, such as leading blindfolded group members around the hotel, the blindfolded not knowing who was leading them.

In the end, the participants listened to each other. And before long a kind of empathy began to flower. The former enemies stopped attacking and competing over who suffered more and thought about how they could make things better. Facilitators Michal Levin and Fakhira Halloun explained that these teachers have access to hundreds of students every year. Ultimately, the hope is that the teachers will act as agents of change within their societies.

In June 2003, a group of about 250 Jews and Arabs from Israel as well as Jews and Muslims from France took part in a two-day visit to Auschwitz-Birkenau and Krakow. The visit, called 'From Memory To Peace',[15] culminated in participants of the delegation reading the names of some of those who died in the camps (a few of the victims were from among the families of the Jewish members of the trip). What's more, the mission walked along the railway tracks at Birkenau, to the same platform where the diabolical selections of Jews had taken place and entered the gas chambers and the crematoria.

At one point, Rabbi Avi Gisser recited the Kaddish, slightly changing the ending to 'He will make peace upon us and upon all peoples of the world'; the Jews and Arabs jointly answered 'Amen'. One of the program's architects, Emile Shoufani, the archimandrite at the Greek Catholic Church in Nazareth and director of the St Joseph High School, said that 'reconciliation between Arabs and Jews would never be possible unless Arabs understood what the Holocaust means to Jews'.[16] Rabbi Gisser added, 'As a Jew, I met with Arabs in a way that I had never met them before, and I allowed them to know me in a way I had never done before. We have deep disagreements about sovereignty, land and resources, rights and history. Yet we have found a deep, common humanity.'[17]

It is unreasonable to think that the mere signing of a peace treaty will result in both sides immediately accepting each other's historical narrative or accepting the justice of the right claimed by the other side. And yet, we must all strive for dialogue, for peace is a noble task.

Sharon's disengagement from Gaza plan: A gamble that might just work

May 21, 2004

The thumbs down by the Likud party's 200,000 members for the withdrawal from Gaza[18] is a setback that should not derail the revolutionary plan of full-scale disengagement from the Gaza Strip. As Ehud Olmert asserted, the withdrawal plan is inevitable and unstoppable.[19]

Remember the days when the Likud position was that the Palestinians did not need a state since Jordan was Palestine? The party was a bulwark for the goal of a Greater Land of Israel. Now it unequivocally accepts the idea of a two-state solution.

In November 2003, four past chiefs of Shin Bet Security declared that the present policy was leading Israel to disaster.[20] The country was in shock, for these were the men who were charged with implementing that policy. In August 2003, Abraham Burg published an article warning the occupation was undermining Zionism,[21] while a month later a group of pilots and navigators signed a letter saying they would refuse to carry out attacks over the territories.[22] Even the late Yitzhak Rabin once said that he wished he would wake up and find that Gaza had been shed.

Things have changed.

Clearly, as many have argued, the status quo is unsustainable, and the cost is too high. The Gaza strip is an area 11.2 kilometres wide and 40 kilometres long. It is under Israeli control because no one else wanted it. Today, it is a hotbed of hatred, crushing poverty and terror. The Israeli settlements situated there are the most unpopular with ordinary Israelis, who believe they are irrationally placed. After an interview Israeli Prime Minister Ariel Sharon gave *Haaretz* on 2 February, a *Yediot Ahronot* poll published the next day revealed that close to 60 per cent backed his exit strategy.[23]

Ask yourself if having 7500 Jewish settlers, living on 20 per cent of the land among 1.3 million Palestinians, makes sense. Both the settlers and the 3000 soldiers installed to protect them are subject to vicious and relentless mortar shells, shootings and bombings. Not to mention the tens of millions of dollars poured into guarding the settlers. At the end of the day, Israel has to do what it has to do to survive, because the demographic implications are worrying.

Sharon, at the moment, has no one to negotiate with and the Arab world has not come up with one credible initiative. Accordingly, he has changed the rules of the Middle East game, saying that since one of the parties to bilateral negotiations has in effect resigned, Israel will act alone. One commentator has asked: Is Israel risking the wrath of the Arab world as a result? It already has. Will this create more suicide bombers? There are enough already. Will political chaos be created in the territories? Got that too. As Paul Romer has observed, 'A crisis is a terrible thing to waste'.[24]

President's Bush affirmation of Israel's right to retain large settlements on the West Bank and his unprecedented rejection of the Palestinian right of return is no small achievement. This is a major change in US policy, which up until now viewed settlements in the West Bank as an obstacle for peace and called for their removal.

I feel for the settlers who will be forced to leave their homes. Still, I agree with Prime Minister Sharon's sentiments that it is his duty to do everything so that the rows of headstones do not get any longer. Listen to his address to the nation: 'We will not allow others to determine our destiny ... we will mould with our own hands a reality which will coincide with the security and political interests which are so important to us.'[25] No doubt, Sharon's move is a practical, sensible solution that will not only break the stalemated peace efforts, but will bring the settlers and the soldiers home out of the most densely populated Palestinian area. And here are Thomas Friedman's sentiments: 'I'm fed up with the stalemate in the Middle East. All it has produced is death, destruction and endless "hit me first" debates on cable television ... everyone is sick of it.'[26]

Head of intelligence, Major Aharon Ze'evi, has told the Knesset Foreign Affairs and Defense Committee that if Israel unilaterally withdraws from the Gaza Strip, there is a 'high probability' that the number of attacks launched by Palestinians from the area would be reduced.[27] Moreover, Israel has announced that even after the withdrawal, the army will counterstrike if Gaza-based terrorism from Hamas and co continues. Similarly, the new barrier, already bearing real security benefits, would be completed before any settlements are evacuated. Also, Gaza will remain landlocked (and probably airlocked) for the time being to prevent its ports from being used for gun smuggling and the accumulation of weapons. Similarly, Israel would continue to monitor activity via sensors, satellites and unmanned aerial vehicles.

Sharon's difficulties bring to mind the formidable opposition Menachem Begin faced from his own government when he decided to return the Sinai. Ultimately, he managed to hold his party together and make a lasting peace with Egypt.

The solution is not an easy one, neither is it risk free. But show me one solution that is. Politics should be pragmatic, never absolutist. Polls indicate that a majority of Israelis endorse the pullout, believing that it is worth a try. So do Netanyahu, Silvan Shalom, Limor Livnat, Ehud Olmert and Tommy Lapid. Oh, and so do George Bush, John Kerry and the Quartet.

So should we.

Israel: The United Nations' punching bag

August 6, 2004

Anyone familiar with the UN's record would not have been surprised at the resolution calling for the security fence to be torn down.[28] Did anyone really think Israel would get a fair go from a Security Council and an international court that include bastions of democracy and freedom like China, Algeria, Angola, Pakistan, Egypt, Sierra Leone and Madagascar?

It is fairly clear that the blistering anti-Israel atmosphere is a key staple in the history of the General Assembly, where even the Jewish state's establishment has come under vicious attack. Incredibly, in the question that the UN put to the International Court of Justice (ICJ), there was no reference to Palestinian terrorism, nor in the December 2003 resolution condemning the fence, nor in the supporting dossier of 88 documents, nor in the written statements filed by most member states. No wonder the ICJ ruled that Israel's building of the barrier was illegal and that Israel must immediately cease construction.

The ICJ gave no serious thought to the killing and maiming of thousands of Israelis over the last four years. The sorry thing is that the UN wants to see the only democracy in the region humiliated time and again.

Since the 1960s, almost 30 per cent of the resolutions passed by the UN's Commission on Human Rights have been aimed at Israel, and of the ten emergency special sessions ever convened, six have been directed at Israel. Israel is the only country with its own UN monitor, the Special Commission to Investigate Israeli Practices Affecting the Human Rights of the Palestinian People and Other Arabs of the Occupied Territories.

In 2003 the General Assembly passed four resolutions focusing on specific countries; Israel received eighteen. China, Syria, Saudi Arabia, UAE, Yemen and Zimbabwe have been spared rebuke. Even a resolution against Sudan, guilty of cross amputation, death by hanging, crucifixion and stoning women to death for adultery, was defeated.

In March this year, after the UN Security Council approved a resolution censuring Israel for the killing of the founder of Hamas, Sheikh Ahmed Yassin (the resolution was eventually vetoed by the USA[29]), Israel was discussed for five straight days under the guise of self-determination and racism, and then the only item on the commission's agenda was dedicated in its entirety to one member state, when all 190 countries were treated jointly under a separate item.

Consider that no report devoted to anti-Semitism has ever been produced by a UN organ. When the first declaration on religious intolerance was passed in 1981, anti-Semitism was excluded, while in the infamous Durban conference references to anti-Semitism were excised from almost all sections of the final declaration.

Israelis are constantly denounced with Nazi terminology. 'Kristallnacht repeats itself daily,' asserted the Algerian representative. 'Israeli soldiers are the true disciples of Goebbels and Himmler, who strip Palestinians prisoners and inscribe numbers on their bodies ... The Israeli war machine has been trying for five years to arrive at a final solution.'[30]

In 2002 John Dugard, charged with reporting to the Commission on Human Rights, seemed to support the carnage inflicted on Israel, testifying that while suicide bombers have sown terror in the Israeli heartland, armed groups with rifles and mortars 'confront the IDF with new determination, daring and success'.[31]

And do I need to bring up the UN's response to Jenin? At first, it described the scene as 'horrific beyond belief',[32] only to admit in mid-summer 2002 that only 52 Palestinians had died, 35 being armed militias. Earlier this year, in the aftermath of a homicidal bombing in Jerusalem in which eleven people were killed, UN Secretary-General Kofi Annan refrained from denouncing the attack outright. He released a statement alluding to 'violence and terror that claimed innocent lives in the Middle East',[33] avoiding direct reference to the murderous assault.

Annan has not been Israel's greatest friend. In November 2003 he refused to publicly support a proposed General Assembly declaration condemning anti-Semitism, but did allow the Security Council to urgently convene when Israel bombed an empty warehouse in Syria.

And when in May 2004, Lakhdar Brahimi, the UN's special

envoy to Iraq (who boasted that he has never knowingly shaken hands with an Israeli or a Jew) told reporters that 'the policy of Israel is a poison in the Mid-East',[34] Annan's spokesman said Brahimi was speaking in his personal capacity and brought to the table strongly held views.

It seems that the UN is not interested in the human rights of Israelis, who have had their rights violated anywhere, anytime – in parks, cafes, discos and hotels. Both Human Rights Watch and Amnesty International have classified suicide bombings as 'war crimes' and 'crimes against humanity', as acts designed to 'destroy in whole or in part, a national, ethnical, racial or religious group'.[35]

One wonders why the UN's founding principles of human dignity and national self-determination don't apply to the Jewish people. Indeed, against the saga of abiding animosity, one journalist has speculated that perhaps the UN regrets its decision to establish the State of Israel in 1948.

Analysing the UN's treatment of Israel, a former US delegate to the UN Human Rights Commission remarked that 'things ain't all on the level down there'.

He couldn't have been more right.

Iran: the hour of reckoning is fast approaching

February 18, 2005

Enoch Powell once said, 'The supreme function of statesmanship is to provide against preventable evils.'[36] Now imagine this climactic moment: John Howard gets a call from President Bush. 'Mr Prime Minister, we have decided to bomb Iran's nuclear sites. I'm counting on your support.'

This might read like an implausible scenario, but there is little question that Iran is today's big story with its clandestine pursuit of nuclear weapons and its dismissive attitude towards the Europeans who are trying to curtail its terrifying aspirations. Indeed, during her recent European tour US Secretary of State Condoleezza Rice delivered an uncompromising warning to the 'loathed'[37] Iranian government, refusing to rule out the possibility of a pre-emptive military strike. And former President Clinton has said that Bush has done the right thing by keeping the military option on the table.[38]

Described in last week's State of the Union address as the world's leading sponsor of terrorism,[39] Iran's continuing and vigorous progress towards producing fissile material that could be used for nuclear weapons was confirmed in September 2004 in a report by Mohamed Elbardei, the head of the International Atomic Energy Agency.[40] Iran has so far given the West the run-around, ignoring calls for it to suspend work on a heavy water reactor and has, according to *Time* magazine, purchased machinery and weapon design from Abdul Qadeer Khan, regarded as the founding father of Pakistan's nuclear industry.[41]

Israeli Defence Minister Shaul Mofaz has warned that the point of no return for Iran's capacity to enrich uranium would be reached within a year. Iran, which refuses to recognise Israel's right to exist, has unambiguously professed genocide against the Jewish state. On December 14, 2001 Ali Akbar Hashemi Rafsanjani (Iran's de-facto leader and former president) said at a sermon in Tehran University that the use of a nuclear bomb on Israel would entirely demolish the Jewish state, whereas it would only damage the Islamic world.[42] Iran's leaders have made many similar statements.

No one doubts that nuclear weapons in the hands of Iran would be a grave danger to the world. Known for its financing of terrorist organisations, a nuclear Iran could transfer its technology to groups such as Hezbollah or Al Qaeda, leading to an atomic attack by terrorist proxies. Furthermore, the ramifications for the region of a nuclear Iran are frightening. There is a high probability that a nuclear-armed Iran will trigger a nuclear chain reaction that could quickly see Egypt, Saudi Arabia, Syria and even Turkey follow suit. In fact, Syria has begun serious nuclear research; Egypt is planning to build reactors to desalinate; the Saudis are interested in importing nuclear arms from China; and Algeria has just upgraded a very large research reactor in a remote location and surrounded it with air defences.

Britain, France and Germany are trying to prove that they can reach a sweetheart agreement with Iran without resorting to force, offering better trade and political relations, although since August 2003 they have been strung along, continuing to negotiate even though Iran reneged on its promises. Iran's Foreign Minister Kamal Kharrazi has insisted that his country would never give up its right to nuclear technologies, adding that 'We won't accept any new obligations. Iran has a high technical capability and has to be recognised by the international community as a member of the nuclear club. This is an irreversible path.'[43] He further explained that no international body can force Iran to legally drop its peaceful nuclear activities.

Although Foreign Minister Downer supports the work of the EU3, the question is whether the Europeans have the teeth to back up their threats. In a 2004 Brookings Institution scenario with mostly former European and American officials, in which Iran actually is about to produce a bomb, the Europeans were unwilling to use force or employ tough sanctions.[44] Madeleine Albright observed, 'Europeans say they understand the threat but then act as if the real problem is not Iran but the United States. We should not forget that it was the United States who brought an end to the mass killings in the Balkans, not a paralysed Europe.'[45]

Appeasement does not always work. The world should learn from the Clinton administration's disastrous 1994 deal when North

Korea promised to halt work on all nuclear weapons in return for American assistance with peaceful nuclear programs. Iran, having had plenty of opportunities to learn how to beat the inspection regime from watching Iraq and North Korea, will continue its nuclear program until it obtains the bomb once and for all. The prospects for derailing Iran's nuclear program through multilateral diplomacy still have some running room, but are growing dimmer by the day.

Still, it would be nice if precision bombing is guaranteed to do the job. Former CIA Director James Woolsey has stated that Iran has had eighteen years to hide its facilities and has dispersed it throughout the country, reportedly submerging their nuclear workshops in densely populated areas that would ensure mass casualties.[46] So, as one commentator succinctly put it, if the horse is 90 per cent out of the barn, it would seem Iran will get the bomb unless the USA invades.

This is simply too big a problem to ignore. Kenneth M. Pollack concludes in his new book *The Persian Puzzle*,[47] 'This is a problem from hell' with no good solution. The clock is ticking fast.

A momentous chapter: the withdrawal from Gaza

August 17, 2005

As dawn breaks over Israel today, one of the most momentous chapters in the Israeli-Palestinian conflict will be written, when the Israeli army begins withdrawing from the Gaza Strip, along with 8000 settlers who have called the overcrowded, impoverished strip of land, less than 200 square miles in area, their home for more than 30 years.[48] The disengagement, as it has come to be known, has been one of the most heated and polarising subjects in the highly fraught arena of Israeli politics, threatening Israel's social fabric as never before. Indeed, anyone recently visiting Israel would find it hard to miss the sea of people wearing orange apparel (against disengagement) or blue (for disengagement), mass demonstrations, blocking of roads and talk of a civil war. The call by extremists for soldiers to refuse military orders to evacuate settlements split the small nation and presented Israelis with a stark choice between two binding authorities – God's law and the state's. Fortunately, the rule of law has prevailed.

The road to disengagement has been long and difficult. Since Israel's cabinet approved the plan in February 2004, the Israeli parliament has voted on the unilateral withdrawal several times and on June 10 of this year, Israel's highest court rejected a bid to stop the pull-out.[49]

Survey after survey has consistently shown that most Israelis support the disengagement from Gaza, while at the same time empathising with the pain of the thousands of residents who for decades had cultivated and turned the sand dunes of Gaza into flourishing agricultural settlements, and who are heartbroken by the dismantling of their enclaves. For some settlers, putting down roots in Gaza meant taking part in messianic redemption, a fulfilment of God's plan. Though most have quietly resigned themselves to the disengagement and will leave quietly with their compensation package, others have vowed to break Israeli law and will refuse to obey the eviction notices and leave Gaza by the deadline.

Prime Minister Ariel Sharon, regarded as the father of the

settlement policy, has staked his political future on pushing through the plan to leave Gaza. Aware that no Israeli government ever intended retaining the Gaza settlements in any future agreement with the Palestinians, the ex-general and Defence Minister realised that the disengagement was necessary in order to reach a different security, political, economic, and social reality in the coming years. Sharon and the majority of Israelis have come to see that since the settlements were first established, after the 1967 Six Day War, Israel's strategic environment, demography and needs have changed.

The most widely accepted explanation for maintaining the Gaza settlements is based on the notion that Jewish settlements on the outskirts of Palestinians villages and towns constitute a buffer zone against attack from Israel's eastern border. But when you consider that Saddam Hussein's regime in Iraq is destroyed, formal peace treaties with Egypt and Jordan are signed, and Syria is militarily weak and isolated, this idea seems outdated. True, Iran is a security threat, but the Gaza settlements will not protect Israel from Tehran's ballistic missiles.

Those who claim that the withdrawal plan rewards the terrorists are mistaken. The terrorist attacks of the last four years have come from the West Bank, not Gaza. Only two of the 100 suicide bombers who infiltrated Israel came from Gaza. Moving a few kilometres will remove the settlers, who live among 1.3 million Palestinians, and the soldiers who protect them, from the constant danger of death and injury. Crucially, the disengagement defuses the demographic time bomb. If Israel chose to remain in the West Bank and Gaza, by 2010 there would be more Arabs than Jews living in Israel, meaning that if demands for 'one man one vote' were to be granted, Israel's status as a Jewish state would come to an end.

Those who back Israel's willingness to make painful concessions for peace cite the pullout from the Sinai Peninsula in the early 1980s, part of the Camp David peace treaty with Egypt, as proof that Israel can give up territory and be more secure as a result. It was only Israel's readiness to relinquish Gaza that resulted in President Bush's affirmation of Israel's right to retain large settlements on the West Bank and his unprecedented rejection of the Palestinian right of return – a major change in US policy.[50]

Ariel Sharon's brave solution is not an easy one, nor is it risk free. What is likely to happen in Gaza after Israel withdraws is unclear. There are concerns that chaos and anarchy will reign in Gaza. Fearing that Palestinian terrorists will increase their operations, Israel will continue to defend its citizens and monitor activity via three security fences and a range of state-of-the-art weapons systems, including sensors, satellites and unmanned aerial vehicles. Also, it will probably retain control of the strategically valuable Philadelphia corridor along the Gaza-Egyptian border.

Yet, one hopes that the Palestinians, free of military rule, will seize this golden opportunity and establish a viable, democratic state that will improve their people's quality of life and show the world they are capable of nation building. Of course, the international community must deliver on its aid pledges and not let the Palestinians off the hook on their security responsibilities. The disengagement creates a new chance to transform the Israeli Palestinian relationship away from confrontation towards negotiation. Perhaps it is exaggerated optimism, but I have a feeling that the day is not too far when Palestinians and Israelis will live side by side in harmony.

The Question of Zion is a case study in anti-Zionism

September 30, 2005

I often despair when I witness the systematic and fashionable hostility towards Israel bubbling within intellectual circles. It has now reached chilling levels (Zionism was last month compared to al-Qaeda in a Melbourne Writers' Festival session), and is deliberately aimed at de-legitimising the Jewish State. One such example is *The Question of Zion*[51] by Jacqueline Rose.

No doubt, it would take a treatise to list the inaccuracies, omissions and misleading analogies in Professor Rose's decidedly biased tract. However, what astonishes me is that anyone is surprised by the slanted views expressed by Rose. Rose is not only a newcomer to Zionist history, but was one of the signatories to a petition calling on European universities to sever all scientific and cultural relations to Israel. She in fact supports an economic, academic and cultural boycott of Israel.[52] Her book *States of Fantasy*,[53] a look at the ills of the nation state, takes as its case studies South Africa, and you guessed it, Israel.

On the eve of the 60th anniversary of the liberation of Auschwitz, Rose took part in a debate for the affirmative that 'Zionism today is the real enemy of the Jews'.[54] She was joined by Avi Shlaim, an Israeli professor teaching at Oxford who has maintained that, 'Israel's illegal occupation of the Palestinian territories inside the '67 borders is the root of all evil.'[55] Rose added that Israel had engaged in ethnic cleansing of the Palestinian people in 1948 and asked, 'How can the creation of a Jewish nation on the back of the suffering, the humiliation of another people, not be dangerous for the Jews?'[56]

In her book, Rose draws analogies between the founder of political Zionism Theodor Herzl and Hitler, remarking that both were inspired to write their fundamental texts by a Wagner performance. Her only logical conclusion is that Israel, which forfeited its soul on the day of its creation, must disintegrate as a Jewish state. She demonises Zionism as a fanatical movement, ignores the historical truth that European Jews immigrated to Palestine because of the pogroms, the unrelenting persecution and virulent anti-Semitism and because they had nowhere else to go – not because of messianic impulses. According to Rose, Zionism is 'corrupt', 'dangerous', 'deadly', 'delusional', 'crazy', 'demonic' and 'defiled'. Like other anti-Zionists, she believes Israel was born in sin.

The Question of Zion is dedicated to the late Edward Said, one time speech writer for Yasser Arafat and professor of English, who while in Lebanon, threw a stone at a border guard post manned by Israeli soldiers. A cursory look at a few of the sources she cites reveals that Rose relies heavily for her information on Israeli and Arab revisionist historians, the radical left, anti-Zionists and notorious anti-Israel propagandists. She quotes John Pilger, the creator of the highly discredited film *Palestine Is Still The Answer*,[57] who in an article last year claimed that the source of the 2004 Madrid train bombing and other western targets is Israel, whom he describes:

> A creation, then guardian of the west's empire in the Middle East, the Zionist state remains the cause of more regional grievance and sheer terror than all the Muslim states combined. Read the melancholy *Palestinian Monitor* on the internet; it chronicles the equivalent of Madrid's horror week after week, month after month, in occupied Palestine. No front pages in the west acknowledge this enduring bloodbath, let alone mourn its victims. Moreover, the Israeli army, a terrorist organisation by any reasonable measure, is protected and rewarded in the west.[58]

Rose relies on Avi Shlaim's book *The Iron Wall*,[59] suggesting that Zionism on the whole is based on Ze'ev Jabotinsky's supposedly militaristic expansionism. Rose totally misses the point that Jabotinsky was in the minority among Zionist thinkers, but shares Shlaim's assertion that Zionism is cruel and that it is the enemy of the Jews, because as he says 'it fuels the flames of virulent and sometimes violent anti-Semitism. Israel's policies are the cause; hatred of Israel and anti-Semitism are the cause.'[60] Rose quotes Ilan Pappe, the historical consultant to Pilger's film and a Haifa historian who says Israeli ethnically cleansed Palestine and who supports a cultural boycott on his homeland.[61] She references *Jenin, Jenin*, a 'film' roundly condemned for claiming Israel committed war crimes in

Jenin even though a UN investigation into the battle found claims of a massacre unsubstantiated.[62]

The problem with Rose is that there is not even a faint attempt to be fair-minded or balanced. Her unashamedly biased book is riddled with disconnected, selective, out-of-context quotations marshalled to illustrate Zionism's violent nature, while at the same time is happy to present a rose-tinted view of the Palestinian leadership and Arab states that ignores their terrorism, rejectionism and intransigence. Everything for Rose is black and white; no effort is made to contextualise or to proffer any big picture perspective that considers Israel's standpoint. *The Question of Zion* is a real disappointment, but no one should be surprised.

Paradise now or propaganda now?

November 25, 2005

After viewing *Paradise Now*, which follows 36 hours in the lives of Said and Khaled, two Palestinian men sent into Tel Aviv on a suicide mission, I walked out recalling the words of Edward Bernays, who explained how propaganda seeks to manipulate the public mind in an attempt to create mainstream acceptance for a particular idea.[63] I then wondered how a film which puts a human face on the inhuman act of terrorism has received such an uncritical reception here and elsewhere.

While it has been playing in Australian cinemas over the last month, organisers of the Cambridge Film Festival back in July this year decided not to screen it out of deference to victims of the London bombings.[64] In fact, a few days after the film was released at the Berlin Film Festival in February 2005, five people were killed and about 50 wounded when a suicide bomber blew himself up outside the Stage Club on the Tel Aviv promenade.[65]

Europe loves *Paradise Now*. Indeed, the film was largely bankrolled by a variety of government-backed European film funds, and has won a slew of prizes. In Germany, the government has produced a companion pamphlet for schools in which one of the assignments asks students to discuss the following three statements: 'Whoever fears death is already dead', 'No freedom without struggle', and 'Resistance can take many different forms'.[66] Further, I learn that the German-French Public Television *Arte* which co-financed the picture has also produced a drama and a documentary that establishes clear parallels between the founders of Israel and the Nazis, equating the Palestinian displacement with the fate suffered by the Jews under the Third Reich.

This one-sided film is at great pains to rationalise senseless slaughter and to create 'understanding' and sympathy for callous, brutal terrorists out to kill innocents. At a time when suicide bombings have left a global trail of blood, do we really need a film that tries to figure out the motivations of a wicked act and places us in the shoes of murderers? Can you imagine an Australian film privileging the viewpoint of the Bali bombers, dressing them in Tarantino like, super-cool outfits and ladling empathy on them like butter on popcorn? Apparently so. The Evangelical Jury awarded it film of the month because it calls on viewers to 'think about the assassin's motives'.[67]

Certainly, spectators are lulled to empathise with these two men despite their savage intentions. Because films often have us sympathise with evil (we instinctively want the assassin to succeed simply because we have been following him or her intimately for two hours) audience members will find it difficult not to identify with the suicide bombers.

Marketed as a 'bold new call for peace', *Paradise Now* subtly makes excuses for the suicide bomber and conspicuously avoids any principled moral argument or criticism of the practice. On reflection, this is not surprising. The film's director, Hany Abu-Assad, has said, 'I do not condemn suicide murders. For me it is a human reaction to an extreme situation.'[68] Assad has further said that a scene in the film where Khaled and Said eat their last meal at a long table in the bomb plotters' cavernous stone hideout should evoke the last supper Jesus ate with his disciples. Perhaps Assad, through such hints of religious symbolism, is trying to infer that like Jesus, the suicide bombers are sacrificing themselves for mankind? Yes, says Assad, 'They are going to sacrifice in order to save.'[69]

The token moderate in the film is Suha, a Palestinian woman who denounces violence. However, her objection is not based on a belief that murdering Israeli civilians in wrong. She claims that the suicide bomber would become 'exactly like' the Israelis if he carries out his deed.

The film also fails to mention the ingrained hatred of Jews and Israel prevalent among the Palestinian population and leaves out scenes of parades filled with calls of 'death to Israel'. The film unambiguously indicts Israel, presenting Israelis as criminal, as intimidating, threatening types who at times seem to possess sadistic tendencies. Likewise, some have suggested that the film skirts along the edge of anti-Semitism, with its employment of classic, age-old myths. Example: in one sequence Jewish settlers are accused of contaminating Palestinian drinking water with poison that causes male sterility.

The picture is replete with political sermons and distortions. One of the designated suicide bombers justifies his actions by claiming that Israel does not accept the two-state solution and that it has carried out ethnic cleansing. Elsewhere, it is claimed that that this specific homicidal operation is the first in two years, though we know that the terrorist attacks against Israel have never stopped.

At film's end, Said decides not to board a bus because he sees a little girl on it. He chooses instead to mass massacre a bus full of soldiers. Such distinctions are false. In reality, suicide killers have purposefully targeted civilians, butchering, over the last five years, 800 Israelis, including young children. Tellingly, the film does not show the consequences – the victims, the carnage – of the suicide bus attack that is foreshadowed at the film's end. No headless bodies or charred pieces of flesh to complicate the film's agenda.

After zooming into Said's eyes, the screen fades into white. At that point, I could only think of Israeli bus-goers in Jerusalem and Australian tourists in Bali.

Peace between Israelis and Palestinians?
It's Hamas's call

January 30, 2006

The Middle East has just become an even more complicated place. Last week, the world awoke to a new reality with the surprising election of Hamas in the Palestinian Authority elections.[70]

This geopolitical earthquake has taught the Bush Administration, which urged the Arab world to accept democracy, the bitter lesson that free elections can produce Islamist regimes opposed to its policies in the region. When a terrorist organisation takes the reins of government it then becomes a terrorist regime unless otherwise proven.

And so the cardinal question is whether Hamas, with a history of rocket attacks and suicide bombings that have claimed the lives of about 600 Israelis, will embrace the rule of law, forswear terror and accept the principle of a two-state Israel-Palestine solution.

There is a thin sliver of hope that this will genuinely happen any time soon.

What is clear is that the new Hamas government cannot have its cake and eat it too. It cannot continue to promote the destruction of Israel and at the same time expect to liaise with the Jewish state on security issues, border crossings, commercial relations, information-sharing and basic utilities, vital for the day-to-day existence of its people.

The US and Europe have demanded Hamas renounce violence and recognise Israel if it wants to keep receiving huge financial aid. Hamas leaders have said they will not. Additionally, Hamas advocates Sharia law, is part of the global Jihad against the West, and supports Saddam Hussein and Osama bin Laden. One of Hamas's elected parliamentarians, Mariam Farhat, is a mother who sent three of her sons on suicide missions, showing one of her boys how to attack and telling him not to return.[71]

Most commentators agree that the trial period for Hamas should be very short and that the ultimatum should be unequivocal – shed your murderous ways or no funds. In this context it's worth recalling that according to the World Bank, The Palestinian Authority will run out of funds by the end of this month. Still, this carrot and stick approach may not be that effective.

Since the 1990s, Hamas has cultivated a strategic alliance with Iran. Hamas's leader-in-exile, Khaled Mashal, recently met with Iranian President Mahmoud Ahmadinejad to discuss how much of windfall profits from oil should be funnelled into the Palestinian economy.[72] Clearly, Iranian money could enable the Hamas-led government to withstand any international boycott for a while.

Optimists say there is the possibility that Hamas may soften its positions and go through a period of reform, adopting a more moderate and practical stance. But if this occurs it will take years, not months.

In any case, Hamas's engagement with the political process may give it new legitimacy in the international arena. Still, it would be a mistake to confuse a calming and deceptive strategy employed over the next few months in order to court the international community, with Hamas's overriding goal of eradicating Israel, as stated in its charter.[73]

The Europeans have said Hamas needs greater encouragement to abandon past practice such as the IRA did. And yes, precedents for optimism do exist. The Islamist government in Turkey has changed its agenda to adapt to the people's desires, making tremendous efforts to convince the European Union to accept it as a member.

Another positive is that Hamas has remained committed to a ceasefire with Israel since last February. The optimists would like to remind us that in the 1980s and earlier the PLO refused to recognise Israel and called for its annihilation but later changed its platform by a process of conditional dialogue. And in Lebanon, the guerrilla group Hezbollah, which fought the Israeli army for years, is now involved in Lebanese politics, though still vowing to destroy Israel.

The Israelis for their part have always been pragmatic. They know that dealing with the men with guns and bombs directly could secure a real peace if Hamas commits itself to an indefinite ceasefire. Even the tough-talking former PM Benjamin Netanyahu has shown a willingness to negotiate with the PLO.

Yet, with chances for peace talks far away, Israel, following the

March elections, may pursue unilateral actions, shaping its own borders and disengaging further from the Palestinians as Ariel Sharon did. Acting Israeli PM Ehud Olmert has said that if Israel has no negotiating partner it will take a go-it-alone approach. One of the outcomes that the Hamas victory has finally achieved is to bury the 1993 Oslo Peace Accords, since that agreement bars the participation of armed groups that do not recognise Israel.

The 2003 Road Map to Peace can also be packed up for good because the fundamental demand for dismantling terrorist groups has been violated.

Nothing in the Middle East has ever been simple.

Only time will tell if Hamas is willing to deal with Israel and cast off its genocidal aims for the sake of a true, lasting peace.

Can anything be done to stop a nuclear Iran?

April 27, 2006

While it may be a year or three years before Iran goes nuclear, another Cuban missile crisis is looming. While most governments agree Iran should not be allowed to build a nuclear bomb, they cannot agree on how to prevent such a chilling scenario.

Iranian President Mahmoud Ahmadinejad has provocatively announced that Iran has succeeded in enriching uranium and has joined the nuclear club.[74] This was after it test fired several long-range missiles in a show of force, and after a Russian offer to allow Iran to enrich uranium on Russian soil was rejected.

But the patience of the Europeans and the Americans, who have been strung along since 2003, is running thin. The UN Security Council has issued an April 28 deadline to Iran for it to show it has suspended any enhancement-related activities, but threatened no consequences if Tehran disobeys.[75] The US, for now, has opted for concerted and coercive diplomacy and alliance building, although experts agree it holds little promise.

Seymour Hersh in the *New Yorker* magazine reports that concentrated planning was under way in Washington for a nuclear strike on Iranian underground facilities,[76] a claim rejected by President George Bush. Still, Bush has stated that all options are on the table.

There is still hope of derailing Iran's nuclear program through multilateral diplomacy and appeasement, but this grows dimmer by the day.

Sweetheart economic and trade packages offered by the Europeans have failed to deter Iran. So what can be done? Large-scale economic and diplomatic sanctions could be invoked as well as naval blockades and border controls. But China, which has concluded a multi-billion dollar trade deal with Tehran and Russia, including arms, is likely to veto such a move.

It would seem a military confrontation is inevitable. The Europeans have gone as far as they can in soft-power negotiations and now look weak. Yet bombing Iran is not guaranteed to do the job. The only military option almost certain to halt Iran's weapons program is a full-scale US invasion and occupation, but no one is publicly touting such a major step. Further, an attack would diminish US support in the Arab world and terrorist attacks would increase.

Iran has ballistic missiles capable of reaching most Middle East countries and a well-developed army of 350,000 soldiers and 125,000 Revolutionary Guards.

The West needs to develop a careful, step-by-step and realistic approach to Iran. It needs to make it clear that if Iran continues on its apocalyptic path it will face dire consequences.

Otherwise, the day when Iran possesses the bomb is not too far off.

The Second Lebanon War: truth gone missing

July 28, 2006

Though much ink has been poured in the Australian media over the escalating situation in Lebanon, most of the core points and various truths have been noticeably missing.

Largely forgotten was the fact that most key players in the region want Hezbollah defanged and know what needs to be done in the critical battle against radical Islamic terror (even the hypocritical Russia, which has agreed to sell missiles to Syria, Iran and Hamas, signed the G8 summit communiqué blaming Hezbollah for the violence) but are busy wringing their hands, happy to let Israel do the job. Israel has gotten the go-ahead from most countries because the world knows that the battle against Hezbollah is part of the global war on terror and that Syria and Iran are the real commanders and transhipment points in Hezbollah's supply chain. What happens in Israel will not stay in Israel.

Also sidelined was the stunning decision by Egypt, Saudi Arabia, Jordan, Kuwait, UAE and Iraq to effectively side with Israel instead of the usual blanket condemnation. The Arab states are concerned about Hezbollah threatening their own regimes.

Very few at the communication forefront mentioned that the timing of the Gilad Shalit kidnapping and the fomenting of this conflagration was directed at diverting attention from Iran's pending referral to the Security Council for sanctions over its nuclear program.

The quartet of Iran, Syria, Hamas and Hezbollah are testing Prime Minister Olmert's nerves and the Israeli people's resolve, thinking that the Israelis will roll over.

Israel is fighting fanatical Islamists with genocidal goals. Therefore, the talk of negotiation or a ceasefire is odd. Is anyone suggesting Australia negotiate with Jemma Islamia or that the US negotiate with al-Qaeda? A ceasefire will not mean an end to hostilities, but rather will provide Hezbollah with a time-out necessary to replenish their stocks and perhaps find a more powerful weapon. Hezbollah cannot be appeased. As World War II has shown, peace usually follows victory.

The lesson to be learned is that no security wall can protect against missiles. Olmert would now be hesitant about withdrawing from the West Bank and putting major Israeli populations within range of destructive rockets. Past unilateral withdrawals have simply emboldened Hamas and its allies who have perceived such steps as signs of weakness and surrender.

Taking a backseat in the media discourse was how Hezbollah thumbed its nose at the September 2004 UN Security Council Resolution 1559, calling for it to disarm and to allow the Lebanese Army to assert control of South Lebanon.[77]

I did not hear anyone mention the one million Israeli Arabs, who enjoy full political and civil rights, more than their brethren in Syria, Iran or Gaza, whom Israeli soldiers are now fighting to protect against the rockets fired by Hezbollah.

During the ABC radio community forum held in Melbourne last week, several participants raised the issue of occupation as precipitating this conflict. Yet, since Israel has withdrawn from Gaza and Lebanon the weakness of this argument has been unmasked. Indeed, analysts have observed that it is precisely Israeli absence from those areas that has created a vacuum leading to this lawlessness. As one Israeli official noted, 'What positive inducement can we give the Palestinians – pull out of Gaza?'[78] Consider, since the disengagement, not a day has passed without rockets being launched at Israel. Hamas, waving Eliyahu Asheri's identity card and demanding concessions, did so while the young man was buried in the ground.[79]

The real occupation that provokes Hamas and Hezbollah is the occupation of Tel Aviv and Haifa by Jews. Certainly, when Hezbollah crossed the UN-recognised border to kidnap and kill Israeli soldiers, it simply carried out Iran's program of obliterating the state of Israel. As Newt Gingrich put it, 'This is the 58th year of the war to destroy Israel'.[80]

Remember that Hezbollah cooperates with Al Qaeda and that before 9/11 it was the group responsible for more American deaths than any other terrorist group. Recall the 1983 killing of 241 marines in Beirut, or the bombing of American embassies in Beirut and Kuwait or the hijacking of TWA flight 847, in which officer

Robert Stethem was shot and thrown out of the aircraft.

Lebanon is not a mere bystander – her US ambassador confirmed Hezbollah is part of Lebanon and the government. I hate to shatter illusions, but when a volley of rockets is fired from your country, you are responsible. Lebanon, squandering the Cedar Revolution, needs to take a hard look at itself and ask how it got here.

Every extremist of every stripe is watching this 'local skirmish' for inspiration to spread more mayhem. It is a waste of time to try to moderate terrorist groups such as Hezbollah, Jemma Islamia, and Al Qaeda or award their militancy with power as is the case with Hamas. A victory for Israel is a victory for Australia and the western world.

Last chance for the United Nations?

September 27, 2006

As the United Nations looks for its next secretary-general to replace Kofi Annan at the end of the year, the organisation is rocked by failures and scandals.

One of the UN's core goals is to protect human rights and yet the UN Commission on Human Rights (UNCHR) has dictators and tyrants deciding on its membership. At one point, Libya provided the UNCHR's chairman, and Sudan, Cuba, Saudi Arabia, Zimbabwe and China were members, refusing to introduce basic respect for human rights as criteria for membership. Finally, The UNHRC was scrapped after Mr Annan dubbed it an embarrassment and called for its replacement.[81] It was replaced by the UN Human Rights Council which, since June, has focused exclusively on Israel. That renamed body too has been impotent regarding events in the Sudan, even refusing to accept that the events in Darfur amount to genocide.[82]

Whereas Israel, the only democracy in the Middle East, is the most condemned nation in UN history, the horrific situation in Burma has not so much as been put on the Human Rights Council's agenda.

Commentator Mark Steyn asserts that the council looks like a lifetime achievement awards ceremony for world torturers[83] while author Joshua Muravchik has declared: 'in 1000 ways the UN acts as a kind of permanent pogrom against the Jewish state'.[84]

The US, the UN's biggest financial supporter, has been the target of rampant anti-Americanism. UN Under-Secretary General Shashi Tharoor, who is a candidate for secretary-general, noted that it was American power that might well be the central issue in the world.[85] Not AIDS, famine, immunising kids, genocide or the environment, but the US. Jean Ziegler, elected to the UN Commission on the Promotion and Protection of Human Rights, has called the US an imperialist dictatorship and denounced the US on food issues.[86]

Last April, Iran was elected as vice-chairman on the UN disarmament commission and a day later announced it had enriched uranium. This year, Kofi Annan has travelled to Iran to shake hands with the Iranian President,[87] a leader who wants to wipe Israel off the map and is a Holocaust denier.

The UN has also been weak on terrorism. UN peacekeepers on the Israel-Lebanon border shared the same telephones and water supplies with Hezbollah, with the two flags flying side by side. Incredibly, the vice-chairman of the UN Counter-Terrorism Committee has refused to condemn terrorism.[88] And a committee established to react to terrorist states has failed to name one terrorist and one organisation in five years. The UN Relief and Works Agency for Palestinian Refugees has hired members of the Fatah, Hamas and Islamic Jihad, despite their terrorist links.[89] Few have confidence in the UN peacekeeping ability and in preventing genocide. Kofi Annan was UN director of peacekeeping when one million were slaughtered in Rwanda and Yugoslavia. He failed to intervene in the massacre of thousands in Srebrenica, which was designated as a haven with Dutch peacekeepers.[90]

The UN-imposed ceasefire in Lebanon last month serves as a reminder that a UN force has been monitoring the border for nearly 30 years with a dismal record. UNIFIL soldiers in Lebanon will not have the power to disarm Hezbollah, search for any arms cache, or patrol the Syrian border to intercept arms smuggling.

The underlying problem with the United Nations is that out of 191 members, only 50 members are democracies. This means that the majority of voting nations are non-democratic and include despotic leaders who are able to outvote the democratic countries and enjoy the same standing as free nations. Perhaps it is time for a council of democracies, the United Democratic Nations, as advocated for by US Senator Bill Frist.[91]

Slowly but surely hearts are turning

March 31, 2008

The heartbreaking and seemingly intractable Israeli-Palestinian conflict seems to embody W. B. Yeats' feeling that 'Too long a sacrifice can make a stone of a heart'.[92] And indeed, the situation in Gaza may have reinforced people's perception that hatred, irreconcilable differences and hopelessness is the prevailing mood between Israelis and Palestinians.

Yet, another tale is slowly emerging. Although the news reports tend to zero in on the religious division, tension and violence, the truth is that reconciliation efforts between Israelis and Arabs are quietly gathering momentum. Small and faithful acts of hope form part of a continuum of peace-making possibilities, propelled forward by tireless warriors who are driven by the belief that the mightiest tree may grow from the tiniest seed.

Determined not to allow extremists such as Hezbollah and Hamas to win, Israelis and Palestinians have been doggedly attempting to build peace from the ground up, breaking through the years of distrust and suspicion and boldly trekking towards co-existence.

Consider the Open House initiative, a centre situated in the Arab town of Ramle that is devoted to building trust and friendships between Muslim and Jewish children.[93] Among its programs is a summer camp for 100 Jewish and Arab teenagers and an Arab and Jewish parents' network, as well as a day-care centre for Arab children.

In Neve Shalom/Wahat al-Salam (Oasis of Peace), a Nobel peace prize-nominated community in Israel founded in 1972, Palestinians Arabs and Israelis live harmoniously side by side and teach their children the histories and national narratives of both peoples.[94]

The eminent Israeli conductor Daniel Barenboim has created the West-Eastern Divan Orchestra,[95] an ensemble of young Jewish and Arab musicians, including participants from the Palestinian territories, Syria and Egypt. The collection of talented players has performed in Britain, Brazil and Argentina.

In the spirit of building understanding and unity, four Israelis and four Palestinians scaled an icy mountain and braved rough seas in Antarctica as part of the Breaking the Ice expedition in 2004. After reaching the top, the group named the snow-capped point Mountain of Israeli-Palestinian Friendship. Their joint statement read: 'We have proved that Palestinians and Israelis can cooperate with one another with mutual respect and trust ... We hereby declare that our people can and deserve to live together in peace and friendship.'[96]

Then there is Hello, Salaam! Hello, Shalom!, a telephone hotline that allows Israelis and Palestinians to talk with someone on the other side. Within the first seven months of the launch, more than 80,000 people from across Israel and the Palestinian areas have called the line talking for a total of about 300,000 minutes.

Particularly significant is the Pathways to Reconciliation project, an inspiring program that sends about 80 Israeli Jews, Israeli Arabs and Palestinian educators to Turkey each year to take part in a conference entitled Continuing Dialogue in Times of Crisis. When they return, the teachers work to strengthen the peace education program that has been running for twelve years in 60 Palestinian and Jewish high schools. Much of the program's power comes from the tremendous change it brings about in the mindset of the participants.[97]

In June 2003, a group of about 250 Israeli Jews, Israeli Arabs, Palestinians, and Jews and Muslims from France took part in a four-day journey to the Nazi death camps of Auschwitz-Birkenau and Krakow. Amid the ghastly images, the group walked along the railway tracks where the diabolical selections of Jews had taken place; they then entered the gas chambers, the crematoriums and prisoners' huts. After hearing the testimonies of survivors, the group erected a small memorial near the Death Wall, where Jews were lined up and shot. Then, Arab participants read out the names of the mission's Jewish members' relatives who perished there. At this moment of shared charity and compassion, the delegation began singing traditional songs of the Holocaust.[98]

One cannot avoid mentioning the bereaved parents who have lost loved ones to spasms of violence. Israeli Roni Hirshenson lost his eldest son, Amir, in a bus bombing, only to lose his second son, Elad, when he committed suicide after his best friend was killed in a bombing. Rather than choose vengeance, the shattered father remarkably chose reconciliation, believing that only by erecting common interests between Israelis and Palestinians can the senseless slayings stop. He heads the Parents' Circle Relations committee,[99] an interfaith organisation composed of bereaved Jewish parents and Palestinian bereaved parents who have lost children to the protracted violence. The group has lectured to more than 50,000 students, in addition to staging political rallies and donating blood to each other's hospitals.

Let's hope that reconciliation continues, an endeavour that, in the words of Abraham Lincoln, 'the world will forever applaud, and God must forever bless'.

Happy 60th birthday Israel

May 8, 2008

Putting aside for a fleeting moment the Israeli-Palestinian conflict, neither simplifying nor exaggerating, you realise that even for the most cynical among us, the rebirth of the modern state of Israel 60 years ago ranks as one of the most inspiring events of the 20th century.

In fact, Israel's triumph rivals the narrative recounted in the Book of Exodus.

Born in the shadow of the Holocaust and from the seeds of the Diaspora, Israel vividly illustrates the triumph of justice over evil, life over death. Carried in the hearts and minds of Jews for thousands of years, against all odds it became a reality in a declaration of independence made from the balcony of a Tel Aviv Art Museum.

Israel's founding fathers took one of history's great gambles and won. Its survival, in a hostile region and through a series of wars, is a feat that could not be, and was not taken for granted for much of its life. It is a testament to the wonders of the human effort.

At first, the so-called experts proclaimed that the creation and arrival of a new state called Israel on the international scene would never take place. And when they were proven wrong and it did happen, they predicted that it would never survive. And when it survived, they said it would never last.

It is small wonder that Nelson Mandela was so moved by Israel's leaders that he required all African National Congress leaders to read the writings of Golda Meir and Menachem Begin. The Dalai Lama, on his visit to Israel, has said how in their struggle for cultural and religious survival, the Tibetans have drawn inspiration from the Jews.

A people who had no military experience, who were subject to persecution by their local governments, and who lived for centuries without a central political authority, have learned to protect their children and to control their own destiny.

The 1976 Entebbe rescue symbolised the importance of Israel as the defender of Jews everywhere. After the spectacular raid the French pilot Michael Bacos was asked if he ever thought the Israeli army would fly thousands of kilometres to rescue the hostages. He looked at the cameras and said, 'Who else?'[100]

And in two operations, Israel airlifted more than 22,000 Ethiopian Jews in peril and brought them to safety in Israel. In 1950, the Israeli parliament passed the Law of Return, the first universal immigration law in history, granting every Jew who needs and wants automatic citizenship. Putting out the welcome mat without hesitation, after the Holocaust, Israel absorbed millions of immigrants from every corner of the globe, including more than one million Soviet Jews in the 1990s.

After its population was reduced by one third between 1939 and 1944 in the murderous hands of the Nazis, Israel rapidly absorbed millions of immigrants so now the population is more than a tenfold of what it was.

In contrast to the stinginess of spirit of the majority of wealthy nations, Israel put out the welcome mat without hesitation. The day is not far off when the majority of Jews in the world will live within the country borders.

A people of many tongues revived a language that was moribund and limited to prayer, breathing new life into this age-old entity, knowing deep in their hearts that the nation needed a vernacular that would unite it.

A tiny state with big problems that, despite having to devote massive parts of resources to defence in six wars, has managed to build a robust democracy, institutions of world renown in the medical, agricultural, scientific and cultural areas and a booming, high-tech economy. It has been noted that parts of Israel are now indistinguishable from Silicon Valley.

Consider inventions developed in Israel and by Israelis: instant messaging, voice mail, Microsoft's NT Windows, small ingestible video cameras used in medical operations, firewall security, drip irrigation, Intel wireless computer chips, the mobile phone (Motorola's biggest R&D centre is in Israel), a fully computerised diagnostic machine for breast cancer, camera phone chip technology, a computerised prescription system, tsunami detection systems, a device that assists the heart to pump blood, smart faucets, and the list goes on.

Israel has developed in every way imaginable, a flourishing oasis in a desert that now produces wines sold in Australia. Israeli art has burst into bloom with undiminished energy, boasting a mosaic of diverse voices and viewpoints that are trailblazing a path in the global arena. Israeli films are screened around the world and are regularly nominated for Oscars. A multi-ethnic, multicultural land of astonishing promises, memories and visions, Israel is endlessly interesting and attractive. A study in contradictions, it is a fusion of the temporary and the eternal, secular and Orthodox.

Nothing has been easy for Israel. On May 14, 1948, as Ben Gurion declared the new state's independence, warplanes rumbled overhead, attacking within five hours.

In a land holy to the three great religions, extremists constantly seek to derail and torpedo reconciliation initiatives, denying the simple pleasure of co-existence to Jews and Arabs who yearn for quiet, normal lives for their families.

The Israeli people have never claimed perfection. Mistakes are inevitable. A democracy in a region where government of the people, by the people and for the people is an alien and often despised concept, Israel has through the last six decades struggled to achieve a secure peace against a backdrop of overwhelming animosity.

Most astoundingly, its passion and yearning for a just peace has never diminished as a range of treaties, peace conferences and territorial withdrawals have demonstrated. Israelis have shown unmistakable courage, putting aside old grievances, resisting the old habits of mistrusts, working to break the cycle of violent provocation and retribution. A country that has a tremendous amount to celebrate but constantly worries about its neighbours gate-crashing with bombs or missiles.

At 60, Israel remains beleaguered, surrounded by an encircling wall of enmity. There is no peace with Syria; beyond the horizon Iran calls for the destruction of the state while pursuing a nuclear agenda; Hezbollah, on the border of Lebanon is re-arming, ready to lob missiles into Israeli cities. And the long twilight struggle against the radical missile builders of Hamas across the border who might be brewing a third intifada in the West Bank and Gaza has compounded Israelis' sense of vulnerability. It has led them to ask whether territorial compromise will finally end the tragic deadlock with the Palestinians or make the next war harder to win.

And still, contrary to its foes' expectations, Israel has not collapsed.

Sixty, a heartbeat in the long sweep of Jewish civilisation, is nevertheless a milestone that would doubtless make Kings Saul, David and Solomon weep for joy.

President Obama and Israel

June 12, 2009

It's a brave new world in US-Israel relations with dark skies replacing the blue skies of the Bush era.

The general consensus from the Netanyahu-Obama May meeting is that the American President gave the Israeli PM the cold shoulder. Indeed, this issue is turning into one hell of a kafuffle. Obama has demanded a complete construction freeze to settlements and has labelled Israel's pro-settlement activities as counter to America's national security. Netanyahu apparently told Obama that Israel cannot 'freeze life' in existing settlements and told the Knesset's Foreign Affairs and Defence Committee that 'there are reasonable requests and unreasonable requests'.[101]

Why is Obama focusing on Israel rather than on de-nuking North Korea and Iran, as well as on a resurgent Taliban, a fragile Pakistan with nuclear weapons, a Turkey vulnerable to Islamism, a still broken Iraq and an intransigent Syria who only this month rejected American gestures?

To many, such a confrontational approach indicates that Obama is trying to bring down the Netanyahu government, knowing that for certain coalition partners, especially Liberman's Yisrael Beitenu, such a move will be a deal-breaker. Commentator Aaron David Miller believes that the current White House:

> may be less concerned with actually getting to negotiations and an agreement and more interested in setting new rules and rearranging the furniture. They may have concluded that they can't get to a real two-state solution with this prime minister. Maybe they want a new one? And the best way to raise the odds of that is to demonstrate that he can't manage Israel's most important relationship: with the US.[102]

Obama's policy represents a blunt and profound departure. Hilary Clinton is now using language such as colonisation in the West Bank. The White House is supposedly weighing up sanctions to compel Israel to sing their tune. They could include an end to near US support of Israel in the UN, re-evaluating loan guarantees and less cooperation with Israel on security matters. As Israeli journalist Eitan Haber put it, 'We're in trouble.'[103]

Obama reminds me of Bill Clinton. Clinton, as Obama now, thought that because he was young and smart he could solve the intractable conflict by imposing his own agenda on the region, instead of realising that this dispute must be worked out by the two sides through reciprocal steps. Obama, who in his speech at Cairo University[104] stressed his vision of reconciliation between the West and Islam, wants to show the Arab world that he can secure a new peace deal by pressuring Israel to come to the party. It's no coincidence that Obama's first trip to the Middle East was to Cairo and not Jerusalem.

There is zero evidence to suggest that a settlement freeze would lead to peace with the Palestinians and would cause Hezbollah, Hamas, Islamic Jihad and the Arab states to accept a Jewish state. Palestinian society is divided with no agreed leadership to represent them. Abbas is idly sitting by, figuring that if he waits long enough Israel will concede more territory. This is after he turned down Prime Minister Ehud Olmert's offer of 97 per cent of the West Bank. Consider that Abbas still, from time to time, calls for armed struggle against Israel and is unwilling to end incitement.

Netanyahu is between a rock and a hard place. He has to contend with a volcanic reaction if he goes against the settlers or defies Obama. Of course, he can point to the understanding reached with the previous Bush administration that permitted Israel to build in East Jerusalem, and within the physical boundaries of existing West Bank settlements as part of natural growth. He could ask Obama why Israel should give up something tangible for nothing of value. Freebies are good for TV game shows, but not when it concerns the future survival of a state. Bibi could also mention the thanks Israel got for its disengagement from Gaza, the wisdom of following US policy (Secretary State Condi Rice insisted on democratic elections in Gaza and left Israel with a Hamas government and rocket bombardment) and the logical expectation that discussion on settlements be part of broad negotiations on a spectrum of issues. He can also appeal to the American Congress which houses more seasoned and sober politicians.

Bibi can also ask Obama what will happen if in two years his initiative fails and Israel is once again left to deal with the fallout.

Will the Israel-bashing ever come to an end?

October 2, 2009

You sometimes have to wonder if Israel-bashing will ever stop. A disturbing campaign, known as 'Boycott, Divestment, Sanctions' (BDS) recently hit the headlines with a LA Times op-ed by Neve Gordon, Head of the Department of Politics and Government at Ben-Gurion University. Gordon labelled Israel an apartheid state that should be boycotted to 'save Israel from itself.'[105]

Gordon was condemned by many, including Rivka Carmi, President of BGU, who wrote that Gordon's article crossed the boundaries of academic freedom and that the boycott would demolish the 'very fabric of the society that he claims to want to protect'.[106] Gordon, who has previously voiced doubts about Arafat's link to terrorism, acted as a human shield in Arafat's Ramallah compound (where he was shown holding hands with him) and wrote a letter to *Haaretz* in which he asserted that Israel and Barak only understand violence and that the Arabs should therefore employ it more often.

Locally, the BDS has been promoted by Associate Professor Jake Lynch of the Centre for Peace and Conflict Studies at Sydney University (who awarded John Pilger the Sydney Peace Prize[107]) and by Anthony Lowenstein.

A closer look at the BDS movement reveals its true intent. It is based on the 2008 Bilbao Initiative that declares that Israel is 'a state which is built on the massive ethnic cleansing of 1948' and that, 'Israel's regime is a system that uniquely combines apartheid, settler-colonialism and belligerent occupation'.[108]

The BDS, which selectively reads history and airbrushes terror against Israel, calls Israel's actions in Gaza genocide, and strives for the 'prosecution and punishment of Israeli perpetrators of war crimes and crimes against humanity'.

Arguing for the right of return of more than four million Palestinians to Israel, if you follow the BDS logic, its proponents envisage Israelis living under a Hamas or Fatah government. The argument that Israel should cease to exist as the Jewish state is very fashionable. The 2007 Haifa Declaration, signed by Israeli Arabs, calls for the abolition of the Jewish state and the return of Palestinian refugees,[109] while Historian Uri Ram maintains that the Jews have no more of a claim to Palestine than do the British to India.[110]

The Gordon episode reveals the deep-seated hostility to Israel to be found among Israeli and Jewish intellectuals. In 2007 *Haaretz* editor David Landau told US Secretary of State Condoleezza Rice that Israel 'wants to be raped by the US'.[111] Canadian writer Naomi Klein, in a recent book-tour to Israel, visited the Palestinian village of Bilin, and observed that the boycott was a tactic to 'threaten the very idea of what the Israeli state is'.[112]

Then there is a group of American rabbis who established *Ta'anit Tzedek* – Jewish Fast for Gaza.[113] It backs dialogue with Hamas and doesn't understand why Israel insists that Hamas recognise the Jewish state's right to exist. Notice that there is no fast for the people of North Korea, Iran or Darfur. Professor Bill Freedman of Haifa University has claimed that Israel is descending into anti-democratic fascism.[114]

The BDS conveniently overlooks the fact that Israeli leaders (Barak and more recently Olmert) offered huge territorial concessions and that the vast majority of Israelis endorse a two-state solution. It forgets to mention that after leaving the Gaza Strip Israel suffered thousands of rocket attacks into its sovereign borders designed to kill civilians, and that Hamas used human shields in concealing its military bases in civilian centres.

The BDS includes an academic boycott, unfairly singling out and castigating scholars based on their nationality, religion and ethnicity. When in 2005, the Association of University Teachers in Britain voted for a similar boycott, Elie Wiesel stated, 'Academic freedom has never been the property of the few and must not be manipulated by them …'[115] If supporters of the BDS were concerned about freedom in the Middle East, wouldn't Israel, which is a democracy, be the obvious starting point?

Israeli intellectuals are at the forefront of actively working for peace, collaborating with Palestinians and fostering dialogue. Consider also that Palestinian academics and scholars in countries with questionable human rights record have not being targeted. The BDS doesn't advocate cutting ties with Russian, Chinese, Yugoslavian and Turkish academics over Chechnya, Tibet, Bosnia and Cyprus.

I wonder why.

O Jerusalem
December 25, 2009

If respected Israeli journalist Yossi Melman had his way, Israel would give up Jerusalem as its capital, albeit temporarily. According to Melman's plan, published this month in *Haaretz*,[116] Israel should move its capital to another city, say Tel Aviv, or Beer-Sheva perhaps. Visiting prime ministers/presidents will be received there and government and Knesset gatherings will be held there too. Melman's rationale is that Jerusalem is the perennial obstacle to settlement, and that 'symbolically, suspension of Jerusalem as capital will neutralise the religious basis of this bloody conflict'.[117] Besides, Melman concludes, the last 42 years of Israeli sovereignty has led to Jerusalem becoming 'one of the poorest, dirtiest and most failed cities in Israel' and even Saudi Arabia did not choose Mecca or Medina, Muslim's holiest cities as its capital, but rather Riyadh.

This kind of a *night shelter* solution should not come as a shock to anyone. The rumblings around dividing Jerusalem are becoming louder and louder. President Obama has this year delayed any moves to relocate the US embassy in Israel from Tel Aviv to Jerusalem, despite assuring the American Israel Public Affairs Committee on June 4, 2008 as a senator that 'Jerusalem will remain the capital of Israel, and it must remain undivided'.[118] No wonder Netanyahu had this to say when he met Obama in May of this year, 'The new US administration informs us with intolerable ease that we have to give up Jerusalem.'[119]

And two weeks ago, European foreign ministers voted for a proposal that envisioned Jerusalem as the future capital of both Israel and a Palestinian state.[120] The EU statement was a softening of a Swedish draft that declared eastern Jerusalem as the capital of a future Palestinian state. The original Swedish draft did not recognise that Israel has any rights in East Jerusalem or Western Jerusalem and would have led ultimately to anyone wanting to visit the Western Wall to produce a passport and cross a border manned by Palestinian soldiers. Its Foreign Minister Carl Bidt has told Israel the EU was united on the issue of Jerusalem and warned Israel not to try and play 'divide and rule'.[121] Sweden, which holds the EU presidency, is hardly an honest broker. When four months ago, the Swedish daily *Aftonbladet* published a blood libel claiming that the IDF was harvesting the organs of Palestinians, the Swedish government stood by and said nothing.[122] Luxemburg's Foreign Minister summed up the European feeling when he told journalists that he could not understand why Israel did not accept that Palestine included the West Bank, Gaza and East Jerusalem.

One wonders why the Europeans feel they have the authority and jurisdiction to decide how Jerusalem should be divided. After all, Europe's record in Jewish history and its concern for Israel's safety are, shall we say, problematic. The EU resolution, coming just days after Netanyahu announced a ten-month freeze on construction in West Bank settlements,[123] is reflective of the international mood and is highly problematic. For one thing, it presupposes the future status of Jerusalem even before negotiations have resumed. Secondly, it does not recognise that there could be changes in the pre-1967 borders, ignoring resolution 242 that acknowledged that the 1967 lines were only armistice lines and may change.

In his response to the Swedish proposal, Jerusalem mayor Nir Barkat called on the EU to back an open city that allows more than the 3.4 billion people 'to visit Jerusalem and practise their faith freely without a division of the sort that devastated the city of Berlin.'[124]

In the same spirit, PM Benjamin Netanyahu has made it clear where he stands. In a 2009 Jerusalem Day ceremony he stated, 'United Jerusalem is Israel's capital. Jerusalem was always ours and will always be ours. It will never again be partitioned and divided.'[125] In September, the Knesset voted to approve a 'continuity law', beginning the process which would obligate any government to go to a referendum before withdrawing from East Jerusalem, giving citizens a say on such a crucial issue.[126]

There is a clear message for the Israeli government. It must increase its diplomatic efforts to explain Israel's rights in the city and to stress the way it has protected the holy sites. A history lesson about the fact that when Jordan ruled the Old City from 1948 to 1967, Jews and Christians were denied access to the holy sites, and a reminder that synagogues were desecrated and destroyed and gravestone were turned into latrines is also crucial. A recent BBC radio documentary that ignored the Jews' ancient connection to Jerusalem and gave the impression that it is the Jews who are the newcomers to the city should set the alarm bells off.

If the government fails to do so, the support for a divided Jerusalem will become the consensus. Even in Israel.

Is it time for the UN to be scrapped?

January 25, 2010

Even those who applaud the work the UN does are honest enough to admit that there is much wrong about the way it behaves and its moral authority.

For those who follow the UN, a recent Associated Press investigation that the UN 'cut back sharply on investigations into corruption and fraud within its ranks, shelving cases involving the possible theft or misuse of millions of dollars'[127] is not surprising.

Even those who applaud the work the UN does are honest enough to admit that there is much wrong about the way it behaves and its moral authority. When its founders met in San Francisco in 1945 they had noble aspirations in mind, hoping, as its charter states, to 'save future generations from the scourge of war'.[128] Sadly, the news is not good. When it comes to global peace and security – the purpose for which it was founded – any assessment of the UN's merits must reflect on its tattered record and its series of failures that have cost millions of lives. Indeed, there are many grounds for reproach and regret in the body's conduct in the face of ethnic cleansing.

The UN's hand-wringing and passive response to the genocide in Darfur, where hundreds of thousands have died and 1.7 million have been driven from their home, has further damaged its fragile credibility. China and Russia, members of the Security Council, reject even threatening sanctions against Sudan because they do not want to jeopardise their commercial relations with the Sudanese government (China has huge oil interests in Southern Sudan). Imagine how many lives could have been saved and can be saved with a modest UN force on the ground.

Equally appalling was the foot dragging that led the UN to sit out the terrible genocide in Rwanda in 1994, where close to a million people were shot and clubbed to death. General Roméo Dallaire, the Canadian commander of the UN force stationed in Rwanda, told the UN that Hutu extremists were getting ready for a campaign of 'extermination'. His proposal to confiscate the weapons stockpiled by the Hutu so as to stop the plan was vetoed by the UN's Department of Peacekeeping Operations.[129] Once the killing began,

Dallaire could have used the forces under his command to stop the massacres, but was instructed by the UN to only evacuate foreigners but no Rwandans. After issuing pious resolutions, the UN withdrew most of its forces instead of sending reinforcements.

As Michael Brandon McClellan has observed, 'In the face of evil, the United Nations encourages good men to stand aside and do nothing'.[130] The UN did nothing in Bosnia when tens of thousands of Muslim were being murdered, watching helplessly until the US began bombing Serbian military positions, forcing the Serbian forces to agree to all allied demands. In fact, the UN forces assigned to protect the Muslims of Srebrenica, who were led to believe they would be safe in the UN declared six 'safe areas', pulled out and abandoned the victims to be slaughtered.[131] And during the second Congo war, in which nearly five million people lost their lives, the UN failed to intervene effectively or carry out humanitarian aid.

Allowing Iraq to defy its will for twelve years without responding, emboldened Saadam Hussein, and left the UN badly battered. The UN's chronic failure to enforce its own seventeen resolutions against Iraq, including UN Resolution 1441,[132] a resolution of last resort, proved that it was clearly not up to the task. Under its watch North Korea has gone nuclear and Iran is soon to follow.

To this day, the UN can't agree on a new treaty against terrorism because member states can't agree on how to define it.

The UN is scandal ridden. In the Congo, Bosnia, East Timor, Cambodia and Kosovo, UN peacekeepers have been accused of raping and sexually abusing the women and children they were sent to protect.[133] Add to this the oil-for-food program which took billions intended for hungry Iraqis and gave it instead to Saddam Hussein and his henchmen to bribe French and Russian businesses and to the UN's own man in charge, Benon Savan, and a disturbing picture emerges.[134]

Consider also the farcical Human Rights Commission, now known as The Human Rights Council (UNHRC). In 2001, the US lost its seat, while tyrannical Libya and slave-owning Sudan, among the world's worst human rights abusers, have served as its chair, along with members that have included Zimbabwe, Cuba, Egypt, Eritrea, Ethiopia, Pakistan, Angola, Azerbaijan, China, Madagascar,

Qatar and Saudi Arabia. These despots and human rights violators sit in judgment on themselves and others. A bad record, it seems, is no bar to membership on this commission.

Kenneth Roth, executive director of Human Rights Watch, has complained: 'The reason highly abusive governments flock to the Commission is to prevent condemnation of themselves and their kind, and most of the time they succeed.'[135] Kofi Annan belatedly admitted that the commission, euphemistically, had a 'credibility deficit'.

There is one country that the UNHRC has focused most on: Israel.

UN scholar Anne Bayefsky has noted that the Human Rights Council has:

> Passed more resolutions and decisions condemning Israel than all other 191 UN members combined. The council has one (of only 10) formal agenda items dedicated to criticising Israel. And one agenda item to consider the human rights of the remaining 99.9 per cent of the world's population ... It has terminated human rights investigations on Belarus, Cuba, Liberia, and the Democratic Republic of the Congo. And all investigations of 'consistent patterns of gross and reliably attested violations of all human rights and all fundamental freedoms' in such states as Iran, Kyrgyzstan, the Maldives, Turkmenistan, and Uzbekistan have been 'discontinued'.[136]

No wonder that the Goldstone report (established by the UNHRC to investigate Operation Cast Lead in Gaza) has been found to be highly problematic and unreliable.

The United Nations General Assembly has been, for the most part, a platform for denunciations of Israel. In 1975, the General Assembly passed the infamous Resolution 3379 that 'Zionism is racism'[137] and which was later rescinded; it marked the anti-Israel campaign that continues to this day.

When the first declaration on religious intolerance was passed in 1981, anti-Semitism was excluded,[138] while in the infamous 2001 World Conference against Racism in Durban, references to anti-Semitism were excised from almost all of the sections in the final declaration, apart from two.[139] In November 2003 Kofi Annan refused to publicly support a proposed General Assembly declaration condemning anti-Semitism. At the 2001 UN Durban Racism Conference, Israel, out of all of the dictatorships and serial rights abusers, was singled out as a racist state.

In 2004, Israel was discussed for five straight days, under the guise of self-determination, racism and then was the only item on the Human Rights Commission's agenda dedicated in its entirety to one member state, when all 191 countries were treated jointly under a separate item.

And when in May 2004, Lakhdar Brahimi, the UN's special envoy to Iraq (who boasted that he has never knowingly shaken hands with an Israeli or a Jew) told reporters that 'the policy of Israel is a poison in the mid-East',[140] Annan's spokesman said that Brahimi was speaking in his personal capacity and brings to the table strongly held views.[141]

Until recently, Israel was the only country denied membership in any UN committees.[142]

In 2000, following Israel's withdrawal from Lebanon, three Israeli soldiers (Benny Avraham, Adi Avitan and Omar Sawaid) patrolling the UN-overseen Lebanese border were kidnapped by Hezbollah terrorists. When Israel learned that Indian peacekeepers from the United National Interim Force in Lebanon (UNIFIL) had videotaped the kidnapping, it asked for the tapes. Both UNIFIL commanders and Terje Roed-Larsen, the Secretary General's personal representative to the Middle East, said no such tape existed.[143] Eventually, the UN admitted it possessed the tape, which could have helped Israel in tracking down the kidnappers, but refused to release it, claiming it wanted to remain neutral. The UN later admitted it had a second tape related to the kidnapping. After ten months of intense pressure, it allowed Israeli officials to view the tapes. Ultimately, the three soldiers were pronounced murdered. When the US House Middle East Subcommittee convened a hearing on the deaths of the three Israeli soldiers, its chair Representative Ileana Ros-Lehtinen lambasted the United Nations for helping the Hezbollah terrorists.[144] The tapes were of vital importance to Israel since it was believed that the Hezbollah terrorists were disguised as UN peacekeepers and were therefore able to lure the soldiers.

Indeed, against the abiding saga of continuing animosity, one wonders if perhaps the UN regrets its decision to establish the state of Israel in 1948.

Believe it or not, but three years ago Zimbabwe was elected to head the UN Commission on Sustainable Development.[145] How anyone could choose the government of Robert Mugabe, a regime that has destroyed the country's human and natural resources and starved its people, is mind-boggling. When you consider that North Korea currently sits on the executive boards of both The United Nations Children's Fund (UNICEF) and the UN Development Program, it's clear that something is not right. Two years ago, on the same day that Iran informed the world that it could now enrich uranium, it was re-elected as vice chair of the UN Disarmament Commission.[146] This was despite the UN Disarmament Commission ruling that Iran violated its non-proliferation resolutions. Eric Shawn, author of *The UN Exposed: How the United Nations Sabotages America's Security and Fails the World*[147] said of Iran's election, 'If there isn't a more blatant example of the hypocrisy and meaninglessness of some of the decisions over there, I don't know what is. You can't make this stuff up.'[148] Syria, on the US State Department's list of terrorist nations for the last 30 years, was elected as the UN Disarmament Commission recording secretary.

The United Nations Educational, Scientific and Cultural Organisation (UNESCO) has also failed to live up to its mission and founding ideals. It awarded Islam Karimov, Uzbekistan's brutal dictator (accused of murder, torture and slave labour of children) the prestigious gold Borobudur medal in 2006 for 'strengthening friendship and cooperation between nations, development of cultural and religious dialogue, and supporting cultural diversity'.[149] This was after the European Union voted in October 2005 to partially suspend its Partnership and Cooperation Agreement with Uzbekistan – the first time it has ever done so with any country.

In 2006, UNESCO awarded another tyrant, Venezuelan president Hugo Chávez, the José Martí International Prize,[150] given to those who have contributed to the 'struggle for liberty'. The prize was personally presented to Chavez by Cuban president Fidel Castro.

Perhaps the prize was for Chavez taking to the UN stage and calling President Bush the devil, saying, 'it smells of sulfur still today'[151] a day after Bush addressed the world body. And just this month, UNESCO sponsored a conference in Beirut that gave international 'resistance organisations' such as Hezbollah a forum to attack Israel and the United States.[152]

Last October, Farouk Hosny, Egypt's Minister for Culture, narrowly lost his bid to become UNESCO's next director-general after he was considered a shoo-in to win the election. In May 2008, Hosny publicly vowed to personally burn any Israeli books found in Egyptian libraries,[153] a pledge that led several leading intellectuals and peace activists, including Nobel Prize winner Elie Wiesel, to call on the UN to 'spare itself the shame' of choosing such a leader.[154] Reporters Without Borders, the journalism watchdog, said Hosni did not show his support for the freedom of expression – one of UNESCO's underlying missions – and said that he was 'one the main actors of censorship in Egypt'.[155] After his loss Hosni blamed 'Zionist pressures' and an unnamed group of Jewish leaders who wielded influence on the elections.

The real problem is that the UN does not distinguish between brutal dictatorships such as North Korea or Syria, and free, democratic societies such as Australia. There are fewer than 50 democracies among its 192 members.

To put it bluntly, any genocidal, theocratic or terrorist state is welcomed. That is why Iran's President, Mahmoud Ahmadinejad, who denies the Holocaust and has openly called for Israel to be wiped off the map, has been twice invited to speak from the United Nations General Assembly podium. His 2009 speech, in which he accused Jews of seeking to 'establish a new form of slavery and harm the reputation of other nations ... to attain its racist ambitions'[156] was full of anti-Israeli and anti-Semitic language which prompted eleven countries to walk out, including Australia, the USA, New Zealand, Great Britain and France.[157]

A few days later Israel's PM, Benjamin Netanyahu, hit back at Ahmadinejad's questioning of the Holocaust. He held up the protocol of the 1942 conference at Wannsee, Berlin, where senior Nazis decided on the extermination of European Jewry, and the blueprints for Auschwitz, including gas chambers and crematoria – where more than one million Jews were murdered. Netanyahu castigated UN delegates who remained for Ahmadinejad's speech:

> To those who gave this Holocaust-denier a hearing, I say on behalf of my people, the Jewish people, and decent people everywhere: Have you no shame? Have you no decency? A mere six decades after the Holocaust, you give legitimacy to a man who denies that the murder of six million Jews took place and pledges to wipe out the Jewish state. What a disgrace! What a mockery of the charter of the United Nations![158]

One of the suggestions put forward is that democracies stand united in campaigning more vigorously for human rights initiatives and attempt to change the membership qualifications so as to exclude cruel and authoritarian regimes. Former presidential candidate, Senator John McCain, has called for the establishment of a League of Democracies, 'a group of 'like-minded nations working together in the cause of peace'.[159] However, the idea of a United Democratic Nations to substitute the UN has not been pursued seriously by any country.

With a budget of $3 billion and a staff of some 15,000 the Secretary-General of the UN does not lack resources to take a strong stance on a host of issues and to act decisively. Money is not the problem.

The UN has often been derided as an ageing toothless tiger in decline, an undemocratic, inefficient, secretive, unaccountable body that needs to take a long, hard, unbiased look at itself. The question is whether the UN's time is up.

Memo to Obama: This is not the way

March 18, 2010

Yes, the timing of Israel's announcement to continue to build new homes for its expanding population in the East Jerusalem neighbourhood of Ramat Shlomo (where 16,000 Israelis already live) during Vice President's Joe Biden's visit[160] was unfortunate.

Yes, many were rolling their eyes at this diplomatic blunder.

But given that the United States has openly said that it is committed to the parties working out the ultimate legal ownership of the land in final status negotiations, why the overly harsh, over-the-top language by Secretary of State Hilary Clinton? The US condemnation is even odder given that the US has exempted Jerusalem from the settlement freeze. Consider also that Clinton knew that Netanyahu was not responsible for the timing, and that he is subject to an unruly coalition.

One can venture the observation that there was no need for Secretary of State Clinton to rebuke Netanyahu during the 45 minute conversation the pair had and then make public the tone and content of that slap in the face.[161] This type of rebuke has not been directed at such dictatorships as Syria, Iran, Hamas and North Korea. Furthermore, when the President of Syria Bashar-al Assad, President of Iran Mahmoud Ahmadinejad, Hezbollah leader Hassan Nasrallah met in Damascus earlier this year and issued anti-American statements and repeated their desire to destroy Israel,[162] Clinton said nothing.

To his credit, Netanyahu has apologised. And several months ago, he agreed to stop construction of settlements in the West Bank. Israel has also consistently stated that it is willing and ready to return to direct negotiations with the Palestinian Authority without preconditions.

But that does not seem to satisfy the American administration. For many, such a confrontational approach indicates that Obama is attempting to bring down the Netanyahu government. Commentator Aaron David Miller believes the White House 'may be less concerned with actually getting to negotiations ... and more interested in setting new rules and rearranging the furniture'.[163]

Sadly, the Palestinians are divided, with no agreed leadership to represent them. Mahmoud Abbas is sitting idly by, after turning down Israeli Prime Minister Olmert's offer of 97 per cent of the West Bank, thinking that he if waits long enough Israel will concede even more territory. Worse, Abbas, from time to time, calls for an armed struggle against Israel, while fanning the flames of rioting on the Temple Mount.

Note that Abbas still refuses to include Israel on the maps in Palestinian text books.

And then there's Hamas, which time and again openly calls for Israel's annihilation and is busy stockpiling Iranian weapons. On the day Biden left the West Bank, the Palestinian Authority celebrated the naming of a town square in Ramallah after mass murderer Dalal Mughrabi with the participation of the Shabiba youth movement of the high schools in the Nablus region. Hasan Fakih, the person responsible for the various activities said, 'this participation was meant to reinforce values of volunteerism and loyalty to the blood of the Shahids, who sacrificed their blood for the sake of the Palestinian cause'.[164]

According to *Time* magazine, in 1978, Dalal Mughrabi 'hijacked two buses filled with tourists and sightseers, took them on a wild ride down the road toward Tel Aviv, shooting along the way at everyone in sight, and finally destroyed one bus in an orgy of fire and death. Official statistics put the dead at 37 (all but a few of them civilians, among them at least ten children) and 76 wounded.'[165]

Why such action was not seen by the American administration as an obstacle to peace is a mystery. We need to remember the understanding that Israel reached with the previous Bush administration, which permitted Israel to build in East Jerusalem, and within the physical boundaries of existing West Bank settlements, as part of natural growth. We should ask why Israel should give up something tangible when the other side will not even acknowledge its existence.

Netanyahu could mention to Obama the thanks Israel got for its disengagement from Gaza in the form of thousands of rockets, or the wisdom of following US policy (Condoleezza Rice insisted on democratic elections in Gaza and left Israel with a Hamas government and rocket bombardment),[166] or the logical expectation that discussion on settlements be part of broad negotiations on a spectrum of issues.

This blow-up by Obama and his administration will not progress peace, only slow it. It seems that what Obama needs is a little more scepticism and even-handedness. Otherwise, his peace plan will be relegated to the graveyard of other presidents' road maps to peace.

The Gaza flotilla

June 11, 2010

Oceans of ink have been poured onto the flotilla incident. By now, with the copious documentation and viewing of the video clips, the facts about the aims of those on board, their terrorist links and about what really happened on board, are gradually emerging.

But the speed and intensity with which the world recklessly rushed to blame Israel, and only Israel, and the scale and venom of the reaction, has left me speechless. Until now.

I don't know how to depict a world that clamours to indict Israel while exonerating its enemies, that uses double standards in promoting false and baseless accusations and that has forgotten history so as to use the language of the Holocaust to portray Israelis as the epitome of evil.

I don't know what to make of a world that is silent when Israelis die in homicidal bombings or rocket attacks, or a Europe that tries to seek forgiveness for its colonial past by defaming Israel time and again and is silent when atrocities are committed against Israelis. I am still shocked by intellectual and cultural figures who relentlessly denounce Israel, leading the charge for boycott and divestment, and who seek Israel's isolation.

It's hard to understand why countries, journalists and commentators have turned a blind eye to the obvious provocative nature of the Gaza Flotilla, or the role Hamas plays in the suffering of Gaza, or to its charter that calls for the destruction of Israel, or to the fact that when Egypt opened its borders with Gaza shortly after the incident, thousands of residents massed at the border, hankering to get out – only to be stopped by Hamas. It's hard to fathom why TV channels, radio stations and newspapers have sought to paint a one-sided picture that takes no account of Israel's defensive needs.

A clear-eyed examination of the facts would ask: if the Turkish convoy was only interested in delivering humanitarian supplies to Gaza, why did it not accept Israel's offer to peacefully off-load the relief in the Israeli port of Haifa for transport into Gaza? After all, Israel ships into Gaza 15,000 tonnes of food and medical supplies every week.[167]

The IHH, the Turkish group who organised the convoy, has been named in a US Federal court as having an 'important role' in the attempt to blow up an LA airport.[168] As organiser Greta Berlin confessed, the flotilla was not about humanitarian aid, but about breaking the blockade.[169] And there are links between IHH, Hamas and global jihad movements.

But beyond the actual incident, another aspect that is becoming disturbingly evident is the blistering demonisation of, and defamation against Israel. And the viciousness of such vilification by the media and international governments, who should know better, is mind-blowing. As philosopher Bernard-Henri Lévy wrote: 'The flood of hypocrisy, bad faith and, ultimately, disinformation, that seems to have just been waiting for this pretext to flow into the breach and sweep across the media worldwide – as is the case every time the Jewish state slips up and commits an error – is by no means acceptable.'[170]

How many journalists have explained that both Israel and Egypt have imposed a naval blockade of Gaza, and that Israel did so to prevent the re-arming of the Iranian-backed Hamas? How many journalists have noted that no country allows ships to enter its waters without inspection for illicit goods of military weapons and ammunition? Elie Wiesel rightly points out: 'We know that the six vessels of the flotilla were chartered by pro-Hamas groups, the initiative coming from the most militant wing of Hamas. How could Israel be sure that they did not carry weapons to kill and destroy'?[171]

How many journalists have written about Gaza being used as a base for launching thousands of rockets into Israeli towns in a murderous and relentless war of attrition? How many journalists have alerted readers to the brutal Hamas regime in Gaza that is stockpiling weapons for eventual targeting of Israeli cities, violently puts down any political opponents, and is slowly imposing fundamentalist Islamic law?

How many readers know that one of the passengers, rejecting an Israeli request to berth the ship for inspection, replied: 'Shut up and go back to Auschwitz' while another blockade runner said: 'We're helping Arabs going against the US. Don't forget 9/11, guys'.[172]

The virulent call for Jews to return to the extermination camp of

Europe provides a glaring and bloodcurdling insight into the mind-set of those on board.

And the hypocrisy is something to reflect on. The unrestrained assault on Israel is unprecedented. No other nation generates such language or focus. Consider that no similar condemnation and media attention has been applied to North Korea's recent sinking of a South Korean boat and its monstrous regime, or to Iran's pursuit of nuclear weapons and oppression of its citizens, or to the Russian invasion of Georgia, or the human rights abuse in Syria, Pakistan, Saudi Arabia, or to the Chinese treatment of the Uighurs in Xinjiang and Tibet, or to India's military occupation of Muslim Kashmir. And the list goes on.

These dictators must be sitting back and laughing at the world's reaction to the flotilla episode, given their crimes. Or as Tom Gross notes about the recent killing of an Al-Qaeda leader, 'plus his wife, three of his daughters, his granddaughter, and other men, women, and children' by an American missile strike: 'No one seems to be getting hysterical about this anywhere in the world. Now imagine if Israel had been involved ...'[173]

The EU representative for foreign affairs, Catherine Ashton, demanded an opening of the Gaza blockade. Yet, the EU, since 2002, has insisted that no one deal with Hamas until it recognised Israel's right to exist and renounced violence. Hamas has not done so. The President of Bosnia compared the Gaza blockade to the siege of Sarajevo of the 1990s where about 10,000 people died.[174]

News agency Reuters has just admitted that it cropped images so as to show Israel in a negative light.[175] In the uncut photo, you can see the hand of an unidentified commander holding a knife over an Israeli soldier lying on the deck of the ship. In the Reuters photo, the knife is missing.

And what was Fairfax Media's journalist Paul McGeough thinking when he described Israeli soldiers as hyenas.[176] Did he not feel that such a description was loaded with inflammatory bias? Could he not think of another turn of phrase? Such language is extravagantly prejudicial and hurtful, drawn from vocabulary and a time we thought had been relegated to the dustbin of history.

Veteran White House correspondent Helen Thomas told Rabbi

David Nesenoff that Israeli Jews should 'get the hell out of Palestine' and 'go home' to 'Germany, Poland'[177] – where six million people were murdered. Her on-camera comments embodied in many ways the disproportionate hostility exhibited towards the Jewish state by intelligent and educated people. Whether Thomas really meant that Israel should disappear, or that a mass expulsion of Jews should take place, is unknown. But her words echo a worrying trend in which people are openly talking about a world without Israel. And I just don't mean the Iranian President who wants Israel wiped off the map. Such incitement only fuels anti-Jewish sentiment.

Over the last week, a Jewish student wearing a yarmulke was assaulted at Sydney University. Unsurprisingly, The Northwest Intelligence Network reports: 'A palpable animosity against Israel and the Jews, most recently exacerbated by media bias with regard to the nature of the aid flotillas to Gaza, are generating a new and vicious level of anti-Semitism worldwide.'[178]

Across the Arab world, hateful and anti-Semitic newspaper cartoons have fanned the flames of intolerance. In Al-Watan, Qatar, a hook-nosed, black-hatted Jew with tentacles, clutches a bloody knife and a gun;[179] in Al Iqtisadiyya, Saudi Arabia, a flag with the Swastika is shown over a Star of David, with an image of a skull and crossbones.[180]

The Turkish government has labelled the Israeli raid a massacre, and likened it to 9/11. Its ambassador to the US said last Friday that Hamas is a key and necessary part of the 'Final solution' to the Israeli-Palestinian conflict.[181] Such comments, inadvertent as they may be, would horrify those who know history. Turkey, part of NATO, who wants to become a member of the EU, would do well to avoid its self-righteous outbursts and look back at its past – specifically the Armenian Genocide and the way it has treated the Kurdish Independence movement that by some estimates has so far led to the death of 40,000 lives.

Thankfully, the history books are slowly being corrected. Here is what Tony Blair, special envoy of the Quartet of Middle East peace mediators said yesterday about the flotilla incident: 'There's no question that there are rockets fired from Gaza and that there are people in Gaza who want to kill innocent Israelis. When it comes to security, I'm 100 per cent on Israel's side. Israel has the right to inspect what goes into Gaza.'[182] Kuwaiti journalist Abdallah Al-Hadlaq agrees, arguing that the outcome of the Israeli navy's operation was, 'in direct proportion to the violence'[183] of the flotilla activists. He further notes that the flotilla organisers are known to have ties with global and regional terror organisations.

Robert Fulford tries to explain the enmity towards Israel by quoting from *The Israel Test*,[184] a book by George Gilder. Fulford writes: 'Without oil, beset by passionate enemies, Israel has nevertheless achieved astonishing, unprecedented success. It now stands second only to the United States in microchips, telecom, software, biotech, medical devices and renewable energy. Per capita, it's easily the most innovative country on the planet.'[185] Fulford ends his article with this question: 'Gilder's "Israel test" asks how others respond to this achievement. Do we study, admire and emulate it? Or do we consider it a devilish trick and hope to see it destroyed?'[186]

I think we all know the answer.

Facing up to a two-state ticking bomb

July 22, 2010

Even for the most starry-eyed, the news that the Palestinian Authority has rejected direct negotiations with Israel after meeting US envoy George Mitchell[187] would have been a surprise. After all, these guys are supposed to be the moderates. For the hard-nosed realists, it was proof-positive that the Palestinians are still squandering golden opportunities.

You can already hear the excuses – they don't really mean what they say; Israel hasn't done enough to address their legitimate grievances; we just need to get the moderates together; we'd like to live in peace so surely they want to also.

The process towards trading land for peace that began with the Oslo Accords in 1993 has failed. Today, still, the widely accepted notion for peace is the two-state solution. Prime Ministers Ehud Barak and Ehud Olmert went that route and were turned down.

The big question is whether this model can actually work.

A sober look at the likely implications of a sovereign Palestinian state is in order, particularly since the stakes are so high. A Palestinian state could, after all, result in a ticking time bomb with massive implications for Israel.

The cold, hard fact of the matter is this: the inexorable process towards trading land for peace that began in Oslo has not opened the road to genuine regional stability. The record so far is not encouraging.

General Giora Eiland, former director of the National Security Council and former head of the Planning Department of the IDF argues that a permanent solution must be sought, but not based just on the two-state solution. In discussing regional alternatives to a two-state solution he writes, 'It is hard to believe that the diplomatic effort that failed in 2000 can succeed in 2010, when most of the elements in the equation have changed for the worse.'[188]

What is he referring to?

Here is a sample from an interview with Abdallah Jarbu, Hamas deputy minister of religious endowments, which aired on Al-Aqsa TV on February 28, 2010:

The Jews suffer from a mental disorder, because they are thieves and aggressors. A thief or an aggressor, who took property or land, develops a psychological disorder and pangs of conscience, because he took something that wasn't his. They want to present themselves to the world as if they have rights, but, in fact, they are foreign bacteria – a microbe unparalleled in the world … May He annihilate this filthy people who have neither religion nor conscience. I condemn whoever believes in normalising relations with them, whoever supports sitting down with them, and whoever believes that they are human beings. They are not human beings. They are not people. They have no religion, no conscience, and no moral values.[189]

How is pint-sized Israel usually rewarded when it concedes land? In 2000 it withdrew from its security corridor in Southern Lebanon and Hezbollah moved in, turning it into a launching pad for a deadly missile campaign that led to the 2006 war. In 2005 it pulled out of Gaza and Hamas seized control and lobbed more than 10,000 missiles into Israeli towns, killed and kidnapped Israeli soldiers.

A two-state model can only work if the other side doesn't want to destroy you. The Hamas charter declares that every inch of Israel should not be given up since it is an 'Islamic Waqf consecrated for future Moslem generations until Judgement Day … There is no solution for the Palestinian question except through Jihad.'[190] Hamas doesn't recognise Israel's right to exist on religious grounds. So unless they violate their theological principles, they cannot sign up to a two-state framework.

Is locking together two states in a tiny territory a ticking time-bomb? Are the Palestinians prepared to 'go all the way' in forging a new relationship with Israel, or are they intent on merely pocketing territorial gains and then going back to the devastating mentality of violence? It's strange that the international community, which should understand that the Middle East is not a nice place – where rules of law, order and democracy do not apply –expects Israel to have an unpredictable genie unleashed on its citizens just on faith and optimism that Arafat and his leadership will turn democratic, abandon their goal of destroying Israel, and not use a state as a springboard for lobbing rockets into Jerusalem or conducting raids into Israel.

No-one wants the next Arab state, likely to be a cauldron of Islamic fundamentalism, next door to Tel Aviv, stockpiling an arsenal of poison gas as well as chemical and biological weapons.

The prospect of a full Palestinian state smack between Israel and Jordan is seen by many as huge risk. It has been said again and again that Israel must not relinquish military control over the West Bank because it has too many vital interests there, including the aquifer which gives Israel 40 per cent of its water. Others point out that it would leave the country too narrow to defend, just fifteen kilometres from the border to Tel Aviv.

Analysts agree that the rough terrain of the West Bank is needed as a barrier against tank attacks as well as the hilltops for early warning stations and the space to buy time to call up reserves. Similarly, any agreements with Fatah will be written on sand because nothing will prevent Hamas from orchestrating another military coup in the West Bank. A Hamas-dominated state carved into Israel's back is a card that cannot be unplayed.

The trouble with conceding strategically significant land for assurances of peace is that while Israel yields something tangible it only gets promises that may prove to be lies. After all, for how long will a Palestinian state accept restrictions on its sovereignty? As Jonathan Rosenblum notes: 'Conditions placed on a Palestinian state would not be worth the paper they are written on. The world does not recognise such a thing as conditional sovereignty. No matter how egregious the treaty violations of the state of Palestine, no country in the world ... would withdraw recognition.'[191]

A sovereign state has the right to enact laws as it sees fit, can control its own borders, is free to invite foreign 'military advisers' from Al-Qaeda, The Taliban and Hezbollah, sign defence agreements with Iran and Syria, eliminate Israel's early warning radar stations on the ridge of the West Bank mountain range and its own air space, thus reducing Israel's air space to that of a mere fifteen kilometres between Israel's densest population centres and the sea.

Liam Fox, the British Secretary of Defence, was told by Iranian politicians that Hamas and Hezbollah are 'part of our defence policy against Israel … Hamas is not part of the Palestinian problem. Hamas is the foreign policy wing of Iran in Israel.'[192]

Although the world is pushing for the quick establishment of Palestinian state, and although Israel has accepted a two-state solution, if rocket attacks or worse take place, the prospects of a Palestinian state anytime soon are growing dimmer.

Time Magazine and Israel bashing
September 15, 2010

As Jews around the world celebrated the Jewish new year last week, they got a hell of a present – a shameful and offensive story from *Time Magazine* that not only engaged in Israel bashing, but also trotted out age-old anti-Semitic stereotypes.

The *Time* cover featured a Jewish star made of daisies, with the headline: 'Why Israel doesn't care about peace.'[193] The story's message is that, for Israeli Jews, making money and partying is more important than making peace.

Here's a sample from the piece, by Karl Vick: 'The truth? In the week that three presidents, a king and their own prime minister gather at the White House to begin a fresh round of talks on peace between Israel and the Palestinians, the truth is, Israelis are no longer preoccupied with the matter. They're otherwise engaged; they're making money; they're enjoying the rays of late summer. A watching world may still define their country by the blood feud with the Arabs whose families used to live on this land and whether that conflict can be negotiated away, but Israelis say they have moved on.'[194]

Time borrowed from Shakespeare's Shylock, that Jewish merchant obsessed with money who takes a pound of flesh from Antonio. Only this time, the nasty and harmful stereotype is applied to Israelis, who are portrayed as greedy and money hungry. The *Time* article typifies the tendency today to take perennial anti-Jewish libels, and to apply them to Israel – the collective Jew.

Anti-Defamation League National Director Abraham Foxman put it accurately: 'The insidious subtext of Israeli Jews being obsessed with money echoes the age-old anti-Semitic falsehood that Jews care about money above any other interest, in this case achieving peace with the Palestinians. *Time* ignores the very real sacrifices made by Israel and its people in the pursuit of peace and the efforts by successive Israeli governments for reconciliation.'[195]

What was this pitiful story based on? 'Representative' interviews with a pair of Israeli estate agents, a survey and some far-left academics and journalists. It is accompanied by pictures of Israelis on the beach, smoking, relaxing on a beach chair and sitting in a café playing with a toddler in a stroller – normal activities that would not rate a mention anywhere else in the world.

Shame on those decadent, cold-hearted, uncaring Jews for having the nerve to live life to the fullest. As one blogger put it, the article paints a picture of 'the villainous Israelis sucking back nargilum (a flavoured smoke) on a Tel Aviv beach, detached from the plight of the Palestinians and letting the world go to hell … while the Middle East peace is a crucial issue to the rest of the world, these hoodlums could care less so long as they can make money and laze on the beach.'[196]

Time has a problem with Israelis because they have survived against the odds. It faults them because they have survived the wars, the suicide attacks, the constant delegitimisation, the hatred and the heartbreaks of failed negotiations for peace. It criticises Israel for weathering the global financial crisis, for being productive, inventive, for building a thriving economy and a modern democracy. Any other people would be praised for such achievements.

Yes, Australians and other nations are allowed to enjoy life, go out to restaurants, have fun on the beach, and lead regular lives. But not Israelis.

Vick conveniently forgets all of Israel's peace offers, starting with Oslo in 1993, Camp David in 2000, the Gaza withdrawal and the evacuation of every Jewish town there, and the generous offer made by former Israeli PM Ehud Olmert in 2008. He forgets that in the past year it is the President of the Palestinian Authority Mahmoud Abbas who has turned down Benjamin Netanyahu's offers for dialogue.

For some reason, Vick does not include the Israeli Democracy Institute and Tel Aviv University 2010 Peace Index that showed that 71.5 per cent of Israelis favour peace talks.[197]

CNN host Howard Kurtz told *Time* managing editor Richard Stengel: 'But the headline is a bit of a marketing gimmick, because it suggests that Israel doesn't want to participate in the peace process, despite the meetings that started this week in Washington. And when you read the story it's as you described. So, obviously, you're trying to draw people in with a provocative headline?'[198]

Stengel admitted that the headline was there to boost sales. 'Yes, it's a provocative headline, it's a provocative thesis. I mean, there are plenty of people who argue, as you know … that, in fact, Netanyahu is just giving the appearance that he actually wants peace, and to negotiate, because really he wants the US to help him with Iran. And that may in fact be true.'[199]

Ah, I see. According to Stengel, Netanyahu, like those other Israeli Jews, also doesn't care about peace.

Israelis may be sceptical about the prospects of peace given the too-many-to-count false starts. They may be fatigued and worried about a Hamas that controls Gaza (and 1.5 million Palestinians), that has vowed to destroy Israel and that has its sights set on the West Bank.

But not a day goes by in which Israelis don't argue, think or reflect about peace. About its absence mostly, but also about the hope that one day peace will come to their neck of the woods.

Time just doesn't get it. Perhaps it chose not to.

No wonder its circulation is in deep decline.

Playing the blame game
June 10, 2011

A pro-Israel organisation recently noted that while the Israeli government and the IDF quickly adjust to new military threats, they don't seem to be able to, 'get a handle on the new way the delegitimisation game is being played globally'.[200] The delegitimisation strategy waged against Israel today is driven by a host of radical-leftist groups, institutions, NGOs and individuals, and is best embodied by the BDS movement, the apartheid tag and by the singling out of Israel by the UN and its agencies. It is composed of bigoted libels, distortions and slanderous assaults. But more disturbing is the frightening myopia.

Have the passengers on the 'peace train' forgotten that the 2005 Gaza evacuation was followed by rockets landing in Israeli towns and villages? Have they asked what other nation would have tolerated such bombardment? That Israel allowed its citizens to be terrorised by Hamas missiles for so many years and did not commence an armed response after the first rocket fell is still puzzling.

When was the last time you heard Israel's critics mention the failure of the UN force in Southern Lebanon in preventing Hezbollah from re-arming, and reconstituting its presence in areas it's supposed to be barred from?

Why has the extreme left ignored the reality that Israel is the lone free outpost in the Middle East? Or that Prime Ministers Ehud Barak and Ehud Olmert offered the Palestinians everything they asked for? Or that Prince Bandar labeled Arafat's 2001 rejection a crime against the Palestinian people?[201] Or that a non-demilitarised Palestinian state will be a significant threat since Israel will not be able to intercept shipments of weapons coming by sea or air from neighbouring states and beyond?

It seems that the Oslo mindset – the one that posits that if Israel makes more concessions, ignores who its 'peace' partners are (even if they are dedicated to your destruction), turns a blind eye to what they say and do, and foregoes defensible borders – than a resolution to the conflict will be achieved. In other words, Israel must cede territory to whomever rules the West Bank and Gaza, just because, well because, it is expected to, even if it's irrational and self-defeating.

One of the most persistent lies in the delegitimisation campaign is that the Israeli-Palestinian conflict is at the heart of the troubles in the Middle East. Or as Anatol Lieven of the New America Foundation argued, the conflict is a 'tremendous obstacle to democratisation because it inflames all the worst, most regressive aspects of Arab nationalism and Arab culture'.[202]

Was Israel responsible for the genocidal gas-attacks against Kurds in Halabja? Or for Iraq attacking Iran and Kuwait and for its deadly campaign against the Shia following the first Gulf War? Or for the sectarian bloodshed in Lebanon? Or for Syria's massacre of 20,000-40,000 people in Hama in 1982? Or for the internal conflict in Algeria that has cost nearly 200,000 lives? Or for the fact that most countries in the Middle East are ruled by despots? Even the 2002 Cairo Declaration, signed by 400 representatives, blamed the USA for the problems of the Middle East, relegating Israel to second place.

Yet, according to Brazilian academic Jose Arthur Giannotti, we should all agree that 'the history of the Middle East would be entirely different without the State of Israel, which opened a wound between Islam and the West. Can you get rid of Muslim terrorism without getting rid of this wound which is the source of the frustration of potential terrorists?'[203] In other words, six million Jews are the reason for Islamist violence and for all the terrorism. Of course, the canard that Jews are at the root of the world's afflictions is not new.

Israel's legitimacy is undermined on every level, from the now discredited Goldstone report, to its portrayal as a racist, illegal occupier, an immoral country which stole land and whose right to exist is still under question.

If you accept those labels, then logically Israel deserves any form of punishment its foes or the international community decide to mete out. As novelist and columnist A. N. Wilson concluded, Israel, by its own actions, does not have a right to exist.

If you read the 2007 Haifa Declaration, authored by the New Israeli Fund backed Mada Al Carmel Centre, the Zionist movement 'initiated its colonial settler project in Palestine' and 'committed massacres against our people ...'[204] Moreover, Israel has 'pursued policies of repression, which at times reached the level of killing... enacted racist land, immigration, and citizenship laws' and 'carried out policies of subjugation and oppression in excess of those of the apartheid regime in South Africa'.[205] The Declaration demands that Israel, 'accept responsibility for the *Nakba* ... and also for the war crimes and crimes of occupation that it has committed in the Occupied Territories'.[206] Finally, Israel must become democratic, recognise the Palestinian Right of Return and abandon 'its destructive role towards the peoples of the region, especially in the context of a hegemonic US policy which supports certain Arab regimes in oppressing their citizens, stripping them of their resources, obstructing their development, and impeding the democratic process in the Arab world'.[207]

No wonder that it's become fashionable to assume the role of a knee-jerk critic of Israel.

I wonder: in the struggle for the hearts and minds of the next generation, what will they think of Israel? I guess it all depends on what they learn from their parents.

Israel under Netanyahu
October 7, 2011

Even his detractors have to admit that Netanyahu's speech to the UN earlier this month,[208] and his May address to the joint meeting of Congress,[209] were moments of sheer triumph. Not surprisingly, the spectacular assuredness he displayed in making Israel's case have boosted his popularity at home.

And though within the 'always criticise' Israel cottage industry it's not trendy to praise any Israeli leader, I wonder whether there is any prime minister, anywhere in the world, who can so eloquently stand up for his country's right to self-defence and principles and receive such standing ovations.

I wonder how many prime ministers would have had the courage to lecture Obama about the dangers of Israel returning to the 1967 borders[210] after the American President ambushed Netanyahu with his Middle East speech just before his arrival at the White House.[211] Yet, throughout the various crises with the American administration, Netanyahu has kept his cool, and was smart enough to heap praise on Obama last week following the President's UN speech.

No wonder that recent polls suggest that the battle between the leftist parties – Kadima and Labor – who are in terminal decline, means that Netanyahu will comfortably win the next election.

Reflect on Abbas's UN speech in which he constantly referenced 1948,[212] demonstrating that it's not the territories that he has a problem with but the state of Israel. Or that Abbas denied that Jews ever lived in Israel. This stance chimes with the declaration last month by Director of Government Media for the Palestinian Authority and Abbas's spokesperson Ghassan Khatib that since there are no Jewish people, how can there be a Jewish country?[213] And what point was Abbas making when he chose Latifa Abu Hmeid, the mother of terrorists convicted of murdering seven Israelis and attempting to murder twelve others, to submit the letter to the UN seeking unilateral recognition?[214]

Reflect that both Arafat in 2000–01 and Abbas in 2008 turned down offers of a sovereign state in the West Bank, Gaza and East Jerusalem. Why? Because to accept a two-state solution would have meant to accept the notion of Jewish self-determination.

Netanyahu has now accepted the Quartet's proposal for kick-starting the negotiations. Abbas has predictably rejected this move. Why? Because he wants Israel to agree to compromise on borders, settlements and Jerusalem even before the negotiations have begun. And what is Abbas offering in return? Nothing.

Netanyahu will not get the credit, but his tough diplomacy is starting to pay dividends. As *Haaretz* has reported, during an address at the UN General Assembly last month, Spanish Foreign Minister Trinidad Jimenez, for the first time, said that Israel is the homeland of the Jewish people, and that 'any solution to the Palestinian refugee issue must preserve Israel's Jewish character'.[215] *Haaretz* went on to explain that Jimenez's statement is 'particularly dramatic because Spain is considered one of the most pro-Palestinian countries in Europe. Its adoption of this new policy could thus lead other European countries to follow suit.'[216] And earlier this year, French Foreign Minister Alain Juppe stated that any solution to the Middle East conflict would need to recognise Israel as the nation-state for the Jewish people.[217]

Is it by chance that such significant shifts in attitudes towards Israel have taken place under Netanyahu's watch?

No one thinks so.

The Israel almost no-one talks about and the one they do

July 12, 2013

This column may come across as the exception to what's cool or fashionable. If so, I'll wear it.

I'd like to talk about the Israel the media rarely reports on and about the perennial critics who feel it's their sacred duty to be the first in line to shout from the rooftops about what's wrong with Israel and why we need a new one.

We should remind ourselves about the achievements of Israel and the Herculean task its people face on a daily basis. It's easy to let slip from memory that this little nation has managed to absorb millions of migrants and is, above all, still a safe haven for Jews. Vice President Jo Biden tells the story of meeting Prime Minister Golda Meir. He was 30, just elected as US senator. Meir looked at the young man and said, 'You look like you're worried'. Biden replied, 'Well, Madam Prime Minister, I am. The picture you just painted – in those days, 60 million Arabs, two million Jews, et cetera.'

Meir put her arm on Biden's arm and said, 'Senator, don't worry. We Jews have a secret weapon in our struggle here. We have no place else to go.'[218]

Even Israel's most vicious naysayers, advocates of the BDS for instance, must recognise that in a part of the world that has no democracy, Israel's citizens are free to speak their mind and to vote for who they want to vote for. Historian Martin Gilbert writes that despite the conflict, economic hardships and social divisions, 'The vision of a forward-looking Israel remains'.[219]

So why am I telling you this? Because far too often I am astounded to see the usual denouncers of Israel's policies get a helping hand from a flock of wannabes who savour the opportunity to partake in the tsunami of virulent verbal onslaught and chronic inversion of fact.

There are even those in the Jewish community who search the newspapers, eager to update their Facebook wall the moment they 'discover' an item that censures the Israeli government, the IDF or any other Israeli institution. Any little shortcoming will do. Among their status updates you'll find beautiful passages from the Torah about the virtues of peace, as if it's the Israelis who need lessons on this point. Some are trumpeted and quoted with respect in the media, paraded as courageous dissidents who want to force Israel to 'pursue peace'.

This is pie-in-the-sky stuff, yet we are told that the animosity in the Arab would magically disappear the moment Israel withdraws again. I wonder: how many more offers does Israel have to make to satisfy its bashers?

Look closely at the familiar denunciators. While they rail against Israeli actions, they neatly overlook the barbaric behaviour of other Middle East states and groups. They paint a dark, grim picture of the Jewish state, depicting the country as the exclusive villain and the Palestinians as the victims. The world's worst dictatorships go under the radar. These unrelenting, 'impartial' voices insist that they are helping Israel, that the severity of their attacks is a sign of a healthy debate and their love for the Zionist ideal.

They are being cruel to be kind.

To them I say: don't bother with this kind of love. Since the vociferous detractors are doing such a fine job, Israel will manage just fine without the additional pillorying by its friends.

Worryingly, young adults may start to believe that those failings are the whole story. Sure, not everyone needs to talk about Israel in warm terms. Mistakes have been made, but never on a scale that has defied morality the way other states have. Criticism about policies is OK, but it has to be proportional, comparative and contextual. An honest presentation of Israel cannot just zero in on its flaws.

Today, the cycle of criticism tends to be self-reinforcing because anything Israel does right is overlooked, and anything Israel does wrong is instantaneously amplified and exaggerated. As Richard Cohen has noted, 'Arab nations have shamefully been granted an exception to the standards expected of the rest of the world, as if they were children'.[220]

On the weekend that the Americans were to make the decision on whether or not the State of Israel should be recognised, presidential adviser Clark Clifford took all the memos that were against recognising Israel to President Truman. When Truman came back from the weekend he said, 'We're going to recognise Israel'.

When asked why, 'Truman simply said – It is the right thing to do'.[221]

Doing the right thing. That's not a phrase you usually associate with the coverage and treatment of Israel.

Twenty years after the Oslo Accords
September 6, 2013

On the 20th anniversary of the Oslo Accords, it is appropriate and timely to declare that Oslo promised much, but delivered nothing.

Fact is, Arafat's true intentions were on display from the very beginning. Problem was, many had blinkers on.

On the same day that he signed the Oslo Accords, Arafat explained to Jordanian TV, 'Since we cannot defeat Israel in war, we do it in stages. We take any and every territory that we can of Palestine, and establish sovereignty there, and we use it as a springboard to take more. When the time comes, we can get the Arab nations to join us for the final blow against Israel.'[222] A month later, in Johannesburg, Arafat again admitted that the Accords were merely a way to facilitate his *jihad* against Israel.[223] And in 2001, Palestinian spokesperson Faisal Husseini revealed:

> had the US and Israel realised, before Oslo, that all that was left of the Palestinian National movement and the Pan-Arab movement was a wooden horse called Arafat ... they would never have opened their fortified gates and let it inside their walls ... The Oslo agreement, or any other agreement, is just a temporary procedure, just a step towards something bigger. ...distinguish the strategic, long-term goals from the political phased goals, which we are compelled to temporarily accept due to international pressure ... Our ultimate goal is the liberation of all of historic Palestine, from the Jordan River to the Mediterranean Sea.[224]

In other words, the Oslo Accords were a ruse to gain Palestinian control of the entire existing State of Israel.

Not many remember that before Rabin's murder, the Oslo Accords had been overwhelmingly rejected by the Israeli public with Rabin's approval rating by April 1994 dropping to 41 per cent. Or that Rabin understood that he was duped by Arafat. A month before his assassination, Rabin told the Knesset that he was aware of the fact that the Palestinian Authority had not kept its promises. Rabin also declared, 'We will not return to the 4 June 1967 lines ... The security border of the State of Israel will be located in the Jordan Valley and in the establishment of blocs of settlements in Judea and Samaria, like the one in Gush Katif.'[225] And, he added, 'We ... committed ourselves before the Knesset, not to uproot a single settlement in the framework of the interim agreement, and not to hinder building for natural growth.'[226]

Oslo did not stop the poisonous brainwashing, or lead to the disarming of terrorist factions running wild in the West Bank and Gaza, or prevent Arafat making speeches asking 'a million martyrs' to march with him on Jerusalem.[227]

The Oslo Accords gave the Palestinian Authority exactly what they wanted – universal diplomatic recognition, billions of dollars and control of the West Bank and Gaza.

Arafat armed and funded Hamas so it could carry out its bus bombings, while claiming that it was Hamas, not the PLO, that was perpetrating those acts of savagery and saying, 'What can I do?'.

More Israelis have been murdered by terrorist attacks since Oslo than in the entire 35 years of Israel's existence that preceded Oslo.

When Prime Minister Ehud Barak put forward a proposal to relinquish 98 per cent of the territories and to divide sovereignty over Jerusalem, Arafat reacted with the Oslo War, or the Second *Intifada*.

Today, rockets still keep raining down on Israeli towns from Gaza.

President of the Palestinian Authority Abbas has not prepared his people for the prospect of peace. Palestinian media continues to broadcast anti-Semitic material. At the same time, the next generation of Palestinians has been infected by an educational system that teaches them to hate Israelis and Jews.

No wonder that Netanyahu rightly insists that the Palestinian Authority first build social, economic and political institutions that will support a state that can actually fulfil its responsibilities in keeping the peace. Given the instability in the Middle East and violent uprisings, he knows that any agreement with the Palestinian Authority could end up as worthless as Oslo.

Those who thought Oslo would improve Israel's international stature have been proven wrong. The BDS, the EU's stance on the settlements, rising anti-Semitism, anti-Israel sentiments around the world and the call for Israel to be replaced by an Arab-majority state are just a few examples.

Oslo has been a complete failure. Yet there are those who still pretend it can work. Dr. Kenneth Levin, in his book *The Oslo Syndrome: Delusions of a People Under Siege*,[228] explains that Israelis, faced with persistent existential attacks from an enemy they were forced to negotiate with, kept blaming themselves as a defence mechanism that one often sees in members of a besieged or abused group.

And in his book, *The Longer Shorter Way*,[229] current Defence Minister Moshe Yaalon details how the policies of Rabin, Peres, Barak and Olmert backfired because they refused to recognise reality and fell for wishful thinking that endangered Israel's security. Yaalon, who was intimately involved with the implementation of the Oslo Accords, now warns Israeli leaders to keep their eyes wide open to the reality surrounding them.

In 1994, former Justice Minister Yossi Beilin was queried as to why the Israeli people were not informed about the secret negotiations with Arafat.

Beilin's response: 'We kept it a secret because they would have stopped us.'[230]

Let's hope this tactic is never repeated.

No quick fix but Gaza peace may be possible

16 September 2009

After the recent conflict in Gaza, the prospects of peace between Israelis and Palestinians look grim. But as Abraham Lincoln once said, 'The probability that we may fall in the struggle ought not to deter us from the support of a cause we believe to be just.'

Along with the tears shed for lives lost on both sides, we must refuse to give in to the short-sighted despair that says that force is the only language Israelis and Palestinians speak. War only produces broken hearts, no winners.

A just peace between the two peoples can be achieved but the business-as-usual of blaming and demonising the other cannot continue. Real security for Israelis and Palestinians is 'shared security'.

No ceasefire will last without a new collaborative path that involves all stakeholders. Violence breeds violence, prolongs suffering and holds back the vital work of building a resolution based on sustained dialogue and painful but honourable compromises.

Primarily, the benefits of peace need to be inculcated among those who have only known guns firing and bombs exploding. The silent majorities on both sides, who are ready to make concessions, need to be engaged for any formal treaties to succeed. Inaction and foot-dragging is not an option.

The two peoples will be neighbours forever and must choose mutually secure ways to share this sliver of land. The lie that Israelis and Palestinians cannot reconcile will not last. How many more mothers must bury their children before the bravado of radicals gives way to new solutions without killing? As John F. Kennedy said, 'Man will put an end to war, or war will put an end to man.'

Israelis and Palestinians, traumatised by war and death, have no choice but to work collectively and purposefully to try to forge a feasible deal of a two-state solution.

In the words of Martin Luther King, Jr, 'We have in our hearts a power more powerful than bullets.' Yes, there is no quick fix. Previous disappointments have produced many cynics and doubters. Yet, any misgivings about the lip service paid to a slew of formulas must take a backseat to the possibility of resolution, denying madness another victory.

Sanity must prevail because if anything, the implications of failure to find peace should prod Israeli and Palestinian parents into action. Otherwise, their children will inherit their conflict.

The global community must invest in people-to-people diplomacy to break down the emotional and psychological barriers. It must stand behind moderate leaders in Gaza and the West Bank. Palestinians must strive for democracy, settle the costly infighting between Hamas and Fatah which divides them and elect a moderate leadership that is ready to consider a future of coexistence with Israel.

Scholar Mark Mathabane urges Israelis and Palestinians to look to South Africa as a model. Mathabane cites Lincoln's second inaugural address which was imbued with pleas of charity for all and malice towards none, and which helped restore a frayed nation.

Recall how Nelson Mandela spoke of the Afrikaners' anguished memories of their own agony at the hands of the British during the Boer War. His appeal was embraced by the resentful black majority largely because he was uttering those words as a human being. Imagine the Palestinians empathising with the Jewish suffering during the Holocaust and Israelis acknowledging the Palestinians' grief.

True peace includes forgiveness and a willingness to put the past behind, as well as an understanding that both sides have been responsible for the injustice and pain. Palestinians and Israelis must set aside decades of atavistic aggression to find the courage to absolve each other of past transgressions and to admit that there has been tremendous hurt.

Only then will they bear witness to an astonishing milestone that will permit the two nations to live side by side, free from terror, in a relationship dedicated to peace and prosperity.

In 1998, Bill Clinton urged Israelis and Palestinians to leave behind 50 years of cynicism and to unearth within themselves the strength to forgive. 'I think the beginning of mutual respect after so much pain is to recognise not only the positive characteristics of people on both sides, but the fact that there has been a lot of hurt and harm,' he said. 'The time has come to sanctify your holy ground with real forgiveness and reconciliation.'

Notes

1   Berel Wein. 'Fight the canard' *The Jerusalem Post*, March 14, 2003.

2   Barbara Demick. 'Israel tries to stem Iraqi 'blood money' *The Age*, October 12, 2002.

3   George W. Bush. 'Remarks on the future of Iraq' Washington, Hilton Hotel, Washington, D.C., February 26, 2003. http://georgewbush-whitehouse.archives.gov/infocus/bushrecord/documents/Selected_Speeches_George_W_Bush.pdf

4   Chris McGreal. 'Israel bows to US and accepts road map' *The Guardian*, May 26, 2003.

5   http://www.un.org/news/dh/mideast/roadmap122002.pdf

6   http://news.bbc.co.uk/2/hi/middle_east/2937030.stm

7   Richard Roth. 'America's road map to peace in the Middle East approved' *CBS Evening News*, May 25, 2003.

8   See: Robert, B. Satloff. (Editor). 'International Military Intervention: A Detour on the Road to Israeli-Palestinian Peace' *Special Studies on Palestinian Politics and the Peace Process*, Number 45, September 2003.

9   Yossi Verter, Amos Harel and David Ratner. '19 dead, 60 wounded in Haifa restaurant bombing' *Haaretz*, October 5, 2003.

10 Elizabeth Matthews (editor). '*The Israel-Palestine conflict : parallel discourses*. Abingdon, Oxon; New York: Routledge, 2011: 7.

11 United Nations. *United Nations Yearbook 2003 Vol 57 (Yearbook of the United Nations)*. Blue Ridge Summit, PA, Brenan Press, 2005: 476.

12 Hope Keller. 'Israel holds the key to ending a war it will never win' *The Baltimore Sun*, January 12, 2003.

13 David Grossman. *Death as a way of Life: From Oslo the Geneva agreement*. New York, Picador: 2004.

14 Joseph Algazy. 'Rabbi Melchior, Latin Patriarch Sabah and Sheikh al-Sider win Coventry peace prize' *Haaretz*, October 15, 2002.

15 http://www.yadvashem.org/yv/en/about/events/event_details.asp?cid=137

16 Yair Sheleg. 'United in pain' *Haaretz*, June 6, 2003.

17 ibid.

18 Yoav Appel and John Vause. 'Sharon tried to regroup after plan's defeat' *Foxnews*, May 3, 2004.

19 Greg Myre and Elissa Gootma. 'Sharon to Alter, Not Discard, Pull-out Plan' *The New York Times*, May 4, 2004.

20 Chris McGreal. 'Israel on road to ruin, warn former Shin Bet chiefs' *The Guardian*, 15 November, 2003.

21 Avraham Burg. 'The end of Zionism' *The Guardian*, 15 September, 2003.

22 Ellen Crean. 'Some Israeli pilots refuse strikes' *CBSNEWS*, September 26, 2003.

23 'Israeli Public opinion Polls: Opinion on Unilateral Measures (2001-2004)' http://www.jewishvirtuallibrary.org/jsource/Society_&_Culture/unilateral1.html

24 Thomas L. Friedman. 'Kicking over the chessboard' *The New York Times*, April 18, 2004.

25 'PM Sharon's Speech at the Memorial Service for Israel's Fallen' April 25, 2004. http://www.imra.org.il/story.php3?id=20563

26 Thomas L. Friedman. 'Kicking over the chessboard' *The New York Times*, April 18, 2004.

27 Nina Gilbert. 'Gaza withdrawal would reduce terrorism – Ze'evi' *The Jerusalem Post*, 21 April 2004.

28 'UN Assembly votes overwhelmingly to demand Israel comply with ICJ ruling' *UN News Centre*, July 20, 2004. See also Aluf Benn. 'ICJ: West Bank fence is illegal, Israel must tear it down' *Haaretz*, July 9, 2004.

29 Shlomo Shamir. 'US vetoes UN resolution censuring Israel for Yassin killing' *Haaretz*, March 25, 2004.

30 Anne Bayefsky. 'Views of a UN 'human rights' body' *The Jerusalem Post*, March 31, 2003.

31 Hana Levi Julian. 'UN Human Rights Envoy Recommends UN Quit the Quartet' *Israel National News*, 15 October, 2007.

32 Phil Reeves. 'Middle East: The crisis continues: Israelis try to pin blame for Jenin on suicide bombers' *The Independent*, April 19, 2002.

33 Press Release 'Secretary-General condemns those resorting to violence, terror in Middle East: call on Israelis, Palestinians to devote all energies to negotiating true, lasting peace' http://www.un.org/

News/Press/docs/2004/sgsm9133.doc.htm

34 'UN envoy condemns Israeli policy' *BBC News*, April 23, 2004.

35 Human Rights Watch. 'Erased In A Moment: Suicide Bombing Attacks Against Israeli Civilians' October 2002. http://www.hrw.org/reports/2002/isrl-pa/ISRAELPA1002.pdf

36 'Enoch Powell's 'Rivers of Blood' speech' *The Telegraph*, November 6, 2007. http://www.telegraph.co.uk/comment/3643826/Enoch-Powells-Rivers-of-Blood-speech.html

37 Steven R. Weisman, Elaine Sciolino and David E. Sanger. 'Rice Says U.S Won't Aid Europe on Iran Incentives' *The New York Times*, February 4, 2005.

38 Charlie Rose. 'President Clinton Tells Some Useful Truths' *Executive Intelligence Review*, February 11, 2005.

39 'Text of President Bush's 2005 State of the Union Address' *The Washington Post*, February 2, 2005.

40 International Atomic Energy Agency. 'Implementation of the NPT Safeguards Agreement in the Islamic Republic of Iran: Report by the Director General' 1 September, 2004. http://www.iaea.org/Publications/Documents/Board/2004/gov2004-60.pdf

41 Bill Powell and Tim McGirk. 'The Man Who Sold the Bomb' *Time Magazine*, February 6, 2005.

42 Richard L. Rubenstein. *Jihad and Genocide*. Lanham, Md.: Rowman & Littlefield Pub. Group, 2010: 121.

43 David Westall. 'Iran rejects curbs and demands to join the 'nuclear club' *The Telegraph*, 13 June, 2004.

44 Fareed Zakaria. 'Iran: The Next Crisis' *The Washington Post*, August 10, 2004.

45 Fareed Zakaria. 'The Stealth Nuclear Threat' *Newsweek*, August 15, 2004.

46 See: R. James Woolsey. 'Iran: Tehran's Nuclear Recklessness and the US Response' US Senate Committee on Homeland Security and Governmental Affairs Subcommittee on Federal Financial Management, Government Information and International Security. November 15, 2005.

47 Kenneth M. Pollack. *The Persian Puzzle: the conflict between Iran and America*. New York: Random House, 2004.

48 Jefferson Morley. 'Israeli Withdrawal from Gaza explained' *The Washington Post*, August 10, 2005.

49 http://int.icej.org/news/headlines/israels-high-court-rules-disengagement-legal

50 'President Bush Endorses Israel's Disengagement Plan' *PBS Newshour*, April 14, 2004.

51 Jacqueline Rose. *The Question of Zion*. Princeton, NJ: Princeton University Press, 2005.

52 Jacqueline Rose. 'Boycotting Israel: a reply to Linda Grant' *Open Democracy*, September 5, 2005.

53 Jacqueline Rose. *States of Fantasy*. New York: Oxford University Press, 1996

54 'Zionism Today is the Real Enemy of the Jews: An Intelligence Squared Debate' Audiobook. Intelligence Squared Limited. 2005.

55 ibid.

56 ibid.

57 http://topdocumentaryfilms.com/palestine-is-still-the-issue/

58 John Pilger. 'John Pilger on terror in Palestine' *The New Statesman*, March 22, 2004.

59 Avi Shlaim. *The Iron Wall: Israel and the Arab world*. New York: W.W Norton, 2000.

60 Avi Shlaim. 'A debate: Is Zionism today the real enemy of the Jews?' *The New York Times*, February 4, 2005.

61 Ayelet Negev. 'Ilan Pappe: I'm not a traitor' *Yediot Ahronot*, March 15, 2008.

62 James Bennet. 'UN Report Rejects Claims of a Massacre of Refugees' *The New York Times*, August 2, 2002.

63 Edward L. Bernays. *Propaganda*. New York : H. Liveright, 1928

64 'Suicide bombing movie is pulled' *BBC News*, July 16, 2005.

65 Jonathan Saul. 'Suicide bomber hits Tel Aviv nightclub: Blast shatters informal truce established at Feb. 8 summit' *National Post*, February 26. 2005.

66 Matthias Kuntzel. 'Suicide Bombing for a Higher Ideal?: Germany's Central Office for Political Education on Paradise Now' *Scholars for Peace in the Middle East*, October 10, 2005.

67 David Medienkritik. 'No to Paradise Now' October 20, 2005. http://medienkritik.typepad.com/blog/2005/10/no_to_paradise_.html

68 Igal Avidan. 'A devil deserving of sympathy' *The Jerusalem Report*, October 31, 2005.

69 John Rosenthal. 'Paradise Now: More Evidence of the European Commitment to Combat Terrorism' *Transatlantic Intelligence*, March 4, 2009.

70 Scott Wilson. 'Hamas Sweeps Palestinian Elections, Complicating Peace Efforts in Mideast' *The Washington Post*, January 27, 2006.

71 Mark Willacy. 'No Ordinary Mother' *Correspondent's Report, ABC Radio*, March 5, 2006.

72 'Hamas chief vows to support Iran' *BBC NEWS*, 15 December, 2005.

73 http://avalon.law.yale.edu/20th_century/hamas.asp

74 'Iran claims nuclear breakthrough' *The Guardian*, April 12, 2006.

75 Gareth Smyth. 'Iran's president dismisses fears of Mideast crisis' *Financial Times*, April 25, 2006.

76 Seymour Hersh. 'The Iran Plans' *The New Yorker*, April 17, 2006

77 http://www.unsco.org/Documents/Resolutions/S_RES_1559(2004).pdf

78 Rich Lowry. 'End of Illusions' *National Review Online*, July 7, 2006.

79 Efrat Weiss. 'Abductors present Eliyahu Asheri's ID card' *Yediot Ahronot*, 28 June, 2006.

80 Tim Russert. 'Former Speaker of the House Newt Gingrich and Senator Joe Biden, Democrat from Delaware, discuss Bush administration and Mideast policies and conflicts, and tension with North Korea' *Meet the Press*, July 16, 2006.

81 Editorial. 'Prodding the UN' *The Washington Post*, February 28, 2006.

82 Rosa Freedman. *The United Nations Human Rights Council: a critique and early assessment*. Milton Park, Abingdon, Oxon: Routledge, 2013: 210.

83 Mark Steyn. 'There is no cure for the UN' *The Spectator* (UK), September 15, 2005.

84 Joshua Muravchik. *The Future of the United Nations: Understanding the Past to Chart a Way Forward*. Washington DC: AEI Press, 2005: 62.

85 Shashi Tharoor. 'Why American Still Needs the United Nations' *Foreign Affairs*, September/October, 2003.

86 Ed Lasky. 'UN 'expert' found abusing mandate to US' *American Spectator*, October 28, 2005.

87 Associated Press. 'Iranian PM snubs Annan over nuclear program' September 3, 2006.

88 Cliff Kincaid. 'Reporter Eric Shawn Outfoxes the UN' *Accuracy in Media*, May 7, 2006.

89 Nile Gardiner and James Philiips. 'Congress Should Withhold Funds from the UN Relief and Works Agency for Palestine Refugees (UNRWA)' *The Heritage Foundation*, February 6, 2006.

90 Julian Borger. 'Kofi Annan's Syrians strategy echoes past failures in Bosnia and Rwanda' *The Guardian*, May 31, 2012.

91 Anne Bayefsky. Goodbye UN hello United Democratic Nations' *The Jerusalem Post*, September 19, 2006.

92 W. B. Yeats. *The Collected Poems of W.B. Yeats*. London: Macmillan, 1952.

93 http://www.friendsofopenhouse.co.il/sections/activities/

94 http://wasns.org/

95 http://www.west-eastern-divan.org/

96 Simon Jeffery. 'An extreme inspiration' *The Guardian*, January 21, 2004.

97 Etta Prince-Gibson. 'Teachers greet "the enemy"'. *The Jerusalem Post*, April 4, 2003: 8-12.

98 Yair Sheleg. 'United in pain.' *Haaretz*. June 6, 2003: 17.

99 http://www.theparentscircle.com/

100 Jeremy Josephs. 'Michel Bacos: the Air France hero of Entebbe' *The Jewish Chronicle Online*, June 15, 2012

101 Amy Teibel. 'Netanyahu: Obama Call For Settlement Freeze 'Unreasonable' *The Huffington Post*, July 7, 2009.

102 Laura Rozen. 'Netanyahu: 'What the hell do they want from me?' *The Cable*, May 28, 2009.

103 Eitan Haber. 'We're in trouble' *Yediot Ahronot*, 20 May 2009.

104 President Barack Obama. 'Remarks by The President On a New Beginning' Cairo University, Egypt, June 4, 2009. http://www.

whitehouse.gov/the-press-office/remarks-president-cairo-university-6-04-09

105 Neve Gordon. 'Boycott Israel' *The Los Angeles Times*, August 20, 2009.

106 Rivka Carmi. 'Neve Gordon's divisive Op-Ed' *The Los Angeles Times*, September 1, 2009.

107 http://sydneypeacefoundation.org.au/peace-prize-recipients/2009-john-pilger/

108 'The Bilbao Initiative – civil society action for justice in Palestine: Final Declaration and Action Plan' http://www.bdsmovement.net/2008/final-declaration-and-action-plan-of-the-bilbao-initiative-213

109 http://mada-research.org/en/files/2007/09/haifaenglish.pdf

110 Meyrav Wurmser. 'Can Israel Survive Post-Zionism' *Middle East Quarterly*, March 1999: 3-13.

111 Gary Rosenblatt. 'Haaretz Editor Urged Rice To 'Rape' Israel' *The Jewish Week*, December 28, 2007.

112 Seth J. Frantzman. 'The colonization of the conflict' *The Jerusalem Post*, July 28, 2009.

113 http://www.fastforgaza.org/about

114 Ofri Ilani. '230 Israeli lecturers vow not to obey law banning Nakba commemoration' *Haaretz*, June 25, 2009.

115 Polly Curtis. 'Union accused of reviving academic boycott of Israel' *The Guardian*, May, 9, 2008.

116 Yossi Melman. 'Israel should give up Jerusalem as its capital' *Haaretz*, December 6, 2009.

117 ibid.

118 'Obama's speech at AIPAC' June 4, 2008. http://www.npr.org/templates/story/story.php?storyId=91150432

119 'Obama postpones US embassy move from T.A. to Jerusalem' *Haaretz*, June 6, 2009.

120 'EU: Jerusalem should be capital of two states' *BBC News*, December 8, 2009.

121 Roni Sofer. 'EU warns Israel not to divide bloc over Jerusalem' *Yediot Ahronot*, October 12, 2009.

122 Roni Sofer. 'Swedish daily: IDF killed Palestinians for organs' *Yediot Abronot*, 18 August, 2009.

123 Barak Ravid. 'Netanyahu declares 10-month settlement freeze 'to restart peace talks' *Haaretz*, November 25, 2009.

124 Tzvi Ben Gedalyahu. 'Jerusalem Mayor to EU: Dividing the City Threatens Peace Process' *Israel National News*, July 7, 2009.

125 Marcy Oster. 'Netanyahu: 'United Jerusalem is Israel's capital' *The Jewish Telegraphic Agency*, May 21, 2009.

126 Amnon Meranda. 'Knesset adopts referendum bill' *Yediot Abronot*, September 12, 2009.

127 UN investigations chief under investigation' *USA Today*, January 19, 2011.

128 http://www.un.org/en/documents/charter/preamble.shtml

129 'A Good Man in Hell: General Roméo Dallaire and the Rwanda Genocide' *United States Holocaust Memorial Museum*, June 12, 2002.

130 Michael Brandon McClellan. 'A Paper Tiger Gone Bad' *The Weekly Standard*, April 15, 2005.

131 Human Rights Watch. 'The Fall of Srebrenica and the Failure of UN Peacekeeping Bosnia and Herzegovina' October 1995, Volume 7, No 13: http://www.hrw.org/sites/default/files/reports/bosnia1095web.pdf

132 http://www.un.org/depts/unmovic/documents/1441.pdf

133 Colum Lynch. 'U.N Faces More Accusations of Sexual Misconduct' *Washington Post*, March 13, 2005.

134 Sharon Otterman. 'Iraq: Oil for Food Scandal' *Council on Foreign Relations*, October 28, 2005.

135 Warren Hoge. 'Officials at UN Seek Fast Action on Rights Panel' *The New York Times*, January 1, 2006.

136 Anne Bayefsky. 'Obama Joins Human-Rights Charade' *National Review Online*, April 2, 2009.

137 http://daccess-ods.un.org/TMP/7496452.33154297.html

138 http://www.un.org/documents/ga/res/36/a36r055.htm

139 http://www.un.org/WCAR/durban.pdf

140 Warren Hoge. 'UN Distances Itself From an Envoy's Rebuke of Israel and the US' *The New York Times*, April 24, 2004

141 ibid.

142 Hannah Newman. 'A Nation that Dwells Alone: The UN-ique Lock Out of Israel from the UN' *Jerusalem Searchlight*, August 2000.

143 Dore Gold. *Tower of babble : how the United Nations has fueled global chaos*. New York: Crown Forum, 2004.

144 Ben Shapiro. 'The United Nations International Terrorism Organization' *Townhall*, June 2, 2004.

145 'Zimbabwe to chair major UN body' *BBC News*, May 12, 2007.

146 Julie Stahl. 'Iran Elected to UN Disarmament Commission' *CNS News*, July 7, 2008.

147 Eric Shawn. *The UN Exposed: How the United Nations Sabotages America's Security and Fails the World* New York: Sentinel, 2006.

148 Cliff Kincaid. 'Reporter Eric Shawn Outfoxes the UN' *Accuracy in Media*, May 7, 2006.

149 'HRW Letter to protest UNESCO Award to Uzbek President Islam Karimov' *Human Rights Watch*, September 13, 2006.

150 Nile Gardiner and Stephen Johnson. 'UNESCO'S Chavez Outrage: *The Heritage Foundation*, February 10, 2006.

151 Ed Pikington. 'Chávez attacks 'devil' Bush in UN speech' *The Guardian*, September 21, 2006.

152 http://archive.adl.org/nr/exeres/7c9ee86b-96fb-4347-b9b7-d4318efe8113,db7611a2-02cd-43af-8147-649e26813571,frameless.html

153 Itamar Eichner. 'Egyptian culture minister: I would burn Israeli books myself' *Yediot Ahronot*, May 14, 2008.

154 Edward Cody. 'Egypt's Farouk Hosni Draws Opposition in Bid to Lead UNESCO' *The Washington Post*, September 9, 2009.

155 ibid.

156 http://www.youtube.com/watch?v=rYKy4dfSF-o

157 Ewen MacAskill. 'Mahmoud Ahmadinejad's renewed attack on Israel hastens walkout' *The Guardian*, September 24, 2009.

158 Benjamin Netanyahu. 'Prime Minister Benjamin Netanyahu's speech to the UN General Assembly' *Haaretz,* September 24, 2009.

159 Liz Sidoti. 'McCain Favors a "League of Democracies"' *The Washington Post*, April 30, 2007

160 Ethan Bronner. 'As Biden Visits, Israel Unveils Plan for New Settlements' *The New York Times*, March 9, 2010.

161 Glenn Kessler. 'Clinton rebukes Israel over East Jerusalem plans, cites damage to bilateral ties' *The Washington Post*, March 13, 2010.

162 Rohee Nahmias. 'Damascus summit: Assad, Ahmadinejad, Nasrallah' *Yediot Ahronot*, February 26, 2010.

163 Laura Rosen. 'Netanyahu: What the hell do they want from me?' *The Cable*, May 28, 2009.

164 Stephanie Gutmann. 'There is a reason Israel doesn't roll over when Mahmoud Abbas bats his eyelashes' *The Telegraph*, March 11, 2010.

165 http://mfa.gov.il/MFA/ForeignPolicy/Terrorism/Palestinian/Pages/32nd_anniversary_coastal_massacre_11-Mar-2010.aspx

166 Steven R. Weisman. 'Rice Admits US Underestimated Hamas Strength' *The New York Times*, January 30, 2006; Glenn Kessler. 'Takeover by Hamas Illustrates Failure of Bush's Mideast Vision' *The Washington Post*, June 15, 2007.

167 Harriet Sherwood. 'Gaza aid flotilla to set sail for confrontation with Israel' *The Guardian*, May 26, 2010.

168 Editorial. 'The nature of the beasts: Gaza flotilla was anti-Semitic, not humanitarian' *New York Daily News*, June 7, 2010.

169 Charles Krauthammer. 'Those troublesome Jews' *The Washington Post*, June 4, 2010.

170 Bernard-Henri Lévy. 'It's time to stop demonising Israel' *Haaretz*, June 8, 2010

171 Elie Wiesel. 'The "activists" wanted violence: Wiesel says we must honestly assess who is to blame' *New York Daily News*, June 6, 2010.

172 Yaakov Lapin. 'Gaza flotilla: Go back to Auschwitz' *The Jerusalem Post*, June 5, 2010.

173 Tom Gross. Videos of today's tragic incident of the coast of Israel' *Tom Gross Mideast Media* Analysis, June 1, 2010.

174 Daniel Henninger. 'Beating up on Israel' *The Wall Street Journal*, June 3, 2010.

175 Natasha Mozgovaya. 'Reuters under fire for removing weapons, blood from images of Gaza flotilla' *Haaretz*, June 8, 2010.

176 Paul McGeough. 'Prayers, tear gas and terror' *The Sydney Morning Herald*, June 4, 2010.

177 David F. Nesenoff. 'I asked Helen Thomas about Israel. Her answer revealed more than you think' *The Washington Post*, June 20, 2010.

178 Rebecca Bynum. 'Threats to Jews at all time high in US and Canada' *New English Review*, June 5, 2010.

179 http://www.tomgrossmedia.com/mideastdispatches/archives/001118.html

180 http://www.adl.org/press-center/press-releases/anti-semitism-arab/arab-cartoonists-turn-gaza-flotilla-affair-into-a-cause-celebre.html

181 Josh Rogin. 'Turkish ambassador calls for engaging Hamas' *The Cable*, June 4, 2010

182 Jennifer Lipman. 'Blair: Israel has right to check what goes to Gaza' *The Jewish Chronicle*, June 9, 2010.

183 http://mideasttruth.com/forum/viewtopic.php?t=9843

184 George Gilder. *The Israel Test* Minneapolis, MN : Richard Vigilante Books, 2009

185 Robert Fulford. 'Failing 'the Israel test' *National Post*, June 4, 2010.

186 ibid.

187 Maher Abukhater. 'WEST BANK: Mitchell fails to get Palestinian approval for direct talks with Israel' *The Los Angeles Times*, July 17, 2010.

188 General Giora Eiland. 'Regional Alternatives to the Two-State Solution' The Begin-Sadat Center for Strategic Studies, Bar Ilan University, BESA Memorandum No. 4, January 2010.

189 http://www.memritv.org/clip/en/0/0/0/0/0/0/2415.htm

190 http://avalon.law.yale.edu/20th_century/hamas.asp

191 Jonathan Rosenblum.

192 Cal Thomas. 'Put the Pressure on Israel's Enemies' *The Sun Sentinel*, May 18, 2009.

193 Karl Vick. 'Why Israel Doesn't Care About Peace' *Time*, September 2, 2010.

194 ibid.

195 Gil Shefler. 'Jewish NGO's slam 'Time' Magazine cover story' *The Jerusalem Post*, September 13, 2010.

196 Martin. C Wincer. 'Why *Time* Magazine's Karl Vick Doesn't Care About Details' *Martin C Winer*, September 16 2010.

197 Lehav Harkov. 'Poll: 71.5 per cent Israelis favor peace talks' *The Jerusalem Post*, July 21, 2010.

198 Howard Kurts. 'Examining the Coverage of Obama's Iraq Speech; Making Up the News; Journalism and the Internet' *CNN*, September 5, 2010.

199 ibid.

200 Press Release. 'Sinking the Gaza flotilla' *Shurat Hadin Israel Law Center*, May 16, 2011.

201 Jamie Weinstein. 'Yasser Arafat's widow admits Palestinian terror campaign in 2000 was premeditated' *The Daily Caller*, 28 December, 2012.

202 Josef Joffe. 'A World Without Israel' *Foreign Affairs*, January 5, 2005.

203 ibid.

204 http://mada-research.org/en/files/2007/09/haifaenglish.pdf

205 ibid.

206 ibid.

207 ibid.

208 Transcript of Netanyahu's UN General Assembly speech, September 23, 2011. http://www.haaretz.com/news/diplomacy-defense/full-transcript-of-netanyahu-speech-at-un-general-assembly-1.386464

209 Israeli Prime Minister Binyamin Netanyahu's address to a joint session of Congress'. http://www.washingtonpost.com/world/israeli-prime-minister-binyamin-netanyahus-address-to-congress/2011/05/24/AFWY5bAH_story.html

210 'Remarks by President Obama and Prime Minister Netanyahu of Israel After Bilateral Meeting' http://www.whitehouse.gov/the-press-office/2011/05/20/remarks-president-obama-and-prime-minister-netanyahu-israel-after-bilate

211 Remarks by the President on the Middle East and North Africa State Department, Washington, DC. May 19, 2011. http://www.

whitehouse.gov/the-press-office/2011/05/19/remarks-president-middle-east-and-north-africa%20

212 Full transcript of Abbas speech at UN General Assembly, September 23, 2011. http://www.haaretz.com/news/diplomacy-defense/full-transcript-of-abbas-speech-at-un-general-assembly-1.386385

213 Dennis Prager. 'Palestinians Want Peace – Just Not with a Jewish State' *National Review*, September 27, 2011.

214 'Palestinians begin campaign for full member status at UN' *The Guardian*, September 8, 2011.

215 Barak David. 'In first, Spain recognizes Israel as Jewish homeland' *Haaretz*, September 26, 2011.

216 ibid.

217 Herb Keinon. 'J'lem greets French edict on Israel as Jewish state' *The Jerusalem Post*, July 27, 2011.

218 Herb Keinon. 'Biden's favourite Israel story' *The Jerusalem Post*, March 6, 2013

219 Martin Gilbert. 'The Rough Road of the First 50 Years' *Los Angeles Times*, May 14, 1998.

220 Richard Cohen. 'Can the Arab world leave anti-Semitism behind? *The Washington Post*, February 28, 2011.

221 'The United States and the Recognition of Israel: A Chronology' Harry S. Truman, Library and Museum. http://www.trumanlibrary.org/israel/palestin.htm

222 Martin Sherman 'Into The Fray: David Harris's 'stunning short-sightedness' *The Jerusalem Post*, August 29, 2013.

223 Raphael, Israeli. *War, peace and terror in the Middle East*. London, Portland, OR, Frank Cass, 2003: 12.

224 'Faysal Al-Husseini in his Last Interview: The Oslo Accords Were a Trojan Horse; The Strategic Goal is the Liberation of Palestine from the [Jordan] River to the [Mediterranean] Sea' *MEMRI, Special Dispatch No. 236*, July 6, 2001.

225 'Prime Minister Yitzhak Rabin: Ratification of the Israel-Palestinian Interim Agreement' *The Knesset*, October 5, 1995. http://www.mfa.gov.il/mfa/mfa-archive/1995/pages/pm%20rabin%20in%20knesset-%20ratification%20of%20interim%20agree.aspx

226 ibid.

227 Robert Zelnick. *Israel's unilateralism*: *beyond Gaza*. Stanford, Calif.: Hoover Institution Press, Stanford University, 2006: 43.

228 Kenneth Levin. *The Oslo Syndrome*: *Delusions of a People Under Siege*. Hanover, NH: Smith and Kraus, 2005

229 Moshe Ya'alon. *Derekh arukah ketsarah*. Tel Aviv: Yediot Ahronot, 2008

230 Emanuel Winston. 'Defensive conquest – (They Attacked; We Advanced)' *Emanuel A Winston*, February 1, 2004.

THE HOLOCAUST

Why we must never forget the Holocaust

January 27, 2005

At a time when Prince Henry, the third in line for the British throne, is photographed at a party wearing a Nazi uniform,[1] the 60th anniversary of the liberation of Auschwitz, commemorated today, has been given additional urgency. The largest cemetery in human history, the notorious Nazi death camp, has no graves, no place to lay a stone or a flower in honour of the one and a half million (90 per cent of whom were Jewish) who were gassed and whose remains were blown from the chimneys of the crematoria into the sky as smoke.

In the spring of 1944, 12,000 bodies per day were incinerated in Auschwitz, the end product of architects, chemists and lawyers operating in the executive suites of the Nazi regime. While accountants calculated the value of gold fillings and hair harvested from corpses, an ambulance outside the infirmary was fitted with a special lever that enabled the driver to divert the exhaust flow to the passenger section, killing the sick who thought they were being taken to a hospital with carbon monoxide.

Describing the Holocaust as a 'clouding of reason, conscience and heart',[2] Pope John Paul II has said that Auschwitz 'is one of the darkest and most tragic hours of our history'. And indeed, as a symbol of soulless, sophisticated industrial extermination by a state, Auschwitz has no equal. What is so horrifying about Auschwitz is that it was set up with the goal of erasing an entire people and culture, to wipe out the Jewish people from this earth.

The Holocaust did not happen in another universe. Less than 80 years ago, Jews were segregated, then dehumanised and then liquidated, by a nation renowned for its art, philosophy and music. As Jews were arrested, placed in ghettos and placed on trains on death journeys to the concentration camps, Germans, and citizens of other European nations, averted their eyes and, in many cases, collaborated with the Nazis.

When the Jews arrived in Auschwitz and walked past the infamous iron gates that read 'Work Will Make You Free' Josef Mengele, the 'Angel of Death', was waiting. He would flick his hand to the left or right, indicating which children were to be 'spared', destined to become the subject of horrendous experiments, and which children would be executed.

One survivor recalls that when Mengele saw him staring at the smoke from the crematorium, he said, 'Look, your friends are going up to heaven'.[3]

Close your eyes and listen to the terrifying screams of the children, picture the tears of mothers torn away from their sons and daughters.

Imagine living through this nightmare, and then carrying it for a lifetime. Imagine seeing children and toddlers walking into the gas chambers thinking they are going into the showers.

Primo Levi, in his recollections of the year he spent in Auschwitz, wrote that our language lacks words to express this offence, the demolition of man.[4] Auschwitz was as close to hell on this earth as man could devise.

As Allied forces overran the camps, the Nazis took thousands of Jews on death marches, hoping that exhaustion, exposure, starvation, drowning and shooting would leave no witness behind. Of those 7,000 left behind in Auschwitz, some, when offered chocolate and sausages by their liberators, couldn't digest the rich food and died on the spot.

Because Auschwitz lacks any measure of sanity, because its barbarity reaches beyond the 20th century, it is impossible for the mind to comprehend its depths of human depravity and monstrosity. Auschwitz brings home the message that right does not always triumph, that decency and goodness can be overcome by chaos. Auschwitz is a sombre warning against the evil man can do and against the dangers of anti-Semitism and racism. It teaches us to never drop our guard.

The Holocaust is beyond politics, and beyond religion. Since not only Jews perished in the Holocaust, it binds all groups, Jewish and non-Jewish. It is our duty to teach succeeding generations that Auschwitz is the direct result of tyranny and intolerance and to remind them of the destruction pure and unbounded hatred engenders. When Laura Bush recently visited Auschwitz and saw the seven tons of hair human (sold by Nazi soldiers for 33 cents per 2.2 pounds), eye glasses and suitcases taken from the victims as they arrived, she remarked that 'the impact of this experience will remain in my memory forever'.[5]

Sadly, Auschwitz did not shock humanity into avoiding the massive crimes of Cambodia, Rwanda and Bosnia. As Australians, we all have a stake in communicating the truth to our children and in guaranteeing that the memory of the Holocaust does not recede from our memory, or is denied. For a people who ignore history are doomed to repeat it.

By remembering the suffering of the victims today, we make sure that their deaths were not meaningless.

Deny these deniers

December 18, 2006

Over the past few days I have had that sickening feeling: here we go again.

The International Conference to Review the Global Vision of the Holocaust was held in Tehran to explore whether the Holocaust really happened.[6]

It included Australians Fredrick Toben and socialite Michele Renouf.

A type of vicious and obscene Jewish hatred, which is a crime in a number of countries and one that we usually equate with cranks and anti-Semites, has been put on display.

Iran is a member state of the United Nations, but its president has vowed to wipe Israel off the map and is cultivating a program to acquire nuclear weapons.

This wilful assault on the truth of the Holocaust should be not relegated to the dustbin of sick jokes. Holocaust denial goes far beyond the claims of Elvis sightings or conspiracy theories about the assassination of JFK.

Holocaust denial deserves the description as an evil act.

Remember the murder of Daniel Pearl? His beheading was caused by the same hatred of Jews that participants in this so-called conference and their ilk have keenly spread worldwide.

This is not just about words. Holocaust denial wants to make Nazism seem not so bad. Its agents must have been wringing their hands in pleasure when they read that an American survey found that close to 40 per cent of high school students did not know anything about the Holocaust, and that 30 per cent of the adults polled thought it was possible that the Holocaust never happened. So, why are some taken in by the Holocaust denial industry and its slick tactics?

Why are some willing to entertain such nonsense?

Commentators have theorised that Holocaust deniers count on fascination with conspiracy theories to account for every major event: the assassination of JFK, the Apollo moon landings, alien abductions, and the death of Princess Diana.

At heart, opposing Holocaust denial is about protecting ourselves from those who promote xenophobia and who wish harm to all Australians. The only reason Holocaust deniers scream about freedom of speech is so that they can manipulate it, deny it to others, and ultimately shut it down.

I have heard people talk about stifling debate regarding the Holocaust. The only debate is among racists, the merely ignorant, and hatemongers who yearn to bring up a new generation of haters.

The Supreme Court of Canada has held that incitement to hatred is not a legitimate expression of free speech, recognising that incitement has led to the death of millions and that it is among the most dangerous activities known to humanity.

And a majority of EU ministers has agreed that freedom of speech is not a shield against Holocaust denial.

Giving a voice to Holocaust deniers is an affront to all those who escaped genocide and tyranny to make new lives for themselves in Australia. Offensive lies are not popular speech and should not be given a public forum. Holocaust denial must be challenged in the strongest fashion possible. The power of evil cannot be underestimated. We all owe a duty to the truth.

Words of hate hurt

June 28, 2007

The report of children as young as eleven racially abusing players on the sporting field should set off alarm bells. Indeed, we should all reflect on why such bigotry still exists in our multicultural and diverse society.

A fourteen-year-old performed a Hitler march during a soccer match against a Jewish team. Another said: 'Too bad the Nazis didn't gas you all.'

In another match, players called African opponents 'darkies' and 'black dogs'. They must have learned such prejudice from someone.

Are such attitudes the fruits of their parents' upbringing, or are they the results of websites, films and music in which such put-downs are used to describe certain groups? Parents often develop bias in their kids. What parents say and do lays down the foundation of their children's values and shapes their responses to people of different ethnic and religious backgrounds.

Research has shown that between the ages of three and five, children notice racial difference, but this curiosity is not linked to any specific qualities.

Whatever negative associations come into their mind are conveyed by parents, relatives, friends and the mass media. Sadly, prejudice is not always high on the agenda of parents and schools, even though it should be a priority.

I have been told by parents they feel uncomfortable discussing discrimination, knowing the questions may be painful or embarrassing.

Respect is the cornerstone of human interaction. Children must practise civility and hospitality and never diminish others by personally destructive remarks.

Suspension and banning are appropriate corrective actions but will not put a stop to disrespect.

Offensive language needs to lead to discussion and counselling. Apathy and silence are not options for parents and educators. Take the initiative and bring up these issues. Ask your kids what they think about racism and offensive phrases.

*

Listen together to Martin Luther King's 'I have a dream'[7] speech, and explore its ideas and themes. Create situations when conversations happen naturally, so your children don't feel as if they are being interrogated or put on the spot.

Most importantly, be mindful of your own behaviour and make sure you instil values through modelling. 'Do as I say and not as I do' won't work.

The messages about respecting others must be demonstrated in your actions. Remain vigilant and persistent. The demeaning words and actions of the young sportspeople I mentioned came from ignorance rather than malice.

As part of a comprehensive strategy, children should be taught about Cambodia, Bosnia, Rwanda and Darfur, and understand that the Holocaust did not begin with the building of Auschwitz. It began with words that dehumanised Jews and other minorities and enabled their murder. Schools and sporting clubs are important allies in raising awareness about the damage caused by biased and insensitive language.

Schools must have initiatives that foster compassion, understanding and acceptance of minorities. Identifying and recognising that there is a problem are key factors in eliminating harassment and establishing a hate-free atmosphere.

Young adults must be taught to treat every person with courtesy and respect. Unchecked use of racial or sexual epithets creates a toxic environment that impedes growth and learning.

Send the message that hateful words are not cool and respond every time you hear a slur whether it was used in a joking or a serious manner. Abusive language is always unacceptable.

Crucially, racial sledging robs not only the victim but also the offender of dignity. Teaching children to value all people is part of our parental responsibilities and should be part of our educational roadmap in raising decent, moral and tolerant adults.

World blind to growing horror

June 23, 2008

After the Holocaust more than 60 years ago, people asked how could we let it happen, how could the world's nations remain silent? They also promised to never again be bystanders when others were attacked because of prejudice and blind hatred.

Well, the 'never again' is happening right now. Who would have imagined that in 2008 similar stories of cruelty and despair would be coming out of Africa?

Indeed, the silence about the bloodshed in Sudan's Darfur region – the first genocide of the 21st century – is deafening.

As JKF commented: 'Dante once said that the hottest places in hell are reserved for those who in a period of moral crisis maintain their neutrality.'

One wonders how the world sits still when an estimated 400,000 people have died in a campaign of ethnic cleansing and 2.5 million people (more than 50 per cent are children) have been uprooted and deported from their homes into refugee camps?

The team of nine Australian Defence Force logisticians sent recently to join the UN mission to Darfur is mere lip service by the Rudd Government.[8]

Memories of the world's apathy during the shameful genocide in Rwanda should have compelled most nations to intervene in this latest bloodbath.

Warnings issued in 2003 about the widespread slaughter went unheeded. In 2004, then US Secretary of State Colin Powell finally admitted genocide had been committed in Darfur, an assessment reiterated by President George Bush.[9]

With the almost total global indifference shown to the one million dead in Rwanda's genocide still casting a giant shadow, the international community continues to remain unconscionably idle. The two top mediators on Darfur have recently painted a grim picture of the prospects for peace, saying that conditions are worse than they have been in some time.

The Arab Janjaweed militias, who are backed by the Sudanese Government, have indiscriminately pillaged and destroyed whole villages and terrorised, tortured and murdered hundreds of thousands of defenceless men, women and children.

Armed bandits and security forces subject girls as young as twelve to beatings, rape and kidnappings. Some experts predict the death toll will pass one million.

Attempts to halt the annihilation have been thwarted by countries with vested economic and political interests – China, with its veto power on the UN Security Council, is Sudan's largest supplier of arms and has oil interests there.

Film director Steven Spielberg this year took a brave stand and resigned as artistic director of the Beijing Olympics, citing China's documented complicity in the genocide.[10]

The toothless UN Security Council has invoked, for the first time in its history, the Convention on the Prevention and Punishment of the Crime of Genocide and threatened strong and effective measures. But this has not stopped the onslaught and the continuing humanitarian disaster.

Holocaust survivor and author Elie Wiesel maintains that what hurts the victim is not only the cruelty of the oppressor, but the silence of the bystander.

Australians must raise their voices in outrage. The public must urge the Australian Government to take a leading role and advocate sanctions against Khartoum's brutal tyrants and the immediate deployment of an effective international force.

Don't play with the memory of the Holocaust

September 2, 2008

We shouldn't be surprised that the Victorian lobby group 'Plug the Pipe' produced a poster featuring parallel images of Hitler and John Brumby (with a crude moustache and fringe drawn on the Premier's face) and grotesquely asking: 'Can you spot the differences between these two dictators?'[11] The linking of the deliberate murder of millions to the issue of water was not just bad taste, but bad morality.

Earlier this year, Australian soccer player Andre Gumprecht attended a post-season party dressed as Hitler,[12] while Sam Leach portrayed himself as Hitler and was rewarded with an Archibald nomination for his 'art'.[13]

The Plug the Pipe episode demonstrates the abhorrent uses of Holocaust symbolism in political life. To borrow from one commentator, what facet of the Holocaust will next become the subject of propaganda – the tattooed arms? The tortures? The gassings themselves?

We live in an age where all bets are off when it comes to the depiction of the Holocaust. Manipulative symbolism and false equivalences have become the trend.

The Holocaust has become a cartoon collection (*We have Ways of Making You Laugh: 120 Funny Swastika Cartoons*)[14]. In one strip a swastika-adorned woman selling matches on a snowy street says to her friend: 'I joined because you get to keep warm during the book burnings.'

An anti-smoking T-shirt on sale in Germany features a yellow star with the word 'smoker' across it; a Brazilian samba group features a Holocaust display; a series of men's striped pyjamas and jackets with boot marks and numbers painted on them are modelled by an emaciated model with closely cropped hair and protruding ears as part of a fashion show.

There is also a *Seinfeld* episode, a Lego set, a campaign that compares the abusive treatment of animals to the Holocaust, and a comedy set in a death camp. Hitler and his genocidal regime are now an all-purpose metaphor, a gimmick, an opportunity to generate publicity.

Feature films about Hitler have either humanised him or turned him into a caricature. In the film *My Fuehrer, the Truly Truest Truth about Adolf Hitler*, the mass-murderer emerges from Berlin's sewer system, where he survived the war. Lying in bed, he cries, 'I'm so alone' while his Jewish acting teacher and wife sing him a lullaby. In other scenes, Hitler is depicted as a pathetic, incontinent wimp who cannot make love to his mistress Eva Braun and plays with toy battleships in the bathtub.[15]

On YouTube, a made-up clip by a student titled 'Hitler Leasing!' has Hitler in a dispute with a car-leasing company. And cabaret artist Thomas Pigor impersonates Hitler, making audiences roar as he sings, 'Hitler, the new perfume for men: smells monumental – and of German shepherd.'

Aren't you laughing?

If this were not enough, even the legacy of Anne Frank has been debased. A musical based on her life that has been playing in Madrid was described by its director as 'a very entertaining musical, with intimate moments and a lot of comedy'.[16]

Holocaust memory and sacredness have been diluted; its desecration is ubiquitous. Sacha Baron Cohen, who grew up in a traditionally Jewish home, should have known better than to perform a honky-tonk tune, *Throw the Jew Down the Well*, to sing-along audiences in Arizona.

The exhibition *Mirroring Evil: Nazi Imagery/Recent Art*, in the Jewish Museum in New York showed a picture of an artist holding a Coca-Cola can superimposed on a photo of emaciated concentration camp survivors saying: 'Just as much of Europe succumbed to Nazi culture ... so does our contemporary culture succumb to consumerism.'

Coke and Auschwitz – same thing, right?

If you want to scold Brumby, don't use an image of Hitler to make the point and in the process trample on the feelings of survivors and the memory of the dead. You can drive home the message without denigrating and demeaning lives lost.

The Holocaust should not just be material for anyone to distort and reinvent as they please in order to suit their own agenda. Plug the Pipe crossed a moral line, wounding people who already experienced unimaginable injury, seeking to sensationalise their cause and counting on society's fascination with shock value.

No one is advocating censorship. Rather, what is pleaded for is the exercising of discretion, understanding and respect for the memory of the dead and the living. The murder of six million Jews and millions of non-Jews, and the man who devastated Europe, are not the subject of levity and should not serve as fodder for crass stunts. When anyone chooses to engage with the Holocaust, the responsibility they carry is of the highest order, born out of the ashes of Auschwitz.

That I have to explain this speaks volumes.

The magnitude and scale of the crimes perpetrated by the Nazis should be depicted authentically through facts and without ambiguity. And the same applies to the suffering of the Armenians, Cambodians, Bosnians, Rwandans, Sudanese and any other group subjected to acts of monstrosity.

A world that now knows what we know cannot afford this trivialisation.

The Holocaust began because words of hate went unchallenged

December 11, 2008

Anti-Semitism often comes from the most unlikely source, such as Australian teenagers at two prestigious private schools who thought it was a 'big in-joke' to create a Facebook site called 'Jew Parking Appreciation Group' – described as an activity that occurs at 'Bellevue (Jew) Hill'.[17]

The site was established and managed by students from Sydney's Scots College and by one student from Kambala School for Girls. It was linked to another network set up and run by Scots College students with postings such as 'Support Holocaust denial', 'Jew Rats', 'F— Mercedes Jews' and a link to another internet address called 'F— Israel and Their Holocaust Bullshit'.

One of the students involved in this shameful episode defended the network by saying that he and the other 51 participants had Jewish friends. Are you shaking with disbelief?

This is not an isolated incident. Last year, players from the McKinnon and Beaumaris cricket clubs posted anti-Semitic remarks against a Jewish sports organisation on a Facebook site called 'FU AJAX Cricket Club'.[18] Comments referred to Jewish players as human goats, with one contributor writing 'AJAX should have won easily but they nearly choked, probably on gas'. Another member, the self-described Deputy Vice-President in charge of Holocaust References, wrote that AJAX should install a 'f— ing Rheem' while another observed that, 'being of German heritage, I think I need to apologise for (AJAX Cricket Club) to still be in existence, my grandparents tried to get them all … but it's easier said than done when they are walking around in sewers trying to find change'.

Every reader should now ask themselves: from whom did these teenagers learn these troubling attitudes? If you are a parent, alarm bells should go off along with the question: Do my children hold similar views?

This latest unsettling occurrence unfolded in a week when an official report revealed that in the past year Australian Jews were the victims of a record 652 anti-Semitic incidents, almost double the average of the past eighteen months. The report said that 'the combined number of incidents involving physical assault, property damage and direct, face-to-face harassment was almost three times the previous average'.[19]

Last month, the world commemorated the 70th anniversary of Kristallnacht – the Night of Broken Glass – a 24-hour spree of destruction that marked the beginning of the Holocaust that resulted in the extermination of six million Jews. Yet, two weeks earlier, in a Richmond Primary School, a project displayed on a classroom wall stated that Hitler was 'one of the many great things about Germany'. It was written by a grade 1 pupil as part of the child's work on German culture. Also featured on the board was a swastika. Neither the teachers nor the principal found any fault with the poster and project and did not remove it.

Consider that young Australians would have learned on Wednesday that a political group compared South Australia's anti-bikie laws to the Nazi persecution of Jews.[20] And in October they may have heard that a Wollongong Baptist minister Kevin Harris said that Jews will suffer a fate 'worse than the Holocaust' because they don't accept Jesus.[21]

Words do matter. Auschwitz, the largest cemetery in the world, happened because of centuries of anti-Semitism and the inaction of bystanders. Glossing over these uncomfortable issues is not an option.

Last month, the Scottish Government provided $450,000 for school pupils to visit Nazi concentration camps,[22] recognising the importance of Holocaust education. Several countries now mandate Holocaust education as part of the general school curriculum, using it to promote respect and to teach students to stand up and speak out when they see something wrong, as well as to stick up for others when they are being persecuted or vilified.

The Federal Government must now act. If we had national Holocaust education, then maybe former national goalkeeping great Mark Bosnich would not have given the Hitler salute while playing for Aston Villa[23] and Australian soccer player Andre Gumprecht would not have shown up at a party dressed as Hitler.

Families also have a role to play in fighting prejudice. When racism causes children to ridicule others, good parents rise up against it and engender a healthy discussion about values. They equip their children with the attitude that judges people based on their integrity and inner qualities, not their religion or ethnic background. Parents also need to watch what they say in front of children, especially when they are angry.

Anti-Semitism has proven to be the most enduring hatred of the 20th century. Only with a legacy of appreciation of all human beings, repeated over and over at home and schools, will our children combat and prevent discrimination and bias whenever it is encountered. This is a cause worth fighting for.

The Reader is pure Holocaust revisionism

April 10, 2009

When *The Reader* was first chosen as an Oprah Book selection and became a bestseller I could not believe it. And when it earned Kate Winslet an Oscar I was filled with incredulity.

The Reader is not a film about the Holocaust. It does not add in any decent way to our understanding of history's darkest chapter. Rather, it distorts and unscrupulously exploits the death of millions for its own cheap box-office purposes.

Further, it's an offensive type of Holocaust revisionism that immorally argues that Germans were oblivious to the liquidation of millions of Jews and only learned about it after the Second World War. It not only misrepresents history but rewrites it, and is the latest in a series of works determined to humanise the Nazis.

The Reader (also a textbook in German schools) inappropriately seduces us to sympathise with a barbaric woman who herded 300 Jewish women into a church and did not unlock it when it was bombed and burned alive its occupants.

Michael, the fifteen-year-old German boy who enjoyed a passionate illicit affair with the 32-year-old Hanna, an unrepentant SS killer on trial years later, believes that her guilt is lessened because she could not read. Got it!? If she could read, she would not have voluntarily joined the SS and would have known that killing is wrong. Illiteracy is a handy excuse for acting as a monster.

The theme of illiteracy in the film stands for something more sinister – the German people's supposed incapacity to 'read' the glaring evidence that industrialised extermination of European Jewry was committed by their government and with their full participation.

The filmmakers present Hanna as simply following orders (she is by extension representative of the beastly SS though most were men and high-school graduates) instead of accurately showing the fanatical hatred of Jews these barbarians held. Winslet herself bought into this insanity when she said on the Charlie Rose show that those who joined the SS were not aware of what they were getting involved with.

Really, Kate?

Hanna, who we are supposed to feel empathy for, is more ashamed of her illiteracy than of guarding the church door so that the hundreds of screaming Jews couldn't escape, or serving as a guard in Auschwitz, or selecting inmates for gassing.

The chilling church scene was omitted from the film so as not to affect our sympathetic view of this sadistic murderer.

When asked by the judge to explain her despicable acts, Hanna slyly asks him what he would have done, insinuating that she only did what any of us would have done in the same situation.

We are supposed to forgive, not punish the helpless Hanna, embrace her, not judge her, since we too would have acted as she did.

Even more troubling, Michael (symbolising the post-war generation of Germans) feels nothing for the dead victims. Perversely, he recalls making love to Hanna while her crimes are detailed. The more heinous Hanna's crimes are, the more that he is sexually aroused.

Michael vilely questions the testimony of the Jewish witnesses, thinking that they are in no position to determine the identity and guilt of the Nazis, and may in fact victimise the innocent, such as Hanna. For him the execution of Jews is like a car accident. Sounds like Holocaust denial, no?

The sinister Hanna's apparent redemption occurs in jail when she learns to read and devotes her reading to survivor-accounts. But she of course need not read Wiesel or Primo Levi. She knows of the terrors that those camps produced because she was there, forcing the young children to read to her aloud before sending them to their ghastly death. The film obscenely turns Hanna from a perpetrator into a victim, even though she shows no remorse and tells Michael that nobody has to apologise for anything.

Manipulatively, the film fills the screen with gratuitous and titillating nudity in which the blond Aryan 'educates' her toy boy in wild sexual sessions. Maybe it's me, but I never associated Nazism with soft-core porn.

The film ups the bad morality scale when Michael visits a Holocaust survivor of the church massacre to hand over Hanna's life savings. In contrast to the suffering Hanna, who is in jail and sick, the survivor is wealthy and elegant. She is portrayed as cold. The unfair conclusion and grotesque stereotype of survivors is easily drawn. The survivor refuses the disgusting attempt at buying her absolution, and the money is donated to a Jewish charity fighting illiteracy. How heart-warming.

Michael takes his daughter to the church cemetery where he buried Hanna and tells her the story, seeking the third-generation's pity for the cruel murderer.

Many may believe that *The Reader*, a glossy, attractive production, aimed at making the viewer feel good about genocide, is fact, rather than fantasy. Those who wish to exonerate the German people for the complicity in the Final Solution must be pleased.

We must never let the Holocaust's grim lessons fade away

April 22, 2009

This week the Victorian Jewish community commemorates Holocaust Memorial Day and says, 'Never again'. And yet we live in a time when the Pope re-admits into his church a bishop who has denied the full extent of the Nazi genocide of six million Jews;[24] and when the Iranian President, whose attitudes have been at the centre of controversy over the UN conference on racism in Geneva this week, denies the Holocaust.

In Australia, the rate of anti-Semitic incidents over the past year is the highest ever.

The Holocaust is one of the darkest, heartbreaking and most traumatic chapters of our history. As a symbol of soulless, sophisticated industrial extermination by a state – as symbolised by the death camp of Auschwitz, where 1.5 million people perished – it has no equal.

Most terrifying about the Nazi regime is that it was established with the aim of extinguishing an entire people and culture, of erasing the Jewish people.

The Holocaust did not take place on another planet. It happened during the 20th century, in the heart of Europe, in a country considered to be the epitome of culture and progress. It was made possible because of a history of terrible anti-Semitism and because Germans averted their eyes while their own citizens were systematically rounded up and shipped in cattle carriages to their deaths.

As one character puts it in Israeli author's Itamar Levy's book *The Legend of the Sad Lakes*: 'Our problem is that we treat the Holocaust like a history lesson. But that's not what it was. The Holocaust was a horrible crime. People were butchered, raped and starved to death in it. It wasn't history that did this to us. It was people.'[25]

British MP Ann Snelgrove noted that 'Majdanek was a camp that was situated right on top of a community in a city. It was not hidden from civilisation. That is shocking … a warning to all of us. If we are not careful, it will happen again among us.'[26]

Because the Holocaust defies any measure of sanity, because its monstrosity transcends the 20th century, it is impossible to under-stand its depths of human depravity and barbarity. One of the hor-rifying messages of the Holocaust is that justice does not always prevail, that decency and goodness can be drowned out by evil.

The Holocaust is a sombre warning against the evil that man can do and against the dangers of unchecked racism. It teaches us to never allow prejudice to go unchallenged.

The time will come when the witnesses of the Holocaust will no longer be with us. Since not only Jews perished in the Holocaust – homosexuals, Gypsies and the disabled were among other victims – it commits all people to action..

We have a shared moral duty to teach future generations that the Holocaust is the direct result of tyranny and discrimination and remind them of the destruction unbounded hatred can lead to. Sadly, the Holocaust did not prod humanity into preventing the genocide of Cambodia, Rwanda, Bosnia, Darfur and Burma.

We need to instil in our children the moral duty to never turn a blind eye to intolerance. As Australians, we have a stake in ensuring that the memory and lessons of the Holocaust do not recede from our memory. A people who ignore history are doomed to repeat it. As Martin Luther King said, 'In the end, we will remember not the words of our enemies, but the silence of our friends.'

By remembering the suffering of the victims, we make sure their deaths were not in vain.

Hollywood – Please stop exploiting the Holocaust!

November 2, 2009

In a 2005 guest appearance on the sitcom *Extras*, Kate Winslet, playing herself as nun on a Holocaust film, is asked 'You doing this, it's so commendable, using your profile to keep the message alive about the Holocaust.' Winslet responds: 'God, I'm not doing it for that. We definitely don't need another film about the Holocaust, do we? It's like, how many have there been? You know, we get it. It was grim. Move on. I'm doing it because I noticed that if you do a film about the Holocaust, you're guaranteed an Oscar. I've been nominated four times. Never won. The whole world is going, "Why hasn't Winslet won one?" ... That's why I'm doing it. *Schindler's bloody List. The Pianist.* Oscars coming outta their ass ...'[27]

Winslet was right, winning the Oscar for best actress this year for *The Reader*.

The commodification of the Holocaust into a profitable, Oscar-reaping enterprise has reached such a nadir that commentators are quoting from Philip Roth's *Operation Shylock*, 'There's no business like Shoah Business.' Though I find this epigram distasteful, it does reflect a disturbing trend in which the Holocaust is being packaged and sold by filmmakers who are using this terrifying dark chapter as a ticket for advancing their own fame and artistic agenda.

These films conveniently skip over the mass shootings, the gas chambers, the ovens, the mounds of naked bodies – filling up the screen with harmful falsifications. The damage Hollywood, with its huge marketing machine, is doing to the memory of the Holocaust is enormous. Think of Hollywood's cowboy and Indian movies and how they shaped our understanding of that episode.

Inglourious Basterds insensitively uses the Holocaust as entertainment. In Tarantino's film, which actor Eli Roth called, 'Kosher porn',[28] it's the bloodthirsty Jewish GIs who are the bastards, torturing and scalping Nazi soldiers. In one scene, the band interrogates a German soldier who comes across as a man of honour refusing to divulge where his troops are stationed. The soldier is then sadistically beaten to death.

Tarantino has offensively stated that this film is the ultimate fantasy of every Jew. Really?

Maybe yours Quentin, not mine.

Besides, what does it say about Jews if all they want is to become carbon copies of the Nazis? Jews have taken revenge on the Nazis through the commemoration and memorialisation of the Holocaust, by saying 'Never Again' and by campaigning to ensure such a genocide never re-occurs. Tarantino works against that aim – glorifying and deliriously celebrating humanity's most animalistic and darkest impulses, which in a perverse way, embody Nazi, not Jewish, behaviour.

This is inexcusable and shock-art at its worst.

I agree with author Daniel Mendelsohn who writes that Tarantino turns the Jews into Nazis, into 'sickening perpetrators'[29] who elicit very little sympathy.

Consider this: The Jews in *Inglourious Basterds* assume the callous characteristics of the Nazis – they take pleasure in their abhorrent violence; they crack skulls with baseball bats just like the Nazis who crushed the skulls of Jewish infants before their parents' eyes; they engrave swastikas onto their victims foreheads just like the Nazis who carved swastikas into the chests of rabbis before slaughtering them.

The end of the film is also an exercise in atrocity distortion. Unsuspecting people are lured into a building, the doors are shut and the building is set alight. But this time the yelling, banging on the doors, the confusion, the despair, the incinerated bodies belong to the Nazis. In Tarantino's nihilist, grotesque alternate universe, it's the Jews who are the villains, who commit the vicious act so familiar from Holocaust history. Would most teenagers who watch *Inglourious Basterds* know that it was actually the Nazis who forced Jews into buildings and burned them alive?

By erasing the Nazi monstrousness, Tarantino, with his World War II spaghetti western has not only rewritten Holocaust history, but has contributed to its forgetting.

And it does seem that our culture has hit rock-bottom when film-makers such as Tarantino are using the Holocaust as a comic-book bloodfest, while audiences help him inflate his bank account.

The insulting and emotionally manipulative *The Boy In The Striped Pyjamas* was described by the *New York Times* critic as 'The Holocaust trivialised, glossed over, kitsched up ... and hijacked for a tragedy about a Nazi family'[30] while Lisa Schwarzbaum of *Entertainment Weekly* called it 'appalling' and 'jaw-dropping'.[31]

The 2009 film focuses on nine-year-old Bruno, a German boy whose family relocates from Berlin to Auschwitz, after his high-ranking SS father is promoted to supervise the wholesale liquidation of Jews in the death camp. The young boy becomes curious about the 'farm' beyond the gate of his new home and befriends Shmuel, the Jewish boy his age who is caged on the other side of the barbed fence. The two boys spend hours talking, playing games, hatching schemes, yet Shmuel never seems troubled by what's happening inside the extermination camp, never talks about the hell the inmates are subjected to.

The whole basis for the film is a fabrication and takes suspension of disbelief too far. Such friendships could never have developed since all Jewish boys who were not old enough for hard labour were immediately gassed upon their arrival, no prisoner was able to stroll around unobserved by the armed guards on the sentry towers, or find the time to have lengthy exchanges with outsiders at the electrified fence.

We are asked to believe that the blissfully clueless Bruno is unaware of what Jews are, or about the bestial nature of the camps, even when he sees through his bedroom window smoke rising from the smokestacks, or when he sees that all the 'farmers' are wearing pyjamas or when he notices that the emaciated, shoeless Shmuel has been physically abused. The Germans knew about the industrialised extermination of their countrymen, but they stood by passively and indifferently. The film provides a defence to that claim of innocence.

Professor Robert Eaglestone has correctly stated that *The Boy in Striped Pyjamas* is dangerously ill-informed and wrongly made Auschwitz 'as unreal as Camelot or Hogwarts School'.[32]

In the film's agonisingly sentimental conclusion, Bruno crawls under the fence and is gassed along with the Jews. His death shatters the family and invites our pity. Never mind about those millions of faceless Jews, about whom the father earlier says to his son, 'Those people – you realise they're not people at all.' The film immorally milks the viewer's emotions so it cares and empathises with the pain of those who actively implemented the Final Solution.

Soon, there will be no eye-witnesses to the Holocaust. Films may replace the testimonies of the victims. Let's hope that when future generations want to understand about humanity's darkest hour that they will not turn to these movies for knowledge.

Blood money: Profiting from death and suffering

February 10, 2010

When I was a kid, we collected stamps. I thought these were the kind of things people collected.

I realised only later that there were other items people were interested in. Abhorrent, grisly collectibles such as medals and daggers carried by SS officers, Nazi officer swords, swastikas, diaries by Hitler and his henchmen.

Last week, the 200-page diary of monster Josef Mengele, nicknamed 'The Angel of Death', was sold by Alexander Autographs Auctioneers House in the US. The buyer of the diary lost a hundred of his close relatives in the concentration camps and will donate it to the Holocaust Museum.[33]

Mengele, who wanted to clone an 'Aryan Race', selected arrivals in Auschwitz for the gas chambers, forced labour or as subjects for his brutal medical experiments. Most of the inmates died in unimaginable pain without anaesthetic on the operating table. Girls were sterilised. Others had chemicals injected to change their eye colour to blue. Those who survived were crippled for life.

I still have not fully come to grips with the worldwide demand that exists for Nazi memorabilia. The recent theft of the Auschwitz gate sign is believed to have been carried out to satisfy the huge and twisted appetite for artifacts from that inhuman period.

Hard to believe, but it's a highly lucrative trade. In fact, it's booming. Just try googling Nazi mementoes or something along those lines, and you'll be shocked by the thousands of sites, and the variety of items for sale. Hitler, Himmler and Goering-related objects are the most sought after.

Some fetch in the millions, especially if they were signed by Hitler. I understand that Hitler's art is particularly popular and attracts high prices. Just ask Texas oil millionaire Billy F. Price.

A tiny sample: Herman Goering's yacht A\$270,000; binoculars used by Hitler A\$53,000; a bottle of Nazi red wine from 1943 featuring Hitler's image A\$7000; an SS Honour ring A\$4000.

Eleven years ago, Atlanta-based Great Gatsby's conducted an

auction of silver pieces, including icecream spoons and lobster forks owned by Hitler.

And it is not just neo Nazis and white supremacists who are willing to shell out large amounts for the chance to display and glorify the emblems of the Third Reich. James Flynn, a Taxing Master in the Irish High Court paid A$305,000 for several pieces of Herman Goering memorabilia.

Mark Garlasco, senior military adviser for the UN's Human Rights Watch was suspended last year for trading and collecting Nazi souvenirs. Garlasco, who penned several reports condemning and accusing Israel of war atrocities, posted the following: 'The leather SS jacket makes my blood go so cold it is so COOL.'[34] Even the UN realised that it would lose any legitimacy if it did not investigate the hobby of its supposedly impartial observer.

And according to newspaper reports, US actor Scarlett Johansson is fascinated by Nazi paraphernalia, a pursuit she developed while looking at items in Bulgarian markets during the filming of *The Black Dahlia*.[35]

Not surprisingly, Holocaust denier David Irving sells Nazi memorabilia on a site, dubbed Naz-eBay. He claims to have a piece of bone from Hitler's body and strands of his hair collected by his barber.

The collectors will tell you that they do not sympathise with the sickening ideology and the genocide carried out by the Third Reich. They are simply history buffs.

Others are honest enough to admit it's purely about the money.

In a three-day grand sale, Jonathan Humbert of JP Humbert Auctioneers in Northamptonshire sold A$160,000 of rare Nazi keepsakes. Humbert noted that the global financial meltdown did not affect his clients. Humbert also noted that the October 2008 sale was his best in five years, and praised the value of investing in 'antiques' or 'chattels' rather than in financial institutions.[36]

I wonder what are the commission fees that Humbert and the other auction houses charge for their services?

And then there are those with more sinister reasons.

The sale of such relics is banned in Austria, France and Germany. But not in Poland. That may explain why today Poland is the biggest producer and exporter of Nazi items, available in markets and shops. An SS officer's uniform sells for about A$1600.

In 2000, a French court ordered Yahoo to stop selling Nazi items, including replicas of Zyklon B poison gas canisters.[37] A cursory search on eBay brings up thousands of Nazi-related items. Some are too gruesome for me to mention.

Why any internet company would allow the hawking of hateful and offensive material to the highest bidder is beyond me. I'm willing to concede that there may be a handful of people who don't fully comprehend the objectionable nature of Nazi memorabilia.

In 2008, swastikas, Nazi armbands and stamps were removed from a Daylesford Mill market.[38] In the same year, concerns were raised about two stores in NSW that were selling Nazi clothing and items. One of the owners said he sold Japanese flags and did not see any difference.

Then there are those who refuse the lure of money. In 2000, the head of the War Museum in Canada refused to sell a bullet-proof Mercedes used by Hitler. The car would have brought in millions.

He lost millions in potential funds. But he retained his morality and principles.

Stopping Genocide in the age of Lara Bingle and Tiger Woods

March 29, 2010

After the Holocaust, survivor, author and Nobel Prize winner Elie Wiesel wrote: 'The victims perished not only because of the killers, but also because of the apathy of the bystanders. What astonished us after the torment, after the tempest, was not that so many killers killed so many victims, but that so few cared about us at all.'[39]

The lasting lesson of the Holocaust is that it succeeded not just because of the Nazi industrialised machinery of death but because of indifference and conspiracies of silence. After 1945 most nations vowed, 'Never Again'. Indeed, President Barack Obama, while visiting the Buchenwald Concentration camp in 2009, stated that 'Never Again' means that 'the international community has an obligation, even when it's inconvenient, to act when genocide is occurring'.

The world remained distant from the atrocities of the Nazis, but we thought we would never see a similar distance. We were wrong. Today the slaughters in Darfur and The Democratic Republic of Congo have gone under the radar. Stories about a model and her cricketer boyfriend, or a golfer and his lovers capture our attention.

In Judaism there is the concept of Tikkun Olam – the mandate for the healing and repair of the human world. And as one who honours Holocaust memory, I am also obligated to take other genocides seriously. For seven years, the Sudanese government has conducted a brutal campaign of genocide. It has murdered hundreds of thousands of civilians in a campaign of ethnic cleansing and destroyed 90 per cent of Darfur's villages. Systematic rape of girls and women is routine. Those who survive the pack-rape are often abducted as slave labour.

Two and a half million people (more than 50 per cent are children) have been uprooted and deported from their homes, living in horrific conditions in refugee camps along the Chad-Sudan border. The US, the only country with real leverage to pressure Khartoum to change its wicked ways, has been feckless. Governments have conveniently turned their backs on the carnage.

Listen to one Sudanese woman tell her story of unimaginable

cruelty committed by soldiers. 'They said to us: "If you have a baby on your back, let us see it." The soldiers looked at the babies and if it was a boy, they killed it on the spot [by shooting him]. If it was a girl, they dropped or threw it on the ground. If the girl died, she died. If she didn't die, the mothers were allowed to pick it up and keep it.'[40] A grandmother, who refused to show a boy to the soldiers, was shot along with her grandson.

Now listen to the story of nine-year-old Chance Tombola. The orphan saw both her parents killed in front of her. Her two sisters, six and twelve, were taken and disappeared. Two months later, soldiers invaded the home of Chance's aunt, uncle and two nieces. They shot her uncle and sliced his belly open, as his widow and daughters watched. They then repeatedly raped Chance and her aunt. The two daughters were taken to the forest, and have not been heard from since.

An International Rescue Committee report concluded that an estimated 5.4 million people died from conflict-related causes in the civil war fought in the Eastern Congo since 1998 – the bloodiest conflict in the world since World War II.[41] The death toll is approaching six million, with 1.5 million people displaced and 500,000 women raped.

In Bosnia, American, British and NATO forces intervened to end the sickening campaign of violence against Muslims, yet in Sudan and in Eastern Congo there has been no such military intervention, only envoys dispatched. Attempts to halt the annihilation have been thwarted by countries with vested economic and political interests. China, with its veto power on the Security Council, is Sudan's largest supplier of arms and has oil interests there.

Very few consumers would know that the Congo is the world's biggest supplier of Coltan, a crucial material in the manufacture of mobile telephones. The campaign against 'blood cellphones'[42] has not been heeded.

Elie Wiesel again: 'It is so much easier to look away from victims. It is so much easier to avoid such rude interruptions to our work, our dreams, our hopes. But indifference to the suffering of others is what makes the human being inhuman. The political prisoner in his cell, the hungry children, the homeless refugees – not to respond to their plight, not to relieve their solitude by offering them a spark of hope is to exile them from human memory. And in denying their humanity, we betray our own.'[43]

Yes, the easy thing to do, our natural impulse, is to turn our minds and hearts away from the needs of others, to place an impenetrable psychological blanket across the heinous crimes. But then we will be doomed. As JKF commented: 'Dante once said that the hottest places in hell are reserved for those who in a period of moral crisis maintain their neutrality.'

Silence hurts the oppressed, the persecuted, the forgotten. In the Book of Micah we read, 'And what does the Lord require of you? To act justly and to love mercy and to walk humbly with your God.'[44]

Actor Ben Affleck recently established the Eastern Congo Initiative[45] to raise money and awareness about the horrendous abuse. If the victims have the courage to tell their stories, surely we have the courage to help them. Standing by idly and observing inhumanity cannot be an option.

Keep the Nazis and their crimes out of comedy shows

March 13, 2012

Seventy years ago, in a villa in the Berlin suburb of Wannsee, in a meeting chaired by Reinhard Heydrich, head of the SS secret police, and attended by Adolf Eichmann along with fifteen high-ranking representatives, the mechanisms for the 'final solution', the systematic, industrialised genocide of eleven million Jews living in Europe was put into play.

Anyone reading the minutes from that gathering, in which gourmet cuisine and fine wine were served, is left breathless by the unimaginable and unbelievable horrors decided there.

Who would have thought that in the 21st century, in the entertainment field, respect for Holocaust memory and for its victims would be so jettisoned?

Hitler is no longer the evil tyrant responsible for the deaths of eleven million people, but an abstraction, a convenient material for comedy, an easy reference for people to make inappropriate comparisons. The trivialisation and merchandising of the Holocaust is everywhere.

There is a new Nazi-chic fad in Thailand with more and more teenagers wearing T-shirts with cartoonish images of the German dictator. Designs include Hitler as Ronald McDonald, as a pink Teletubby with a swastika as antennae, and in a panda costume with a Nazi armband.[46] In London's Madame Tussaud, tourists have their pictures taken beside a waxwork of Hitler, with many doing Nazi salutes.

And comedian Ricky Gervais, following his hosting of the Golden Globes, posted on his Twitter account photos of himself dressed up as Hitler and wearing a swastika.[47]

Maybe it's just me, but I don't find Hitler and the murder of millions funny.

The creators of the SBS comedy program *Danger 5*, Dario Russo and David Ashby, have recently pushed the envelope of Holocaust commodification and trivialisation. I wonder whether Russo and Ashby thought about the feelings of Holocaust survivors and their children when they came up with their Nazi sci-fi spoof. The twenty-something writing team quotes Mel Brooks, who 'believes it's everybody's right to portray the Nazis as idiotically as possible … to make fun of them'.

What they should have quoted is Charlie Chaplin's 1964 autobiography in which he says that if he had known of the true horrors of the Nazis, he could not have made *The Great Dictator*.

The first few episodes of *Danger 5* mix a lascivious Hitler, a buffoonish Mengele, Nazis, eroticised wrestling, bedroom scenes, cartoonish violence and lots of sex. Television critic Graeme Blundell has written: 'I can't get enough of this nutty action/comedy series.'[48]

I find it disturbing that Russo and Ashby, and by extension SBS, The South Australian Film Corporation and the Adelaide Film Festival, who financially backed the series, felt it was OK to capitalise on the Shoah for entertainment and cheap laughs. *Danger 5* and other films, musicals and books of its ilk are not just in bad taste, they are morally wrong because they exploit the horrendous killings of the Jews, Gypsies, homosexuals and other 'undesirables', and use them as backdrop for their comic payoff.

Russo and Ashby are not alone. *Iron Sky*, a Finnish-Australian comedy about Nazis living on the dark side of the moon who plan to invade Earth to avenge their loss in World War II, was a hit in this year's Berlin International Film Festival.

We are now reaching a stage where entertainment and commerce have come together to diminish the crimes of the Nazis by using them for money-making entertainment. What frightens me is that distasteful comedies such as *Danger 5* will redefine and shatter the memory of just who the Nazis really were, desensitising audiences and causing cultural and historical amnesia.

Ask yourself: is it really appropriate for us to laugh about a man who was responsible for the death of millions and who devastated Europe? Or to reduce the memory of the Holocaust to comic fodder?

For me it is clear that you don't laugh about the suffering, torture and death of so many.

The prevailing view seems to be that as long as it's funny, as long as the audience is getting its money's worth, who cares if Hitler's barbaric actions are reduced to a harmless romp.

So, is anything taboo any more?

It is not unreasonable to ask whether future television shows may include episodes that poke fun at Jews being gassed, or their bodies burned at the crematorium, or parents and children shot in the fields by the mobile execution units, or babies' heads being smashed against the wall, or the medical experiments Mengele conducted on his victims.

What facet of the Nazis' monumental crimes is beyond laughter and fun?

Vulgar and offensive comedies such as *Danger 5*, whose sole purpose is to wring a chuckle from viewers, pollute society's understanding and sense of the Holocaust. The problem with *Danger 5*, as well as with music cartoons, video clips, exhibitions and stand-up comedians who try to make us laugh about the Holocaust is that they are eviscerating history by taking Hitler and the Nazis out of context, stupidly diluting the evil they spawned and throwing away the past.

Given that more and more people learn their history from popular culture, and given that coarse comedies and art about the Holocaust are proliferating, I have a real concern that schoolchildren will not know what happened in the Holocaust. At the end, youngsters may not believe that Hitler is guilty of what he did, or believe that the Holocaust wasn't so bad after all.

The Holocaust is such a vast tragedy, still affecting lives today, that anyone wanting to approach it must do so with great emotional respect, historical authenticity, humility and caution.

And for the record, as I have stated on previous occasions, I would say the same thing if a comedy about the Cambodian killing fields, Bosnia, Rwanda or Darfur were screened by SBS.

Triple J Holocaust joke sickening

August 10, 2012

By now it's clear that nothing is off-limits when it comes to the Holocaust. It seems that there is no aspect or symbol of the darkest episode in human history that is not subject to perverse abuse and cheap trivialisation.

And this dangerous trend is hitting new lows.

Yesterday, on the *Tom and Alex* show on Triple J, a truly appalling and bizarre segment was broadcast in which a 'game' was made of linking things to Hitler; the final item in this 'game' was a wind farm.

Why a wind farm, you ask? Because it contains fans, which is linked to fan-forced ovens, which in turn connect to the Holocaust and Hitler.

Got it? Fan-forced ovens were the ovens in which the corpses were burned after the victims were led into the gas chambers where they were told they were going to have a shower.

Tom Ballard and Alex Dyson probably thought this was hilarious and would elicit chuckles. I was speechless.

With this beyond distasteful episode, Tom and Alex crossed so many red lines I stopped counting.

In response to an irate listener, Ballard on his Twitter account replied: 'Dude, if you don't like the show, just don't listen. It's profoundly easy.'[50]

I wonder what makes certain 'entertainers' feel that making jokes out of the death and suffering of millions acceptable?

Maybe Tom and Alex can explain to us what is remotely funny about the gassing of millions of men, women and children and the burning of their bodies?

Perhaps if the two visited the death camps of Auschwitz, where 1.5 million people were exterminated, where mothers with their babies clutched to their breasts went into the gas chambers, they could enlighten us about the humour in it.

What right do Tom and Alex have to re-traumatise survivors and trample on their feelings?

They, and the producers of the show, should have known that

the horrors of the Holocaust must be approached with respect and sensitivity and that there is nothing funny about Hitler.

Would they have played the same game if their grandparents, parents, siblings or uncles were executed and their naked corpses incinerated in the ovens?

Triple J may think that any publicity is good publicity and will lure listeners. But yesterday's hurtful and sickening prank showcases a disturbing abdication of responsible judgment and a troubling lack of sensitivity. Was there not a single person to tell them that this was a terrible idea, that there was no humour to be milked from mass murder, that trivialising genocide for outrageous comic pay-off is inexcusable and will be a kick in the stomach to survivors?

Surely someone at Triple J knew that comedy does not bring with it unlimited licence.

Is this what tax-funded broadcasting has sunk to?

Tom and Alex, please leave the Holocaust, its victims and survivors out of your stupid comedy routines. Instead, I suggest that you go away and learn about the history of the Holocaust. Visit the Holocaust Museum here in Melbourne. Sit down and listen to the horrifying and heartbreaking stories of the survivors and their families. Maybe you'll then realise that some things aren't funny.

It's time for both of you to grow up. And to apologise.

Shoah amnesia at Triple J

August 17, 2012

It was a monument to trivialisation and to abuse of the Holocaust.

The *Jerusalem Post* picked it up.[51] So did the *Herald Sun* and an array of other publications. Even *The Warrnambool Standard* carried the story.

I received scores of emails. Some overtly anti-Semitic. Most supported my position.

And Alex and Tom's Triple J show Facebook account posted hundreds of comments.

What was it all about?

Last week, Tom Ballard and his co-host Alex Dyson played a game called 'Six Degrees of Hitleration'. The aim of the game was to link objects to Hitler in six steps. Ballard was the last one and had to connect Hitler to wind farms. He did, linking them to fan-forced ovens, which in turn connected to the ovens in which the corpses were burned after the victims were led into the gas chambers.

I thought the 'game' and Tom Ballard's so called wind-farm joke was just a plain, mean thing to do to the victims, the survivors and to their families. It was outrageous and perverse.

So I wrote an op-ed for *The Age* taking them to task for the reckless and appalling behaviour.

Here is some of what I wrote:

> By now it's clear that nothing is off-limits when it comes to the Holocaust. It seems that there is no aspect or symbol of the darkest chapter in human history that is not subject to perverse abuse and cheap trivialisation.
>
> 'And this dangerous trend is hitting new lows … With this beyond distasteful episode, Tom and Alex crossed so many red lines I stopped counting … Perhaps if the two visited the death camps of Auschwitz, where 1.5 million people were exterminated, where mothers with their *babies* clutched to their breasts went into the gas chambers, they could enlighten us about the humour in it.[52]

I asked if Tom and Alex would have 'played the same game if their grandparents, parents, siblings or uncles were executed and their naked corpses incinerated in the ovens?'

Tonedeafcom reported on my article: 'His incendiary *Age* piece goes on to flame the radio hosts for their insensitivity and the production crew at Triple J for allowing their segment to be approved.'[53]

I concluded my editorial by telling the hosts to, 'Please leave the Holocaust, its victims and survivors out of your stupid comedy routines.

'Instead, I suggest that you go away and learn about the history of the Holocaust. Visit the Holocaust Museum here in Melbourne. Sit down and listen to the horrifying and heart-breaking stories of the survivors and their families. Maybe then you'll realise that some things aren't funny. It's time for both of you to grow up. And to apologise.'

It didn't Triple J long to issue an apology. Tom Ballard also apologised.[54] Sort of.

The idiocy displayed on the Triple J show proved once again that Holocaust exploitation continues to spread.

This disgusting gag was not just a failure of the imagination.

It was evidence that moral parameters have so shifted to the point where nobody bothers to question whether basing radio skits around the horrific tragedy of the Holocaust is crass and highly offensive.

And it's not just the Holocaust. It applies to any type of genocide.

To put it in a different context, does anyone think a woman or a man who had been raped found it funny? Or think it's funny and worthy of jokes?

It has now become commonplace for people to enjoy and laugh about the Nazi crimes against and about those who perpetrated them.

The most shattering event in modern history is treated as entertainment, as material for comedy, as an opportunity to generate laughs.

It is as if we have become afflicted with historical amnesia.

In my opinion, there can never be any justifiable purpose for using Hitler, or the Nazis, or their industrialised killing machine to elicit chuckles. It debases and degrades the memory of six million Jews and millions of others who perished in the Holocaust.

As Hitler and the Holocaust become increasingly associated

with laughter, I fear that we might get soon get to the point when anyone who claims that the Holocaust is about the inhumanity of man rather than about entertainment, will be accused of being over-sensitive. Or old fashioned.

In the end, will anyone remember who Hitler and the Nazis really were?

Notes

1   Neil Tweedie and Michael Kallenbach. 'Prince Harry faces outcry at Nazi outfit.' *The Telegraph*, 14 January, 2005.

2   Celestine Bohlen. 'Pope issues warning against a modern-day Auschwitz.' *The Ottawa Citizen*, January 30, 1995.

3   *Life Magazine*, Volume 8, 1985.

4   Primo Levi. *If this is a man.* New York: Orion Press, 1959.

5   Kalman Sultanik. 'Auschwitz-Birkenau: A Sacred Zone of Inviolability.' *Midstream*, September/October, 2003.

6   Nazila Fathi. 'Holocaust Deniers and Skeptics Gather in Iran.' *The New York Times*, December 11, 2006

7   https://www.youtube.com/watch?v=smEqnnklfYs

8   'Australia to join UN mission to Darfur: Rudd.' *Hindustan Times*, June 8, 2008.

9   Rebecca Hamilton. 'Inside Colin Powell's Decision to Declare Genocide in Darfur.' *The Atlantic*, August 17, 2011.

10 Helene Cooper. 'Spielberg Drops out as Adviser to Beijing Olympics in Dispute Over Darfur Conflict.' *The New York Times*, February 3, 2008.

11 Naomi Levin. 'Foolish poster condemned.' *The Australian Jewish News*, 28 August, 2008.

12 http://www.abc.net.au/news/stories/2008/02/26/2172655.htm?site=nsw

13 Lorna Edwards. 'Archibald Hitler portrait stirs up fury.' *The Age*, February 29, 2008.

14 Sam Gross. *We have Ways of Making You Laugh: 120 Funny Swastika Cartoons* New York: Simon Schuster, 2008.

15 Eric Hansen. 'My Führer – the Really Truesy Truth About Adolf Hitler.' *The Hollywood Reporter*, January 9, 2007.

16 Steve Lipman. 'Can a Swastika Be Funny?' *The Jewish Week*, 13 February 2008.

17 Anna Patty. 'Facebook scandal shames students.' *The Sydney Morning Herald*, December 9, 2008.

18   Miki Perkins. 'Cricket club under fire for anti-Semitism' *The Age*, August 19, 2007.

19   http://www.antisemitism.org.il/eng/2008%20Report%20on%20 antisemitism%20in%20Australia%20-%20By%20Jeremy%20Jones

20   John Wiseman. 'Jewish outrage at bikie laws analogy' *The* Australian, December 10, 2008.

21   http://www.antisemitism.org.il/article/26893/australia-baptist-min- isters-hellish-comments-spark-jewish-ire

22   http://www.het.org.uk/index.php/component/content/article/11- cat-news-cat-news/262-news-lfa-scotlandas

23   Simon Rocker. 'Bosnich apologises to Jews over his Nazi salute at Spurs' *The Jewish Chronicle,* 18 October, 2010.

24   Sam Edmund. 'Racism just not cricket' *The Herald Sun*, August 9, 2007.

25   Itamar Levy. *Legend of the Sad Lakes* Tel Aviv: Keter, 1989.

26   http://www.publications.parliament.uk/pa/cm200809/cmhansrd/ cm090129/debtext/90129-0010.htm

27   Bradley Burston. 'Winslet, 'Waltz', and how Hollywood likes its Jews' *Haaretz*, February 23, 2009.

28   Jeffrey Goldberg. 'Hollywood's Jewish Avenger' *The Atlantic*, Sep- tember 1, 2009.

29   Daniel Mendelsohn. 'Tarantino Rewrites the Holocaust' *Newsweek*, 13 August, 2009.

30   Mahola Dargis. 'Horror through a Child's Eyes' *The New York Times*, November 6, 2008.

31   Lisa Schwarzbaum. 'The Boy in Striped Pajamas' *Entertainment Weekly*, November 5, 2008.

32   'Jewish paper attacks Boy in Striped Pyjamas film version' *Sunday Business Post*, September 21, 2008.

33   Jesse Leavenworth. 'Auctioneer Says Death Camp Doctor Mengele's Journal Bought By Holocaust Survivor's Grandson' *Hartford Cou- rant*, February 3, 2010.

34   John Schwartz. 'Rights Group Assailed for Analyst's Nazi Collec- tion' *The New York Times*, September 4, 2009.

35 http://www.novinite.com/articles/69739/Scarlett+Johansson+Fascin ated+by+Nazi+Souvenirs+in+Bulgaria

36 Kerry McDermott. 'Fury as Nazi Memorabilia is sold off at auction house on the most solemn day in the Jewish calendar' *Daily Mail* (Australia), 6 October 2012.

37 http://news.bbc.co.uk/2/hi/europe/760782.stm

38 http://www.theage.com.au/news/national/anger-at-nazi-market-stall/2008/05/26/1211653914879.html

39 Rittner Myers. *The Courage to Care: Rescuers of Jews During the Holocaust* New York: New York University, 1986.

40 Bob Herbert. 'Holding On to Our Humanity' *The New York Times*, May 29, 2009

41 http://www.rescue.org/special-reports/special-report-congo-y

42 http://www.dw.de/the-campaign-for-clean-mobile-phones/a-15982934

43 Elie Wiesel. ' The perils of indifference' April 12, 1999 included in James Daley (editor) *History's Greatest Speeches*. USA: Dover Publications, 2013.

44 Micha, Chapter 6, verse 8.

45 http://www.easterncongo.org/

46 Tibor Krausz. 'Bangkok's 'Hitler chic' trends riles tourists, Israeli envoy' CNN, 2 February 2012.

47 http://www.mirror.co.uk/3am/celebrity-news/ricky-gervais-dresses-as-hitler-for-no-169736

48 http://www.safilm.com.au/library/Nutty%20and%20sexy%20in%20 the%20hunt%20for%20Hitler%20The%20Australian%205%20 March%202012.pdf

49 http://www.uws.edu.au/ssap/ssap/research/challenging_racism

50 https://twitter.com/TomCBallard/status/233415043268616192

51 http://www.jpost.com/Breaking-News/Radio-host-finally-apologizes-for-Hitler-oven-game

52 http://www.smh.com.au/federal-politics/society-and-culture/triplej-holocaust-joke-sickening-20120810-23yem.html

53 http://www.tonedeaf.com.au/187423/triple-j-radio-host-apologises-after-holocaust-joke-misfires.htm

54   http://www.fasterlouder.com.au/news/33402/Tom-Ballard-sorry-for-Hitler-gag. See also this interview with Tom Ballard. Meg Watson. 'Q&A with Tom Ballard: rape, the Holocaust, and the politics of comedy' *Meanjin*, September 3, 2012

ANTI-SEMITISM

The best of friends: anti-Zionism and anti-Semitism

January 23, 2001

In his latest article 'The Jewish Answer',[1] Geoffrey Wheatcroft traverses a path well trodden, asserting that Zionism has failed because censure of Israel is construed as anti-Semitism and that therefore Israel, whatever else it may be, it is not a nation like all others, and maybe never can be. It's a clever, albeit morally bankrupt argument, too hard for many to rebut, expose or tackle, but it is nonsense.

Anti-Zionism gives old-fashioned anti-Semitic intent a sheen of civilised discourse, but we should not be too deceived or intimidated to deal with it. As they say, the devil is in the details. Principally, anti-Zionism is an accurate reflection of unbridled street level anti-Judaism feeding on anti-Semitic myths, that in turn nurture the battle against the existence of Israel. Obviously, it's easier to disseminate age-old anti-Jewish feeling cloaked as anti-Zionism. But in no way should anti-Zionism serve as a convenient cover, a euphemism, a loophole for those spewing and fomenting anti-Semitic slander.

For the record, not every criticism of Israel is anti-Semitic. No one wants to stifle a free, honest and open debate on all sides. It's all about the pitch the criticism reaches. I also have no problem with champions of the Palestinian cause who use industrial-strength criticism to make a point about the specific policy of the Israeli government. As long as they recognise Israel's right to exist, do not deny individual Jews self-determination and the right to live, and do not seek Israel's destruction because it is 'a racist entity' guilty of genocide and crimes against humanity'.[2] To wit, who can forget the blatantly hypocritical circus of the 2001 Durban conference where a considerable number of nations insisted that every reference to anti-Semitism be linked with the 'racist practices of Zionism' while simultaneously arguing that Zionism was a movement based on racist supremacy akin to apartheid.

For Gabriel Schoenfeld, editor of *Commentary*, anti-Semitism is 'the right and the only word for an anti-Zionism so one-sided, so eager to indict Israel while exculpating Israel's adversaries, so shamefully adroit in the use of moral double standards, so quick to issue false and baseless accusations, and so disposed to invert the language of the Holocaust and to paint Israelis and Jews as evil incarnate.'[3] Ruth Wisse reveals that, 'Contemporary Anti-Zionism has absorbed all the stereotypes and foundational texts of fascist and Soviet anti-Semitism and applied them to the Middle East.'[4] Swedish statesman Per Ahlmark wisely doubts that anyone would believe this declaration, 'I am against the existence of Great Britain, but I'm not anti-British.'[5]

History has shown us that rarely has there been anti-Zionism without anti-Semitism. Take Resolution 3379 (Zionism = racism),[6] a strategy to delegitimise Israel's right to exist. Arab historian Bernard Lewis has written that the insidious resolution was chosen as the best stand-in for a vicious anti-Semitic campaign by Soviet and Arab ideological goals. Once accepted, it erased the taboo against publicly expressing anti-Semitic sentiments in the wake of the Holocaust. And as then US Ambassador to the UN Senator Daniel Patrick Moynihan recalled in his book *A Dangerous Place*, the shameless resolution was not only aimed against Israel but also against world Jewry.[7]

Intellectual William F. Buckley observed at the time that the UN had become 'The most concentrated gathering of anti-Semitism since the days of Hitler's Germany'[8] while Lionel Trilling maintained that with this legal travesty the ghost of Hitler haunted the halls of the UN. Recognising the interdependence of anti-Zionism and anti-Semitism, the US Senate passed a resolution condemning the vote as an encouragement of anti-Semitism, as did the Australian Parliament. In 1991, President Bush in an address to the UN assembly stated, 'Zionism is not a policy, it is the idea that led to the creation of a home for the Jewish people in the state of Israel ... To equate Zionism with racism is to reject Israel itself, a member in good standing of the UN.'[9] Even the Vatican, in its document *The Church and Racism: Towards a more Fraternal Society* (part II, no. 15) acknowledged that, 'Anti-Zionism ... serves at times as a screen for anti-Semitism feeding on it and leading to it.'[10]

People of conscience should not let anyone turn truth squarely on its head. Consider that anti-Zionism is the first type of Jew hatred to deny that it hates Jews. Indeed, we live in a world where those who hate Jews and who fan the flames of bigotry call themselves anti-Zionists, seeking new modes of packaging their virulent ideology and knowing that 'if one tells the same lies long enough', as Goebbels stated, 'people will begin to believe them'. Yet, it is beyond dispute that throughout the world, classical anti-Semitism is being dressed up as anti-Zionism, a more respectable, but no less poisonous and vile, type of hate.

In 1994, a journalist who lived in the Gulf states pointed out that he would often be told by officials that they were hostile to Zionism but not to Jews. Yet, he couldn't work out why even a foreign encyclopaedia in Bahrain not only had the Israel entry and map ripped out, but also had the section on Judaism missing.

There is hard and fast evidence that all too often anti-Semitic figures brand themselves anti-Zionists. Consider Kwawe Ture. When speaking on American campuses, the Black Nationalist figure's favourite punchline is: 'The only good Zionist is a dead Zionist.'[11] Ture asserts that he is not anti-Semitic, merely anti-Zionist, although he heads the AAPRP, one of the most radical anti-Semitic groups on the left, tells audiences that Jews dominated the slave trade and that Zionists collaborated with the Nazis to create the Holocaust. Clearly, animosity towards Zionism by high profile hatemongers is always bonded to smearing against Judaism. Robert Wistrich remembers an interview with Valery Emelianov, a leading member of the ultra-right wing Russian group Pamyat in which Elianov kept using the word Zionists where it was plain it was a transparent codeword for Jews, also repeatedly employing the term 'Jewish Nazis'. And what about Syrian Defence Minister Mustafa Tlas and his 1983 book *The Matza of Zion*,[12] a blood libel cloaked as insight into Zionist behaviour and intention. One could also add the Peronist congressman in Argentina who classified Zionism as a device for taking over Latin America and the court in Crete that ruled in 1984 that Jehovah's Witnesses are part of a Zionist conspiracy to rule the world, as prime examples.[13]

True, the establishment of a Jewish state has not erased anti-Semitism. There is still a need for a demonised scapegoat and Israel itself has become the world's Jew, its favourite scapegoat. Anti-Zionism is an ingenious way to defame Israel and the Jewish people.

And for that very reason, anti-Zionism should not lose its seat on the bus of political correctness that protects certain groups; it should never be made acceptable, tolerated, ignored or hushed up.

J'accuse: The academic boycott and the politics of prejudice

May 31, 2002

Dark times are upon us. A new war has been declared, and this time it is against the Israeli academic community. A vicious anti-Israel campaign, in the guise of an Australian boycott petition, has been circulating, seeking to isolate Israel and make it a pariah state. It proposes to sever joint cooperation between Australian universities and Israeli universities, freeze academic exchange programs and deny scholarship funds to prospective students who want to travel and study in Israel.[14] Gradually, a deep and worrying hostility towards Israel has been reaching chilling levels. This crudely sensationalist political agenda, that deliberately aims at delegitimising the Jewish state, is another stage. It demonstrates the pervasive nature of a highly intemperate circle of prejudice that refuses to accord Israeli academics the same respect their international colleagues receive.

Using intellectual coercion to intimidate Israel and its educators must not be tolerated. A gross violation of academic freedom, this shameful planned boycott works on the assumption that immoral pressure will somehow cause Israel to abandon its war on terrorism. Likewise, there is something bigoted about applying the rule of a collective ban to punish all Israelis without regard to who they are and regardless of their political views. Unfairly singling out and castigating scholars based on their nationality, religion and ethnicity is menacingly slanted and makes me uneasy.

It is no surprise that this McCarthy-like petition lays the blame for the current escalation only at the feet of Israel, blatantly ignoring Palestinian use of terror. No suggestion has been put forward of suspending ties with Palestinian members of the Academy. Clearly, the initiators of this petition are opposed to any type of understanding of the Israeli side in this crisis. Imagine the anger and outrage if a call to boycott Australian academics because of mandatory detention of illegal immigrants was sent out.

If we don't come out strongly against this call, it could snowball. Just last month, a routine request to the Norwegian Veterinary School by Jerusalem scientist Eithan Galun for DNA clone material to aid anaemic Palestinian children was refused.[15] In an email, the institute explained that due to the situation in the Middle East, it would not be sending any material to an Israeli university. Similarly, two Hebrew University researchers have had their papers refused by an editor of an international journal who explained he was a signatory to the European embargo.[16]

Aside from its moral bankruptcy, the petition ignores the fact that Israeli academics are at the forefront of actively working for peace, collaborating with the Palestinians and fostering dialogue that ultimately will bring the parties to the negotiation table. Rather than cultivating reconciliation, the petition will create a greater split between the two cultures. Consider also that academics in countries with questionable human rights records have not being targeted in this way. Do the initiators of the petition here advocate cutting ties with Russian, Chinese, Yugoslavian and Turkish academics over Chechnya, Tibet, Bosnia and Cyprus? Of course not.

And how about Edward Said? Last year, while in Lebanon, the Professor of English threw a stone at border guard post manned by Israeli soldiers,[17] in effect committing an act of violence against Israeli society. Was he hounded out of his university, banned by other campuses or arrested for his assault? No, he got off scot-free. Which only goes to show the old double standard that has always applied to Jews and Israel is still at play. I protest that the Jewish state has always been held to a standard no other people have. This petition is a gratuitous display of hypocrisy that captures the essence of what Israel's opponents stand for.

We cannot afford a certain detachment. The politics of prejudice have no place in academia where the common pursuit is the championing of truth and discovery. One of the cornerstone values I cherish most is my right to think, publish and teach independently, without restraint and without the threat of a sanction hanging over my head. As such, I condemn this unprecedented call as an extreme, partisan, bullying political tactic, and would remind all that this issue cuts to the heart of what are fundamental values of fairness and equality in a civilised world. A letter in the British newspaper *The Independent* stated, 'Jewish academics were among the first to be persecuted by the Nazis'. There is something very wrong when in 2002 a concerned reader feels the need to invoke this frightful episode.

Coming to this country, two little girls and their ... sad songs of hate?

November 3, 2005

Watching the angelic looking Lamb and Lynx Gaede, the thirteen-year-old twins who make up the teeny duo Prussian Blue, I could not help thinking that racism has some strange faces.

The twins smile so wholesomely while spewing out hate and modelling Hitler happy-face T-shirts.

As one character in the movies observes, there's wrong, and there's wrong, and there's this.

The blonde-haired, blue-eyed, sweet-faced sisters from Bakersfield, California, give 'Heil Hitler' salutes during their concerts on stage and belt out pop songs about Nazis.

Labelled the Aryan Olsen twins, they plan to tour Australia.

Marketed in a perversely alluring fashion, running through fields of wild flowers and wearing tartan miniskirts, the band's name is a nod to the girls' blue eyes and German heritage. It is also a reference to the residue left by the Zyklon B used in the Nazi gas chambers, although they claim it is a myth.

Performing since the age of nine, the darlings of the Neo-Nazi movement headline Holocaust denial events and like to relax by playing a video game called *Ethnic Cleansing*, where players try to kill as many black people as possible.

Their website comes complete with a blog and forums, and contains links to clothing company Aryan Wear and other white supremacist sites. Surprisingly articulate for their age, in one interview Lamb said that men such as Adolf Hitler and his deputy Rudolf Hess were heroes.

Lamb's sister Lynx said the twins did not believe that six million Jews were executed. 'We know there were concentration camps,' she said, 'but they had swimming pools and tennis courts there.'[18]

When asked what was the most important social issue facing America, Lynx replied that there were 'not enough white babies born to replace ourselves'.[19] Recently, the twins offered to help Hurricane Katrina victims, but demanded that the money they would give go to whites only.

Yet, beyond their sickening world view, the Gaede twins serve as a cautionary tale about the significance of parental influence and its potential to corrupt the innocent. The twins' twisted outlook was learned primarily from mother April and grandfather Bill. They were schooled at home by their mother, who also writes some of their lyrics. She is also working on an alphabet book for toddlers titled, A is for Aryan.

The girls have been nourished on a steady diet of vitriolic bigotry. April's repellent views were shaped by her father, who wears a swastika on his belt, has a swastika on the side of his truck and a swastika registered as his cattle brand.

Prussian Blue hopes to cross over to mainstream audiences, offering albums over the net as a tool to recruit school-aged children. Looking to the future, April says: 'What red-blooded American boy isn't going to find two blonde twins singing about pride in your race very appealing?'[20] And if you are thinking, surely this can't be real, ask yourself when was the last time you checked what your kids were listening to or what internet sites they have been visiting?

Instead of shrugging our shoulders and adopting the just-ignore-them strategy and hoping this will go away, we must continually educate our children against such shockingly offensive and dangerous ideologies.

Parents are the first and best line of defence, and the best way to respond to racism is to inform our children with facts and knowledge. Unreason must be fought with reason. Tolerance must be fostered. Diversity must be celebrated. This is a battle worth fighting for.

Parents must be aware that throwaway lines that teach kids to treat races and religions differently are harmful. Prussian Blue is proof that racism is a learned characteristic and that children parrot what they hear at home.

Families need to drown out the message of blind hatred with lessons about respect for people of all backgrounds. Only then will children turn away from racist propaganda, even when it lies behind the face of a thirteen-year-old.

Fight cyber hate on the home front

July 2, 2006

Racist websites are proliferating unchallenged, spreading their venom to such an extent that cyber hate is at an all-time high.

Hate and racist sites are targeted at the young and are predatory in the worst way. There are extremist sites that provide visitors with links to games that allow players to shoot and kill caricatures of non-whites. In *Ethnic Cleansing*,[21] players are instructed to kill 'subhumans' – blacks and Latinos – and their 'masters', the Jews, depicted as the personification of evil.

While hate sites mushroom, accessing those sites has become easy for children. So parents must come to grips with how this sophisticated technology threatens to corrupt young minds.

It is crucial to remember that prejudice is learned in childhood – no one is born with awareness of ethnic and religious stereotypes. And it is stereotypes that underlie hate and lead to racial violence.

Parents have a duty to fight prejudice at home. They need to foster tolerance in their children. When racist views cause children to ridicule, or hold ill feelings, or feel hostility towards people of other faiths, good parents rise up against it.

The best way to do that is through honest conversations that are measured and infused with conscience and love. This can neutralise the bigotry that young people confront online.

Homes are an ideal environment to combat bias because most kids trust and respect their parents. If racism is tackled correctly, children will internalise their parents' views.

The core message is that children should celebrate the uniqueness of everyone. If they do look at demeaning stereotypes purveyed by the internet and the media, then they should do so with a critical eye and with empathy for people who are different.

Families need a long-term strategy that deals constructively with eradicating the toxic ideologies that the internet contains. Families need to devote time to lessons about respect for people of all backgrounds and religions. The lesson could be delivered in a lively, informative way over dinner.

In dealing with racism, it is important that parents are never dismissive or too defensive. Affirm your children's curiosity about race and ethnicity, and explain that people come in many shades and with different religious beliefs and views. Regularly take the family to an ethnic restaurant where all the family can learn about the food and, more importantly, the culture. Sit with your children and visit websites that describe other countries' religions and history. Consider the cultural diversity reflected in the art, music and literature in your home. Perhaps it is time for something new?

Encourage your children to take a stand against everyday prejudice. Instead of allowing them to passively consume words and images they encounter online, teach them to be discerning and to apply the values they learn at home.

If your child repeats what he or she has read on a racist website, or makes a disparaging, racial or religious-based remark, simply denouncing that remark won't do. You need to start a sensible discussion about why such an observation is wrong and perhaps, as mentioned earlier, a wider discussion about respect for all people.

All too often, parents think, 'What can I say in response to that?' Or laugh along, uncomfortably, or are frustrated or angry. But employing the just-ignore-them tactic sends the message that this attitude is acceptable.

Above all, parents must remain vigilant about what sites their children are viewing. They also need to watch what they say in front of children, especially when they feel angry.

In building a harmonious future, parents are crucial in ensuring that hatred is not allowed to be embedded in the hearts of our children.

Hate crimes require a special unit

April 29, 2008

Swastikas smeared across a synagogue and a Jewish restaurant;[22] obscene graffiti painted at an Islamic college; a Jewish teenager hit with a baseball bat[23] and a Jewish father punched in front of his children; a Sudanese-born youth viciously attacked by a gang; rocks and eggs hurled at Hindu devotees at a temple in Carrum Downs;[24] Indian taxi drivers in Geelong bashed;[25] threatening letters and e-mails received by ethnic organisations; windows smashed at a kosher bakery.

This is not a list from Europe or the US. These events took place in Victoria over the last year. Clearly, racially motivated violence is dramatically on the rise.

Hate-crimes are the most pernicious expressions of prejudice. Heartless and unprovoked, they inflict enormous psychological harm, inspire vulnerability in the victim and intimidate an entire class of people.

Hate-crimes are an offence against all that Australians cherish, tearing at the very fabric of our society, endangering deeply held beliefs in principles of individual liberty.

They remind us that the dark forces of division still exist.

Admittedly, hate crimes occur in every country. To combat this insidious and abhorrent behaviour, many police departments in Britain, Canada, the United States and elsewhere have taken the enlightened step of establishing dedicated hate-crime units. Victoria Police is yet to set up one, but it should.

This is how the units work overseas. Any cases identified as hate offences are given priority, and specially trained officers are brought in to look at secondary and collateral activity related to the crime and to act as a liaison with the people suffering from the devastating effects of the assault. It has been proven that hate-crime units investigate racial attacks that might have gone unattended and have generated a greater number of indictments. Indeed, no one knows how many hate cases are under-reported or are buried in reports classified as simple assaults.

Police are the evidentiary gatekeepers. Prosecutors can only work with the evidence that they receive. The Director of Public Prosecutions relies on motive and the key lies with the hate-crimes unit that can collect the evidence that the offence was motivated by hate.

The significance of a hate-crime unit is not limited to just arrests. The concern shown by the unit will underscore the positive message that government and police are sensitive to victims. Studies of the efficiency and success of hate-crime units reveal that such units have enhanced the credibility of police among ethnic communities.

Experience shows that hate-crime units get better results, since they break down traditional barriers and gain the trust of victims who are willing to report incidents. Canada has introduced a 24-hour telephone hotline that allows victims to communicate such crimes, and in England there are 'third party' reporting centres where people, who may not feel comfortable going to a station, can report hate-crimes that are then passed on to police.[26]

If the Holocaust and other genocides have taught us anything, it is the grave consequences of apathy and indifference in the face of such violence. The battle against racism never ends. Australia is a multicultural and multiracial society – it is the source of our strength as a nation. We must never allow the extremists to determine how we socialise with each other and defend those who cannot protect themselves. The police are our greatest ally in this mission.

The establishment of a hate-crime unit is not a quick-fix solution, but rather a comprehensive, long-term strategy that will provide law enforcement with new tools to use in wiping out hate, and enable it to go head-to-head with racists in our community.

When *Family Guy* crossed the line into anti-Semitic caricatures

November 27, 2009

Although I appreciate clever, edgy humour, last month's episode of American sitcom *Family Guy* crossed the line into offensive anti-Semitic caricatures that skewered Jews and Judaism.

The episode, entitled 'Family Goy', dredged up age-old stereotypes about Jews and money and reinforced deeply embedded prejudices that still abound today.

And before anyone thinks, but it's just one half-hour show, consider this: *Family Guy* has been on air for ten years with more than eight million people regularly tuning it. As well as garnering three Emmys, it has given rise to a cottage industry of products: a soundtrack, six books, a video game, a TV spin-off, and a planned feature film. Its reach and popularity among teenagers is enormous.

So offensive was the program that Jewish groups in the USA wrote to The Fox Broadcasting Company expressing their dismay at its excessive employment of false and hurtful perceptions of Jews.[27]

The storyline revolves around the mother Lois, who during a breast cancer check finds out that she is Jewish and that her mother is a Holocaust survivor. The revelation serves as an opportunity for the creative team to load up the show with a plethora of anti-Jewish images and jokes.

* Peter, the father, decides to become Jewish and decrees his family will attend synagogue. In one scene, sixteen-year-old Meg is propositioned by a young man to engage in sodomy, while at school baby Stewie asks the Jewish teacher, 'How long before we play pin the eviction on the black guy's door'.

* Barbara tells her daughter Lois that her grandmother's original name was Hebrewmoneygrabber.

* Lois' father ties a dollar to a string and throws it next to the mother and daughter, laughing, 'C'mon you know you Jew girls want that dollar'.

* It recreates a scene from *Schindler's List*, where Nazi officer Amon Goth (Ralph Fiennes) would shoot Jewish prisoners from his balcony. Here, Peter, sitting shirtless at his bedroom window with a

cigarette in his mouth shoots at Lois as she stands near the mailbox. He then shoots at Mort, their Jewish neighbour. Mort is not bothered, telling Lois that that's usually how people say hello to him, at which point, neighbour Joe shoots at Mort and, Mort responds by saying, 'Hi Joe!'

Family Guy has form in depicting violence against Jews. As an opener to the eighth season, the writers turned the entire cast into Disney characters, transporting them to that magical world. Mort Goldman, the Jewish pharmacist, comes to the door. He is drawn with classic anti-Semitic features – the big nose, crooked teeth and a large yellow Star of David around his neck. Together the characters turn angry, shout 'Jew' and proceed to beat him up. While I understand that the reference was to Walt Disney's reputed anti-Semitism, is using extreme violence against Jews an effective way to discuss anti-Semitism?

The show's creator, Seth MacFarlane, also has a history of ridiculing the Holocaust. Earlier this month, fox aired MacFarlane's special *Family Guy Presents Seth & Alex's Almost Live Comedy Show*. When his co-star, Alex Borstein, whose mother and grandmother escaped the Nazis, refused to sing 'Edelweiss' from the *Sound of Music* because of Austria's complicity in the Holocaust, MacFarlane cracked an offensive joke, telling Borstein, 'But if none of that happened how many Jewish comediennes would you be competing with? Right now, it's you and Sarah Silverman.'[28] Microsoft pulled its sponsorship of the special because of concern over its contents.[29] Fox executives did not demonstrate the same level of good judgment.

But while Fox let this latest anti-Semitic *Family Guy* episode to air, in 2000 Fox executives did shelve the episode, 'When You Wish Upon a Weinstein' for concern that it would be construed as anti-Semitic. In that episode, Peter begins to believe that to make money he needs a Jew to manage his finances. He chases Max Weinstein, a Jewish accountant, and forces him to aid him in balancing his cheque book. When Max asks Peter, 'How did you know I was an accountant?' Peter responds: 'Hello, Max Weinstein', emphasising the name to suggest that since Max is Jewish he must be good with money.

In one scene, Peter breaks out in a song 'I Need a Jew', which includes the line, 'Hebrew people I adored, even though they killed my Lord'.

Fox Executives had a change of heart about this episode, allowing its broadcast in 2004 after selling millions of DVDs of it. The producers of *Family Guy* were later sued by music publishing house Bourne Company who claimed that 'I Need a Jew' was an anti-Semitic parody of its classic tune from Walt Disney's *Pinocchio*.[30]

Not all jokes are funny.

South Park and Kick a Jew Day

January 5, 2010

Those who think *Family Guy* and *South Park* are just moronic, harmless shows that have no social impact, think again. Last month, students at Florida's North Naples School decided to launch their own 'Kick a Jew Day', asking children if they were Jews and then kicking them if they said yes.[31] The ten high school students who participated in this vicious assault were given one day 'in-school suspensions'. *Naples News Daily* stated that this outrageous event 'is one of our community's ugliest stories of 2009'.[32]

So where did they get this idea, and how did they know who in their school was Jewish? After all, it wasn't their features, language or clothes that labelled them as Jewish.

Apparently, one source that provided them with 'inspiration' was a 2008 Facebook group named 'National Kick a Ginger Day, are you going to do it?', modelled after a *South Park* episode called 'Ginger Kids'.[33]

In the *South Park* episode, one of the characters, in a hate-filled speech, tells his classmates that red-haired kids are genetically defective, inhuman, soulless and should be gotten rid of. The fourteen-year-old administrator of the Facebook page claimed that it was just a joke, even though the group encouraged its more than 20,000 members to 'get them steel toes ready'.

In fact, in the same week of 'Kick a Jew Day', red-haired students were targeted in a California Middle School. According to the Los Angeles County Sheriff, seven red-haired boys and girls were assaulted because they were 'gingers'.[34] The investigation revealed that the redheads were shoved, punched and bloodied; one twelve-year-old boy was surrounded by fifteen boys and was kicked in the stomach, groin and head. The boy is now scared to go to school.

The offenders were detained and two were booked by police for battery.

The *South Park* episode seriously misfired. It was meant as satire and supposedly contained a message about tolerance, but it was obviously lost on some. In Calgary, Canada, one parent whose twelve-year-old son was kicked again and again because of his red hair, was considering a lawsuit against *South Park*. This was after numerous students were suspended and the police were called in.

Naples Middle School administration, where 'Kick a Jew Day' took place, said that the first 20 minutes of classroom meeting will now be devoted to sensitivity training, and a greater focus will be placed on respect. However, the ultra-lenient reprimand given to the students is worrying. What is an 'in-school suspension?' By any measure it is a slap on the wrist. Given that physical assault is a criminal act, and that the offenders singled out Jewish students for violence, an 'in-school suspension seems hardly adequate.

Unless serious and substantive penalties are imposed on such hateful outbursts, hooliganism of this type will continue. As *The Purdue Exponent* newspaper noted: 'Negatively targeting members of a certain group is a hate crime, even if it is meant as a joke. Harsh punishments for those who use violence against these groups is valid and merited.'[35]

This is not an isolated occurrence. In 2008, in Parkway West Middle School in St Louis, a Jewish student was slapped in the face while others were struck on the shoulders and back in after some students decided it was 'Slap a Jew Day'.[36] The principal, Linda Lelonek, denied the 'hitters engaged in anti-Semitic action since you've got remorse, you've got tears, you've got embarrassment. Not anti-Semitic behavior at all.'[37] Remarkably, students who verbally harassed and taunted other Jewish students, and spurred their friends on, were not punished at all.

Paul Tandy, the district spokesman, observed that there is a 'mix of sadness and outrage. The concern is a lot of kids knew about it and they didn't take action or say anything.'[38] Perhaps those teenagers who created the mayhem with their unprovoked actions thought their antics would be a funny take off on *South Park*, but the question needs to be asked: where did they learn the attitude that it was OK to abuse their fellow students? Was it at home? One grandparent interviewed by the local TV station said, 'This is just kids being kids' while the County's Superintendent claimed the 'prank' was not about 'picking on Jews' but about copying what they saw on TV.

There is no excuse for racism and it's not only schools that need a long-term strategy to deal with eradicating the toxic ideologies that can be found on the internet and in the media. Parents, too, have an obligation to combat and counter any form of hate and bigotry.

The myth of the Jewish Lobby
February 18, 2010

In a post last week, Professor Stephen Walt, co-author of *The Israel Lobby and US Foreign Policy*, declared that his thesis that the Israeli lobby in the US played a key role in the decision to invade Iraq has now been confirmed.

Here's why:

> I hope readers will forgive me if I indulge today in a bit of self-promotion, or more precisely, self-defence. This week, yet another piece of evidence surfaced that suggests we were right all along ... In his testimony to the Iraq war commission in the UK, former prime minister Tony Blair offered the following account of his discussions with Bush in Crawford, Texas, in April 2002. Blair reveals that concerns about Israel were part of the equation and that Israel officials were involved in those discussions.[39]

Yet, a close reading of what Blair actually said ('the Israel issue was a big, big issue at the time') reveals that he was referring to Israel's actions in the West Bank during Operation Defensive Shield, not to the decision to invade Iraq.[40]

In *The Israel Lobby and US Foreign Policy*, Walt and his co-author John Mearsheimer argued that if the US attacks Iran it will not be doing so independently – it would be because of the Israel lobby and its backers, including neoconservative newspaper columnists: 'If the United States does launch an attack, it will be doing so in part on Israel's behalf, and the lobby would bear significant responsibility for having pushed this dangerous policy.'[41]'

They also argued that American politicians are so fearful of 'The Lobby' that they cannot vote according to their conscience. Other assertions are that the US invaded Iraq because of Israel and a cabal of mostly Jewish, neoconservative intellectuals who coerced the administration into the war: 'Within the US, the main driving force behind the war was a small band of neoconservatives, many with ties to the Likkud.'

The Israel Lobby and US Foreign Policy has been labelled the modern *Protocols of the Elders of Zion* and *The International Jew*.[42]

White supremacist David Duke has applauded it;[43] The Holocaust-denying Institute for Historical Review has published it on its site; Hamas, the PLO, Iran's press service, Egypt's Muslim Brotherhood and Al Jazeera have been giving the paper heavy airing.

The book argues that US support for the Jewish state has endangered American domestic security, leading to terrorism and hatred against the American nation. Why has the most powerful nation in the world been willing to neglect its own security for the sake of another state? Because of the all-powerful, nefarious Israel lobby, referred to ominously as 'The Lobby' (their capitalisation), comprised of American Jews who 'make a significant effort ... to bend US foreign policy so that it advances Israel's interests'.

The book argues that the 'unmatched power' of the Israel lobby has hijacked American foreign policy, noting that the American-Israel Public Affairs committee 'is a de-facto agent of foreign government and has a stranglehold on the US congress'.

According to the authors, 'The Lobby' is everywhere, controlling the media and academic publications and silencing debate on Israel, although they fail to explain the rampant and pervasive anti-Israel sentiment spreading on almost every campus and permeating global newspapers. The book seeks to explain most of America's misfortunes in the world through a shadowy, sinister Israel lobby. This is quintessential conspiracy theory, combining 'blame-the-Jew' with antiquated 'Jews seek world domination' myths. Although the American Israel Public Affairs Committee (AIPAC) is singled out as a lobby with vast tentacles of damaging influence reaching across all sectors of government, other Jewish bodies are roped into the mix.

The allegations that American Jews, and by extensions other Diaspora Jews, have a double loyalty, are subversive, even treasonous, and are working harmfully for another country, is an alarming imputation to make. To question the loyalty of Jews who are devoted to America, or Australia, or any other country, and suspect them of disloyalty is wrong and unfair. History tells us that in times of national predicaments and crisis, Jews have frequently been accused of such betrayal.

The book is so overflowing with factual errors that even Noam

Chomsky, no supporter of Israel, ridiculed the work, saying the authors, 'have a highly selective use of evidence (and much of the evidence is assertion)'.[44] Christopher Hitchens mocked the 'over-fondness for Jewish name dropping'.[45] Abe Foxman, in *The Deadliest Lies: The Israel Lobby and the Myth of Jewish Control*[46] explains the danger of such myths being promoted and demolishes the authors' contentions.

The book's core formulation – powerful Jews behind the scenes – is the staple of the radical fringe and anti-Semitic propaganda. But to have such charges aired with a tag of academic respectability in a style affiliated with serious, objective scholarship and to have them enter mainstream discourse is alarming. If Chicago and Harvard intellectuals accept these absurd convictions and beliefs, anyone may.

Mearsheimer opposed the Iraq War, believing it would provide Israel with the chance of ethnically cleansing the Palestinians. In December 2004, he offered diametrically different opinions to that of his book, stating that the Americans went to the Iraq War in good faith, believing they would find weapons of mass destruction, fearing that Saddam Hussein could become a serious threat to the US and believing in the power of democracy – that is, rather than acting in the interests of Israel. How does one explain such contradictions?

As Senator Moynihan once said, 'Everyone is entitled to his own opinion, but not to his own facts.'

When Comedy Central became anti-Semitism central

May 18, 2010

At the risk of being told I don't get cutting-edge, shock humour, a new online game from the folk at American TV Cable channel Comedy Central has crossed the line into anti-Semitism and Israel -bashing.

Just to remind you, Comedy Central screens *The Daily Show* with John Stewart, *The Colbert Report*, *Futurama*, *The Sarah Silverman Show*, *Reno 911* and other comedy shows.

The channel was in the news recently because it altered a *South Park* episode featuring the Prophet Mohammed after death threats were received against the show's creators.

Back to the offensive web game – I.S.R.A.E.L. Attack. The game is part of a promotional campaign for the DVD release of the now cancelled animated television series *Drawn Together*.

The game opens with an evil looking, long-nosed character screaming at a faceless figure, 'You lied to me, Jew producer'. The blabbering, squirming, frightened 'Jew producer' at first denies the accusation and then admits that he's 'busted'. And what did the 'Jew producer' fail to do? He did not kill each one of the *Drawn Together* cartoon characters after the show was taken off the air.

So, to finish the job the 'Jew producer' was supposed to carry out, the giant robot I.S.R.A.E.L. – Intelligent Smart Robot Animation Eraser – is dispatched by the villainous mastermind to wipe out every character. Forever.

The blue and white (the colours of the Israeli flag) murderous female robot, equipped with a machine-gun, a rocket and eraser bombs, goes on a rampage and destroys everything in its path, including animals and plants in addition to children.

Got it? ISRAEL is the cold, efficient, homicidal automaton that is programmed to indiscriminately annihilate without mercy. The game borrows heavily from the classic anti-Semitic blood libel of Jews as baby-killers.[47]

The aim of the game is to eradicate anything in sight – birds, cows, old people, young girls and boys. The highest amount of points

(700) is awarded for killing a little girl; for some reason killing a little boy earns players only 500 points. An old man gains the player 400 points.

I understand that the game is a huge success – it's been played 43,894 times. It's impossible to tell how many have downloaded it onto their computer to share with friends. I guess most have accepted the game's anti-Semitism as a given.

Interestingly, as the game loads, a line on the right side of the screen informs us that the *Drawn Together* DVD was released on April 20. In case the date's significance has escaped you – April 20 is Hitler's birthday. Must be a coincidence.

The unmistakable message is that when there's any slaughtering of children to be done, it's I.S.R.A.E.L. that does the job. According to the creative team at Comedy Central, that's the natural association we should all make when we think of the Jewish state and its people.

That not one executive found anything objectionable, defamatory, tasteless and hateful about the game speaks volumes about how entrenched and mainstream the vilifying of Israel and Jews has become. It seems that the notion of self-censorship did not apply when the demonising of Jews was on the agenda.

As one online commentator noted, imagine the firestorm if the menacing robot's acronym was made up of the N word, the racist epithet for African Americans..

All in all, what the kids playing the game will take away is this – Israel is a violent, relentless, immoral, child-killing machine. Come to think of it, it almost sounds like the nasty propaganda one encounters on the most bigoted, racist sites flooding the net.

What was Comedy Central thinking? Why anyone would want to perpetuate such vile stereotypes and prejudices, as well as inject this type of toxic incitement into the minds of young and old is beyond me.

I'm not laughing.

Uncovering the mask of anti-Zionism
April 29, 2011

I am no longer the youngest child at the Passover table but I still ask what is it about Israel that generates such unique contempt and such disproportional sympathy for one cause, and indifference to others.

Call me naive, but I am still bewildered by how the Israeli-Palestinian conflict seems to be always more important and urgent than the mass murder of Africans by Muslims in Darfur and the mass rape of women in the Congo, or the widespread ownership of slaves by Muslims in Niger, or the denial of freedom for the female half of the population in many nations, or the persecution of Arab homosexuals (so much so that Palestinians escape to Israel) or the disappearance, torture and murder of journalists and political activists in Gaza or in countries like Pakistan and Turkey.

Or did I miss the discussion of these issues by the Marrickville Council who adopted a motion to support the boycott of goods and services from Israel?[48]

Why is Israel singled out for special censure, when we all can list countries that are truly guilty of appalling human right abuses? Why the obsessive focus on Israel, when serious scrutiny of regimes that are astoundingly repressive takes a back seat? Do the Tibetans under Chinese rule, the Muslims in India, the Kurds in Iraq, the Animists in Sudan, to name but a few atrocities, receive such obsessive focus? Why are Jews forced to defend Israel's right to exist again and again? Are the Spanish, Danish, Syrians, Egyptians required to do so too?

As former NSW premier Bob Carr wrote earlier last month, discussing Marrickville Council's proposed boycott of Israel, 'There are numerous regimes in the world guilty of oppression and breaches of freedom worse than any committed by the Netanyahu government which, at the very least, faces a free media, parliamentary opposition, regular elections and a Supreme Court that has disallowed torture.'[49]

Singer Macy Gray appealed to her fans in January of this year, asking whether she should perform in Tel Aviv despite Israel's apartheid and the government's disgusting treatment against the Palestinians.'[50] Has she questioned the human rights record of every country she has performed in?

It begins to feel like the radical left has made attacking Israel the very reason for its existence, a pursuit that is so fashionable and comforting, that the facts and logic are sidelined in favour of demagoguery. It is so 'in' to criticise Israel that the catchphrase 'I am Zionist, I have to judge Israel' is now a cliché. To quote Edgar Bronfman, president of the Samuel Bronfman Foundation, who this month wrote in *Haaretz*, 'I do not criticise Israel because I wish to separate myself from it. I speak up because I am a committed Zionist who loves Israel.'[51]

I guess it's easy to criticise sitting in front of a laptop in a cafe, far away from the rockets and terrorist attacks.

Professor Ruth Wisse, in her book *Jews and Power*[52] argues that Jews in the Diaspora have practised a politics of accommodation to the powers of the day as they have made new homes for themselves in countries not their own. This continuous accommodation, she argues, is harmful, because it has inevitably led Jews to look inward for culpability rather than blaming those whose goals are to destroy them: 'The unfortunate consequence is that we become a no-fail target and can never protect what we achieve. While Israel has given the Jews the wherewithal to fight back, the fight becomes debilitating. Why should we alone of all the people in the world have to continue to defend ourselves?'[53]

It is now accepted in certain circles that as long as you are talking about Israel, not Jews, you can say whatever you want. Anti-Zionism is the convenient mask.

Question: who said the following: 'Instead of attacking Jews they are attacking Zionism, and this is the way because you cannot attack Jews anymore openly.'[54] Answer: Author, A. B. Yehoshua, March 2007. Anti-Zionism is underlined by a denial of Jewish national self-determination and of Israel's right to exist as a Jewish state in the Middle East.

What other country is more closely monitored and censured than Israel? If you Google 'Israel' and 'illegitimate' or 'racist' or 'rogue' your computer might blow up or you might cause an electricity shortage throughout the city. I can't think of another state that has so many groups and individuals wishing to see it disappear.

The disturbing element is that there is hardly any recognition of violence and terror against Israel – the BBC did not even cover the Fogel murders.[55] Zionism and Israel are judged according to one standard and everyone else to another – but of course it's easier to lay all the blame at Israel's doorstep.

The constant Israel-bashing may have people believing the lies.

Israel is not perfect and is not a saint. But what other country is?

Facebook should be a force for good,
not a home for hate

August 2, 2011

A few weeks ago, 21 survivors of the death camps who witnessed the murder of their families by the Nazis wrote to Facebook asking the organisation to take down pages that promote Holocaust denial.[56]

Last week, Facebook refused to remove the pages stating: 'We think it's important to maintain consistency in our policies, which don't generally prohibit people from making statements about historical events. No matter how ignorant the statement or how awful the event.'[57]

Facebook is very wrong in where it has drawn the line and on what side it has chosen to stand. For some reason, Facebook seems to be impervious to its own Statement of Rights and Responsibilities, which prohibits the posting of hateful material. Of course, they will remove sexual content or pictures of mothers breastfeeding, but do not feel hate speech is worthy of the same treatment.

You decide: do lines, posted on a Holocaust denial pages, that call Jewish people 'snakes', 'liars', 'a disease', 'not really human beings' and 'children of Satan', not amount to hate speech?

The agents of this invidious and wilful assault on the truth should not be given a forum on the world's most popular social networking website to preach hate, to gain legitimacy for their sickening canards and to attract new members to their cause. The denial of the Holocaust is employed as a pretext and a springboard to peddle and encourage hatred towards one group – the Jews.

By allowing these pages to stay, Facebook is enabling the flourishing of a type of vicious and bone-chilling Jewish hatred that is a crime in a number of countries and which is part of a long campaign of nasty falsehoods and incitement that have led to the deaths of millions.

In the past few years, Facebook has become incredibly powerful, with 750 million users. That's more than the combined populations of the US, Australia, Canada, Britain, New Zealand, France, Russia and Germany (to name but a few). With such power, comes great responsibility and accountability. Nothing in life happens in a moral vacuum and Facebook's lack of action will contribute to the social acceptability of anti-Jewish sentiment and racism.

I have no doubt that Holocaust deniers are smiling, emboldened by the knowledge that they can continue to exploit this new technology to demonise Jews, to label survivors as liars and hoaxers, and to keep inflicting grief and suffering on the victims. The Nazis, who provided Germans with free or cheap radios so they could bombard their citizens with their vile ideology, would have found much to like in the way Facebook has allowed hatred to invade its reputable space.

Perhaps Facebook should listen to US President Barack Obama, who at a Days of Remembrance ceremony in 2009 remarked, 'To this day, there are those who insist the Holocaust never happened; who perpetrate every form of intolerance – racism and anti-Semitism, homophobia, xenophobia, sexism, and more – hatred that degrades its victim and diminishes us all.'[58] Further, giving a voice to Holocaust deniers is an affront to all those who escaped genocide and tyranny to make new lives for themselves in Australia and around the world.

In one sense, I say to Facebook, 'Thanks for reminding us' that it is time for everyone to reassess their standards, to look into their heart and to reflect on the principles that guide them. Holocaust denial tests our values and contravenes the moral code Australians have always cherished.

Facebook should be a vehicle that champions social values and human rights, and builds a civil society online, rather than be a facilitator for the proliferation of hate.

Instead of shrugging their shoulders and adopting a 'just-ignore-them' strategy, Facebook must stop giving access to deniers who trample on the memories of the Holocaust and who stain our children's minds with putrid and pernicious falsification. It must take the moral, honourable and ethical path and never again permit its site to become the disseminator of harmful and hate-filled content of the kind that you would expect to see on the wall of a public toilet.

Otherwise, Facebook will confirm Edmund Burke's dictum that, 'All that's necessary for the forces of evil to win in the world is for enough good people to do nothing'.

Global anti-Semitism: making sure 'Never Again' is not a hollow slogan

April 14, 2013

A recent report shows that anti-Semitic attacks worldwide were up by 30 per cent last year,[59] and that the number of anti-Semitic incidents in Australia in that time almost doubled.

The report – released by the Tel-Aviv University's Kantor Centre for the Study of Contemporary European Jewry – noted that 2012 saw 'an alarming rise in the number of terrorist attacks and attempted attacks against Jewish targets, and an escalation in violent incidents against Jews worldwide'.[60]

The head of the Kantor Center, Dr Moshe Kantor, said: 'As a Jewish leader, I can say that the [Jewish communities] in Europe are in danger. People are afraid to go to synagogue, to go to Jewish school – this is a new phenomenon and it is joined by several other trends we haven't seen before, like the fact that neo-Nazi [parties] have not only become legal in Europe, they're already holding parliament seats in Hungary, Ukraine and Greece.'[61]

This news came as communities around the world observed Holocaust Memorial Day honouring the six million Jews who were murdered by the Nazis and their collaborators simply because they were Jews. The solemn occasion also honoured those who survived, and the courageous rescuers and liberators of the death camps.

In Europe, anti-Semitism is rearing its ugly head again to frightening levels. In France last year there was a disturbing 82 per cent rise in physical and verbal assaults against Jews;[62] in Hungary, the neo-Nazi Jobbik Party is now the third-largest political party in the country. Marton Gyöngyösi, one of its members, has argued for the establishment of a 'registry' of Jewish MPs and government officials in Hungary since they constitute a 'national security threat'.[63]

There are daily reports of Jewish cemeteries and memorials being vandalised and desecrated, and the UK[64] and Belgium[65] recorded one of their worst years for anti-Semitic incidents and complaints.

Meanwhile, a report released last month by the Australian Online Hate Prevention Institute notes that anti-Semitic activity on social media like Facebook is a growing phenomenon.

Worryingly, the report also found that while some Facebook 'hate sites' are taken down almost immediately, others remain online, some for more than six months. The report identifies what Facebook removes and what sort of content Facebook does not consider hate speech and refuses to remove.[66]

And this month, in an interview with a Polish historical magazine to mark the 70th anniversary of the Warsaw Ghetto Uprising, Polish professor Krzysztof Jasiewicz stated that 'the dimensions of the German crimes were only possible due to the active cooperation of the Jews in the process of the slaughter of their people'.[67] Jasiewicz went on to say that he was not willing to debate these issues, since: 'it's a waste of the time we would devote to a dialogue with the Jews, whose sense of superiority and confidence that they are the chosen people are leading them to oblivion'.[68]

The Holocaust is unique in human history. For the first time, a war of industrialised, institutionalised extermination against an entire population of men, women and children became state policy.

The Final Solution was planned in the 1942 infamous Wannsee Conference. In a polite atmosphere and setting, fifteen Nazi politicians and administrators – in just two hours – planned the total eradication of the Jews of Europe and endorsed their murder by poison gas.

The Holocaust was conscious, it was deliberate, and it was funded and carried out as a top priority by a government elected by its citizens in a country renowned for its contribution to science, literature, music and philosophy.

Hell-bent on destroying every single Jew in Europe, Nazi Germany executed the Final Solution using its modern industry and military. Their national project of liquidation slaughtered one and a half million Jewish children, as well as millions of Poles, Soviets, the Roma, Jehovah's Witnesses, homosexuals, the handicapped and the mentally disabled: anyone deemed less desirable.

As Jewish philosopher Abraham Heschel once said, his problem was not so much where was God, but where was man during the Holocaust.[69]

The Holocaust was the darkest instance of man's inhumanity to its fellow man. It still serves as a stark reminder about the deadly consequences of intolerance.

The Holocaust teaches us that 'Never Again' means standing firm and taking decisive action to fight prejudice, bigotry and hatred whenever and wherever it happens.

The Holocaust also teaches us that it happened because of the inaction of bystanders who were complicit by their silence. We learn that indifference is the final element for mass murder to prevail.

All Australians must actively rededicate themselves to make certain that hatred and bigotry against a Jew, a Christian, a Muslim – against any race, creed or colour – is never left unchecked or unchallenged.

There will be those who will say that the Nazi atrocities happened so long ago, that they happened in Europe, that it happened to Jews and others but not to us.

So why should we care about the suffering there and then, or about Darfur now? What does this have to do with us here in Australia?

The answer is that if we remember the Holocaust, we can prevent such horrendous acts occurring in the future by reflecting on our own moral responsibility.

Over the last few weeks, MTV has been airing a range of commercials. One of them, titled *Subway Roundup*, is set on a NY underground train. Suddenly, the lights go out; the passengers are frightened, unsure of what is happening. The car moves from side to side, evoking memories of the trains that took Jewish people to the Nazi death camps. When the train arrives at its destination, officers with machine guns and dogs are waiting outside. They order and push the riders to form an orderly line. The final image of the modern day passengers dissolves into that of the Jews in Nazi Germany.[70]

As the commercial ends, the message across the screen is: 'The Holocaust happened to people like us.'

We must choose to act. Inaction is not an option.

Free speech is not absolute
March 28, 2014

Unless you've been living on Mars, you would know that the issue of Section 18C of the Racial Discrimination Act has been debated openly and passionately.

In fact, a few days ago, Attorney-General Brandis, in promising to repeal parts of that section, said that 'People do have a right to be bigots'.[71]

This is a complex moral issue on which good, intelligent people can disagree. I'm certain that Australian Human Rights Commissioner Tim Wilson and columnist Andrew Bolt, who want 18C amended, understand that racism is a growing societal problem.

Where we differ is on how to best tackle it. There is a lot at stake here. And context is important. I don't believe that 18C should be repealed and don't subscribe to the hands-off approach when it comes to hate speech.

You hear people talk about freedom of speech and how it must not be limited by laws. What is not often spoken about is the huge toll that hate speech takes on its victims. The aim of vilification is to wilfully promote, stir up and generate hatred against one or more groups.

When bias-motivated speech and racial vilification are allowed a free reign, this slow-acting poison robs the intended victims of their dignity and sense of security. Be it against Muslims, Hindus, Jews, women and the LGBTI community, it creates a climate of intolerance and prejudice.

One argument is that the marketplace of ideas will take care of bigoted and hateful rhetoric because there is enough space for counterpoints and ideas. Problem is that the devastating harm has already been done and no amount of counter-arguments will remedy the victim's real fear, ordeal and grief.

Simply sitting back and saying, 'Suck it up and learn to live with it' is not the way to go. In the end, it comes down to what kind of society we want to live in. Do we want to live in a society where vulnerable groups are protected by law from hate speech that threatens their safety and rights?

Do we want to live in a society where everyone is accorded respect and equality, and can go about their daily lives without facing a verbal onslaught that expresses wanton hostility, hatred and discrimination?

Do we want to live in an Australia where the weak can take comfort in knowing that when they are explicitly demonised, abused, stigmatised, denigrated and dehumanised because of their skin colour, sexual orientation, religious, national or ethnic orientation, the legal system will come to their aid.

Do we want to be part of a community that assures vulnerable minorities that they and their families can walk the streets and live their lives free from deliberate and unreasonable humiliation, knowing that they truly belong here, and that they will not be emotionally and mentally scarred by unbridled, toxic hate-filled expression?

Or do we want to live in a country that is a haven for hate-speech dissemination, where our children's minds are polluted by hateful speech like Holocaust denial that destroys the very fabric of tolerance, diversity and mutual respect our co-existence is founded upon?

On any analysis, hate speech devalues and injures human beings. It says that that minorities or anyone different don't have the right to live among others. It shuts them out. It brands them as undesirable. And it's just plain dangerous.

The FBI has drawn a direct link between vilification and crimes when it stated several years ago that 'groups that preach hatred and intolerance plant the seeds of terrorism here in our country'.[72]

And in its 2011 Law Enforcement Report, the FBI noted that a hate group that is not stopped will inevitably commit violent hate crimes.[73]

If history has taught us one lesson, it is that bigots at first preach their warped falsehoods, and in time, act on them. Verbal violence and physical violence are intimately connected, one preceding the other. Racist speech justifies bullying, beatings and murder.

So maybe it's time to think about the rights of the victims. Advocates for doing away with 18C usually cite the USA as a place where free speech is almost absolute. Yes, the USA is the odd country out.

Even so, in 1952, the Supreme Court held that group libel – when you attack the dignity of a group – is illegal.[74]

And eleven years ago it ruled that speech aimed at intimidating, such as cross burning, might not receive First Amendment protection.

Every western-liberal democracy has some kind of hate-speech regulation. There is a recognition that this kind of speech causes real trauma and suffering that is long-lasting and is enormously damaging.

The message we must send to young people is that intimidating and insulting anyone because of their race, religion, gender, sexual preference or ethnic orientation is unacceptable in Australia. And that names, not just stick and stones, can hurt.

Europe vs Israel

May 16, 2014

It is now accepted that the age-old hatred of Jews is once again coming to the surface in Europe. Hitler's *Mein Kampf* is a best-seller;[75] the Quenelle, the modified Nazi salute, has become increasingly popular;[76] neo-Nazi demonstrations are becoming a common occurrence, while violence against Jewish communities and individuals has dramatically increased and intensified; and a recent survey found that 76 per cent of Jews felt that anti-Semitism had worsened across Europe in the last five years.[77]

According to the book *Demonizing Israel and the Jews*[78] by Manfred Gerstenfeld, 150 million Europeans still retain and hold anti-Semitic and anti-Israel beliefs. And earlier this month the United Nations Human Rights Council passed a series of anti-Israel resolutions which included a vote that bolstered the vile BDS campaign by encouraging businesses to boycott Israeli settlements. Shamefully, not a single European member of the UNHRC objected to this blatant demonisation, instead voting to egregiously castigate Israel.[79]

It wasn't always that way. The decimation of European Jewry left anti-Semitism, in Western Europe, at least, as a spent force. The new State of Israel was seen by many in Europe's emerging democratic classes as a role model for nation building. Yet, as Alan Dershowitz rightly noted, 'Why are so many of the grandchildren of Nazis and Nazi collaborators who brought us the Holocaust, once again declaring war on the Jews? Why have we seen such an increase in anti-Semitism and irrationally virulent anti-Zionism in Western Europe?'[80]

It's here that we might bring in the psychologists, because what has transpired over these past nearly five decades cannot simply be ascribed to 'the occupation' and 'the settlement question'. Before the Oslo Accords, we had lived through PLO terror and hijackings, brought about with broad Arab support, always focused on Israel's 'illegitimacy'. And since Oslo, we've witnessed enhanced terrorist activity, marked by suicide bombers and super-negationist, terrorist organisations like Hamas and Hezbollah.

Add to that the now 35-year sustained Iranian call for Israel's demise and the outbreak of total chaos in Israel's neighbourhood and you'd have thought that Israel would be looking pretty good these days to Europeans looking for stability and like-mindedness, and recalling – while there are still survivors to bear witness to the Holocaust – the near destruction of the Jews of Europe while governments and tens of millions of Europeans looked on.

Over the years, there has been building in Europe a certain impatience with Israel – and with those who support it. It's hard to put your finger on it, and it cannot be simply explained away by the settlement issue, which has become the go-to, convenient excuse for all of Israel's perceived ills.

This 'impatience' has now found its way into new and troubling forms. The global BDS campaign seeks to marginalise Israel as a 21st century South Africa. And Europeans, who should know better, are buying into it.

Most disconcerting of all has been the EU's attitude toward all of this. Though official statements disavow boycotts, the Council of Ministers issued a declaration last year – on the very day that US Secretary of State John Kerry was announcing a resumption of Israeli-Palestinian negotiations – which prevented Israeli ministries, public bodies and businesses operating beyond the Green Line from receiving grants from the European Investment Bank. Now, there is talk of EU demands that products which originate in the 'occupied territories' be labelled. This is an invitation to boycott, much as labelling a cigarette pack as being injurious to one's health is a warning not to buy. Rather than encouraging the peace process, some EU figures – including its envoy to Israel – are being publicly quoted as assigning blame to Israel should the talks break down.

If that were not troubling enough, a perfect storm of anti-Semitism is brewing across Europe in large countries and small. Some of it comes from the rise of the extreme right, particularly in former Central and Eastern Europe, but not only there. Paramilitary uniforms, marches in the streets of major cities, and anti-Semitic (and anti-immigrant, anti-Roma) rhetoric has become a familiar feature in a number of countries. 'Anti-Semitism without Jews', used at one time to describe lingering anti-Semitism in Eastern

Europe, can rightfully be applied today, as between the Holocaust and emigration, smaller Jewish communities find themselves particularly vulnerable. A rise in Holocaust revisionism, including the veneration of pro-Nazi, fascist leaders, is being reported in a number of places. Elsewhere, anti-Semitic intimidation has been carried out by Islamic extremists; the killing of students at the Jewish school in Toulouse, France, may be the best known of these, but not the only one.

And, adding insult to injury, there are the dual campaigns in Europe against kosher ritual slaughter[81] and circumcision.[82] This intrusion into the millennia-old customs of the Jewish people is often masked as a call of protection of the rights of animals and children, but in fact is both an affront and, assault on religious freedom. That most Jews are also supporters of Israel and carry out 'inhumane' practices in their daily lives, proffers a field day to those who wish to delegitimise Israel and its backers via a one-two punch.

Of course, not all Europeans engage in this kind of activity, but there is enough of it around to make one feel uneasy. Israel enjoys good bilateral relations with a number of countries in Europe, which is its biggest trading partner. A number of European airlines serve Israel, and investor interest from Europe in its many hi-tech start-ups is high. Israelis are inveterate tourists, and are always finding the 'next place' to vacation in Europe. But with all of that, there is a palpable unease in the air. Is it really just about 'occupation' and 'settlements,' or is there something else bothering Europe?

Surely, policy makers in Europe know it's more complicated than that. Dealing with the rise of the extreme right, with Islamic extremism, with the casual and dangerous calls on the left for Israel's demise, demands courageous and focused leadership. In democracies, 'stand-up' leaders use the bully pulpit to speak out against the inciters and to protect the vulnerable. The media should be doing the same, instead of publishing editorial cartoons that equate Israelis with Nazis. And, European leaders should stop seeing Israel as an alien, uncomfortable implant among the community of democracies. If shared values mean anything, then Israel must be a member of the club. That doesn't presuppose agreement on every issue, but rather a full appreciation that, despite repeated attempts to destroy it by war or other means, and notwithstanding the absolute chaos which surrounds it now, Israel is today, what it was in 1948: a robust democracy that has, in its brief history, contributed so much to the betterment of mankind.

Is that asking too much?

Hatred such as anti-Semitism is a virus that weakens the nation

August 12, 2014

Over the past two months, we have all woken up to a new, frightening reality. There are alarming developments and chilling signs that are making the Jewish community here less comfortable, less confident and very worried that the flames of anti-Semitism are burning more furiously at home. This hatred is so vitriolic and so insidious that it is hard to take. The ugly demon of anti-Semitism has risen with such a searing intensity that I am worried.

I shuddered when I learned last week that teenagers boarded a school bus in Sydney, screaming 'Heil Hitler' and 'kill the Jews', and threatened to slit the throats of Jewish students as young as five,[83] or that anti-Semitic graffiti was daubed on the Carmel school in Perth,[84] or that Jewish students were verbally abused, intimidated and physically harassed on our university campuses and excluded from entering a meeting because of their religion,[85] or when a visiting rabbi was assaulted in Perth,[86] or when a Jewish man was slashed by two men who shouted 'Jewish dog' in Arabic and made references to the Gaza conflict.[87]

It's amazing how anti-Semitism is excused when the atmosphere allows it to masquerade as criticism of Israeli policies. Since the onset of Operation Protective Edge, Australian Jews have been unfairly blamed and singled out for events unfolding in Gaza and Israel.

The cumulative effect of such contemptible behaviour, and its sharp escalation, is that Australian Jews are increasingly feeling insecure about their safety. It should come as no surprise that some are scared to admit that they're Jewish, or visit Jewish places, or wear religious clothing and items that identify them as Jews. This is simply unacceptable.

Anti-Jewish prejudice, mingled with inflammatory, obsessive Israel demonisation and defamation, has been mainstreamed, finding ready acceptance in large parts of social and traditional media. I could not believe my eyes when I saw a Fairfax cartoon depicting a Yarmulke-wearing, hooked-nose old Jew, comfortably sitting in a chair emblazoned with the Star of David, holding a remote-controlled detonator in his hand, bombing Gaza.[88] All Jews were now being portrayed as cold, heartless murderers with a lust for blood.

A box of lies, libels and stereotypes has been opened, and it's not closing any time soon.

Public displays of hate have become disturbingly prevalent. In pro-Palestinian rallies across Australia, Israel is frequently likened to Nazi Germany and accused of perpetrating a new Holocaust, with posters intertwining the Star of David with a Swastika. In a protest in Melbourne over the weekend, Adam Bandt charged Israel with committing a massacre while surrounded by banners labelling Israel a terrorist state, calling for its boycott and proclaiming 'from the river to the sea, Palestine will be free' – a well-known call for Israel's annihilation.

*

Globally, violent anti-Semitic rhetoric and acts are exploding. In France, Jewish areas have been subjected to mob-like looting, synagogues have been firebombed and shops smashed, while cries of 'Death to the Jews' were chanted in Paris;[89] in Germany crowds howled 'Jews to the gas', while Molotov cocktails have been hurled at synagogues;[90] in Belgium, a woman was turned away from a shop and told: 'We don't currently sell to Jews.'[91] And the list goes on.

Two days ago, Rabbi Joseph Raksin was fatally shot while walking to a North Miami Beach synagogue.[92]

Hitler is dead but, as one commentator observed, his children are thriving throughout.

Anti-Semitism contravenes the moral code of inclusiveness and a fair go which Australians have always held dear. It doesn't have a place in our country. And this is not just about the Jewish community. Anti-Semitism stirs up and promotes racial hatred that is harmful to Australian society as a whole. Because where Jewish-hatred flourishes, you will always find racism, religious bigotry, Islamophobia, ethnic purity, homophobia, misogyny and loathing of minorities.

Anti-Semitism undermines our proud social cohesion and leads to violence. One writer noted: 'Hate incubates. It festers and grows

– multiplies exponentially until words become chants, lies become truths and ideologies that seemed ridiculous no longer do. And when poisonous ideologies pervade and consume, blood will be spilled. And will continue to be spilled.'[93]

A civilised society that cherishes democracy, multiculturalism and equality simply cannot look away from this threat and allow it to be normalised. Anti-Semitism is a virus that spreads, and the only way to pulverise this evil is to fight back through education. That is why the B'nai B'rith Anti-Defamation Commission, through its *Click Against Hate* program, equips students with the tools and knowledge to stand up and speak out against bullying, racism and discrimination.

One of the lessons of the Holocaust is that we must all be vigilant and be mindful of the perils of unchallenged extremism and of words that stoke the flames of intolerance and division.

There is no other choice.

Universities must protect students from anti-Semitism

September 2014

Here we go again.

The 50-day conflict between Israel and Hamas has spurred a dramatic and chilling increase in anti-Semitic incidents as campuses have become extensions of the virulent and irrational Jewish-hatred infecting our community.

The gloves have come off as thuggish behaviour, bullying, propaganda parades and circuses, indefensible Student Council motions, graffiti, calls for BDS, and verbal assaults have poisoned the atmosphere at several Australian universities.

And yes, it is ironic that the supposed oases of education, open dialogue and reason, are also hotbeds and hotspots for shocking racist behaviour. It's not surprising that our collective anxiety level has been ratcheted up several levels as young people, who have come to university to learn and grow, have had to run the gauntlet and confront an ongoing and rampant anti-Israel campaign that is vicious, organised and multilayered.

This is not crying wolf. The blatant and purposeful escalation has caused state and federal politicians Christopher Pyne, David Southwick and Michael Danby to express their deep concern, as a troubling picture has emerged of a hostile and harassing environment which presents us all with a unique challenge.

This hurtful behaviour is part of a broad, unrelenting, multidimensional global effort to normalise and mainstream the vilification and undermining of Israel. The line between anti-Zionism, anti-Israelism and anti-Semitism has become increasingly blurred with the three D's – double standards, demonisation, and delegitimisation – now commonplace.

The aim of the extremists on campus is fivefold: to damage and erode Israel's image, to intimidate anyone who stands up to defend the Jewish state against these grotesque slanders and libels, to influence other students who may not be knowledgeable about the situation, to foment intolerance against Israelis and Jews, and to export this menace to other student centres.

The impact of this Israel-bashing should not be underestimated. I have spoken to many students. who feel isolated and emotionally depleted to the point that they are afraid to confront those groups for fear of violence or abuse and who feel unable to participate fully in campus life.

What has compounded Jewish students' sense of vulnerability and frustration is not just personally experiencing or witnessing anti-Semitism, but the perception that university administrators have not responded swiftly and effectively to this serious problem. Indeed, as one student told me, 'The ugliness of the last two months has happened under the gaze of university bureaucrats who have gone missing in action'.

This is a wake-up call for everyone since anti-Semitism is not just a problem for Jewish students. It is a virus that endangers every minority, for where anti-Semitism thrives, so does every type of bigotry, prejudice and discrimination.

The primary responsibility for clamping down on anti-Semitism on campus rests with university administrators.

The Anti-Defamation Commission has heard the pleas of students. It has been partnered with the Australian Union of Jewish Students, which should be commended for its initiative and efforts.

We have spoken with and called on university leaders to counter hateful speech and behaviour, and to ensure that Jewish students are physically and emotionally secure.

There is something very wrong when students are targeted and threatened because of their views about Israel, or because of their religious appearance, or because of their affiliation. In short, for simply being who they are.

Stemming the tide and mounting an effective fight-back response requires a multipronged strategy that may require throwing out the old playbook and embracing new methods.

Pro-Israel student activists need to create their own positive message about Israel and to drum the truth as an antidote to the defamation and distortion. Strategies include op-eds, letters to the editor, inventive social media platforms and online petitions, public lectures, information stalls, their own programming to correct the misperceptions about Israel and to trumpet its achievements, hold

Shabbat dinners with non-Jewish leaders, and enlisting other student associations as allies in the fight.

And they need to be informed and skilled.

Also, university administrators and staff need to understand the difference between acceptable criticism of Israeli policies and hate speech, and know that anti-Israel activity is not about political protests, but is grounded in age-old Jew-hatred. A university resource guide fact sheet on the basic aspects of anti-Semitism is now warranted.

Universities must take every measure and every step to protect Jewish students. They can start by taking a leadership role and issuing a public statement that explicitly and unreservedly condemns all forms of anti-Semitism.

Second, they must be unequivocal that language and conduct that demonises Israel, labels it a racist or a Nazi state that has no right to exist, is an expression of anti-Jewish bigotry.

Third, denounce the employment of anti-Semitic images and symbols.

Fourth, acknowledge that anti-Semitism is a real problem and pledge to vigorously tackle this scourge.

Fifth, integrate into university policy a clear and working definition of anti-Semitism.

Sixth, commit their administration to quickly investigate and prosecute those individuals and groups who violate university guidelines and outline the harsh penalties involved.

Seventh, inform all students of their legal rights and educate them about the avenues available to them to bring complaints.

Eighth, implement a wide-ranging campus strategic plan that delivers anti-bias training, explores the hurtful results of anti-Semitism and effectively responds to reporting of incidents. Workshops that inspire students and staff to become champions and voices of positive change and foster a welcoming, inclusive and respectful environment are an imperative.

Only when there is zero-tolerance of anti-Semitism, will the hate-mongers know that they will be held to account and will not be able get away with their destructive crusade.

Notes

1   Geoffrey Wheatcroft. 'The Jewish Answer' *The Spectator* (UK),
    December 17, 2002.

2   http://i-p-o.org/racism-ngo-decl.htm

3   Gabriel Schonenfeld. 'Israel and the anti-Semites' in Ron Rosen-
    baum. (editor). *Those Who Forget the Past: The Question of Anti-Semi-
    tism.'* USA: Random House, 2004.

4   Ruth Wisse. 'On Ignoring Anti-Semitism' in Ron Rosenbaum.
    (editor). *Those Who Forget the Past: The Question of Anti-Semitism.'*
    USA: Random House, 2004.

5   http://www.jcpa.org/phas/phas-gerstenfeld-s05.htm

6   http://daccess-dds-ny.un.org/doc/RESOLUTION/GEN/
    NR0/000/92/IMG/NR000092.pdf?OpenElement

7   Daniel Moynihan. *A Dangerous Place.* Boston: Little, Brown, 1978.

8   Avi Beker. *The Chosen: The History of an Idea, and the anatomy of an
    Obsession.* New York: Palgrave Macmillan, 2008.

9   http://www.presidency.ucsb.edu/ws/?pid=20012

10 http://www.ewtn.com/library/curia/pcjpraci.htm

11 Philip Herbst. *Talking Terrorism: A Dictionary of the Loaded Lan-
    guage of Political Violence.* Westport, Conn: Greenwood Press, 2003.

12 The actual book is available here: http://www.jrbooksonline.com/
    PDFs/Matzo%20of%20Zion%20JR.pdf

13 http://www.jta.org/1984/12/28/archive/greek-jewish-community-
    is-angered-and-disturbed-court-in-crete-rules-that-jehovahs-wit-
    nesses-sect

14 Philip Mendes. 'Much huffing but no puff: the proposed Australian
    academic boycott of Israel' *Australian Quarterly*, Volume 75, No. 6
    (November-December 2003): 18-40.

15 Tovah Lazaroff. 'Far from academic' *Jerusalem Post*, May 3, 2002.

16 Peter Foster. 'Academia split over Boycott of Israel' *The Daily Tele-
    graph*, 16 May, 2002.

17 Dinitia Smith. 'A stone's throw is a Freudian slip' *The New York
    Times*, March 10, 2001.

18   Lynn Crosbie. 'Sweet, melodious and Nazi to the core' *The Globe and Mail*, January 7, 2006.

19   Carolyn O'Hara. 'From Prussia with hate: Lynx and Lamb are Californian twin sisters hoping to become stars. But, as Carolyn O'Hara reveals, their pop-country ballads represent the latest strategy of America's white supremacists' *New Statesman*, November 14, 2005.

20   Louis Theroux. 'Raising Hate' Sunday Mail (Queensland, Australia), March 7, 2004.

21   http://www.adl.org/combating-hate/domestic-extremism-terrorism/c/racist-groups-use-computer.html

22   http://www.theyeshivaworld.com/news/general/13914/anti-semites-target-australian-synagogue-kosher-bakery-and-restaurant.html

23   Natasha Robinson. 'Teenager bashed in anti-Semitic attack' *The Australian*, August 20, 2007.

24   http://www.rediff.com/news/report/aus/20080311.htm

25   Britt Smith. 'Cricket fuels race attacks on cabbies' *Geelong News* February 6, 2008.

26   http://www.northumbria.police.uk/campaigns/never_too_late/third-partyreporting/index.asp

27   http://archive.adl.org/media_watch/tv/fox_family_goy.html#.VBFo_fmSy_g

28   Barry Garron. '*Family Guy*: Seth & Alex's Almost Live Comedy Show – TV Review' *Hollyywood Reporter*, 8 November 2009.

29   Gina Serpe. 'Microsoft Not Amused by Family Guy, Pulls Plug on Sponsorship' *eonline*, 27 October, 2009

30   Larry Neumeister. 'Show accused of anti-Jewish spoof of `When You Wish Upon a Star' AP, October 3, 2007.

31   Katherine Albers. '10 North Naples Middle students suspended for taking part in 'Kick a Jew day' *Naples News Daily*, November 23, 2009.

32   Editorial. 'North Naples Middle School … lessons in responding to schoolyard ugliness' *Naples News Daily*, November 30, 2009.

33   Ken Meaney. 'RCMP investigating Facebook group over 'Kick a Ginger' day' *Vancouver Sun*, November 20, 2008.

34 'Ginger Day' Attacks: Boys Arrested For Bullying Redheads' *Huffington Post*, May 25, 2011.

35 Editorial Board. 'Online jokes can lead to real-life, dark interpretations' *The Purdue Exponent*, November 30, 2009,

36 Jim Salter. 'Hit a Jew Day' at St. Louis School: Students Face Punishment' *Huffington Post*, 21 November, 2008.

37 David Hunn. '3 students suspended over 'Hit a Jew Day' Principal of Parkway West Middle School says the youngsters are not anti-Semitic' St. Louis Post-Dispatch (Missouri), October 24, 2008.

38 'Students face punishment for 'Hit a Jew Day' AP, 23 October 2008.

39 Stephen Walt. 'I don't mean to say I told you so, but ...' *Foreign Policy*, February 8, 2010.

40 http://www.martinkramer.org/sandbox/2010/02/chronologically-challenged-professor-walt/

41 John J. Mearsheimer and Stephen Walt. *The Israel Lobby and U.S Foreign Policy*. New York: Farrar, Straus and Giroux, 2007.

42 Melanie Phillips. The *World Turned Upside Down: The Global battle over God, Truth and Power*.New York: Encounter Books, 2010.

43 Eli Lake. 'David Duke Claims to Be Vindicated By a Harvard Dean' *The New York Sun*, March 20, 2006.

44 Noam Chomsky. 'The Israel Lobby' *Znet*, March 28, 2006.

45 Christopher Hitches. 'Overstating Jewish Power' *Slate Magazine*, March 27, 2006.

46 Abe Foxman. *The Deadliest Lies: The Israel Lobby and the Myth of Jewish Control*. New York: Palgrave Macmillan, 2007.

47 Maayana Miskin. 'Comedy Central's I.S.R.A.E.L Draws fire for Anti-Semitism' *Israel National News*, May 21, 2010.

48 Simon Benson. 'Marrickville Council faces $4million bill for Israel boycott' *The Daily Telegraph*, April 4, 2011.

49 Bob Carr. 'Don't sack Marrickville: It'll help the dopes' *Thoughtlines with Bob Carr*, April 15, 2011.

50 Or Barnea. 'Macy Gray consult fans on Israel gig' *Yediot Ahronot*, 20 January 2011.

51 Edgar Bronfman. 'Supporting Israel means questioning its policies' *Haaretz*, April 18, 2011.

52 Ruth R. Wisse. *Jews and Power*. New York: Nextbook: Schocken, 2007.

53 Ruth R. Wisse. *Jews and Power*. 60.

54 Aimee Rhodes. 'A. B Yehoshua: 'Anti-Zionism: Mask for anti-Semitism' *Jerusalem Post*, January 1, 2001.

55 Neil Rubin. 'BBC official admits the network 'got it wrong' on Fogel murders' *Jewish Telegraphic Agency*, june 22, 2012.

56 http://www.wiesenthal.com/site/pp.asp?c=lsKWLbPJLnF&b=7548639#.VBIpD_mSy_g

57 Miriam Grossman. 'Facebook firm on Holocaust denial pages, despite survivors' letter' *Jewish Telegraphic Agency*, July 28, 2011

58 http://www.ushmm.org/confront-genocide/speakers-and-events/all-speakers-and-events/president-obamas-days-of-remembrance-address

59 Sam Sokol. 'Study: Global anti-Semitism rises by 30 per cent' *Jerusalem Post*, July 7, 2014.El

60 Eldad Benari. 'Report: Alarming Rise in Anti-Semitic Incidents in the World' *Israel National News*, 27 January, 2013.

61 Yael Branovsky. 'Report: Anti-Semitism worldwide up by 30 per cent in 2012' *Israel Hayom*, April 7, 2013.

62 'French Jewish Leader: 'The Number of Anti-Semitic Acts Has Exploded' *The Algemeiner*, February 20, 2013.

63 Martin Dunai. 'Anger as Hungary far-right leader demands lists of Jews' *Reuters*, November 27, 2012.

64 ' UK report: Slight rise in anti-Semitic incidents' *Jerusalem Post*, 2 October, 2013.

65 Jspace staff. 'Complaints of anti-Semitic incidents up 30 per cent in Belgium' *Jspace*, 28 February, 2013.

66 http://ohpi.org.au/reports/IR13-1_Recognizing_hate_speech_anti-semitism_on_Facebook.pdf

67 Roman Frister and Saviona Mane. 'Leading Polish Professor blames Holocaust on the Jews' *Haaretz*, April 2013

68 ibid.

69 Bob Abernethy. 'Abraham Joshua Heschel' *PBS*, January 18, 2008. http://www.pbs.org/wnet/religionandethics/2008/01/18/january-18-2008-abraham-joshua-heschel/1789/

70 Derek Beres. 'MTV Recreates the Holocaust – for Teens' *The Huffington Post*, 25 May, 2011.

71 Gabrielle Chan. 'George Brandis: 'People have the right to be bigots' *The Guardian*, March 24, 2014.

72 http://www.fbi.gov/about-us/investigate/civilrights/hate_crimes/overview

73 http://www.fbi.gov/news/stories/2012/december/annual-hate-crimes-report-released/annual-hate-crimes-report-released

74 http://www.law.cornell.edu/supremecourt/text/343/250

75 '*Mein Kampf* makes comeback in Germany' *Associated Press* February 2, 2014.

76 Deborah Lipstadt. 'In Europe, elites create the atmosphere that allows popular anti-Semitism to grow' *Tablet* Magazine, January 2, 2014.

77 https://www.jewishvirtuallibrary.org/jsource/anti-semitism/euantisem2013.pdf

78 Manfred Gerstenfeld. *Demonizing Israel and the Jews. New York: RVP Publisher, 2015.*

79 http://blog.unwatch.org/wp-content/uploads/Israel_settlements1.pdf

80 Alan Dershowitz. Europe's Alarming Push to Isolate Israel' *Newsmax*, March 11, 2014.

81 Jacob Aril Labendz. 'Move To Ban Kosher Slaughter Really Not About the Animals' *The* Forward, June 18, 2014.

82 Cheryl Wetzstein. 'To cut or not to cut? That is the circumcision question roiling Europe' *Washington Times*, January 28, 2014.

83 Ben Mcclellan, Ian Walker and Bruce McDougall. 'Bondi racist bus attack: Jewish schools on alert after eight males threaten to cut schoolchildren's throats, five teenagers arrested' *The Daily Telegraph*, August 7, 2014.

84   Peter Kohn. 'Zionist scum' daubed on Perth Jewish school' *Australian Jewish News*, July 31, 2014.

85   Zoe Kron. 'Jewish students feel the heat' *Australian Jewish News*, August 11, 2014.

86   Caroline Frank. 'Visiting Jerusalem Rabbi attacked at Australian mall' *Jerusalem Post, May 8, 2014.*

87   David Hurley. 'Ex Israeli Defence Force soldier beaten up in alleged racial attack in Melbourne' *The Herald Sun*, July 13, 2014.

88   Sarah Dean. 'The way-too-far side: Sydney newspaper apologises for 'anti-Semitic' cartoon after Attorney-General brands it 'deplorable' *The Daily Mail*, August 4, 2014.

89   Jessica Elgot. 'France's Jews flee as rioters burn Paris shops, attack synagogues' *Huffington Post*, July 23, 2014.

90   Jon Coates. 'How Gaza has unleashed new Nazism on Europe's Jews' *Express*, 10 August, 2014

91   Jon Henley. 'Antisemitism on the rise across Europe 'in worst times since the Nazis' *The Guardian*, 8 August, 2014

92   Edgar Sandoval and Reuben Blau. 'Orthodox rabbi from New York gunned down on his way to Miami temple' *New York Daily News*, August 10, 2014.

93   Simon Goldberg. 'Why safeguard a tortured history' *Jerusalem Post*, December 3, 2012.

PEOPLE AND EVENTS

Ariel Sharon: Peacemaker

November 12, 2004

Forget the simplistic accounts in the media. You don't have to be an extreme supporter of Ariel Sharon to admire the Prime Minister's resolve in pushing through his historic disengagement plan. Just last week, former leader of the Labor Party, Amram Mitzna, claimed the Knesset's approval of the evacuation proposal was the most important since the foundation of the Jewish state in 1948. This is no hyperbole.

Sharon's tenacity in ploughing on regardless of the hurdles his party places in his path, and the virulent verbal attacks from radical segments in Israel, demonstrate the breathtaking ability of this leader to walk a tightrope and win. Like Nixon visiting China, he is relying on the will of the majority of Israelis to back his own reversal over the settlement issue. Over the last two years, Sharon has suffered setback after setback. In 2002, the Likud's central committee rejected his endorsement of a two-state solution. Then, in May 2004, a party referendum voted down his Gaza plan. And on August 18 this year, the Likud convention refused his idea of bringing Labor into his governing coalition.

Yet Sharon, far from being the poster boy of the peaceniks, is risking it all in the battle of a lifetime, out of a pragmatic realisation that Israel cannot hold on to all of the land it captured in 1967. What is even more remarkable is that Sharon has adopted Labor policies, namely Ehud Barak's call for a security fence and Amram Mitzna's 2003 single-issue platform of unilateral withdrawal from Gaza. As the election slogan said, 'Only the Likud can'. Yes, the Right has a better record in making peace – after all it was Israeli Prime Minister Menachem Begin who made the painful concessions in response to Egyptian President Anwar Sadat's advances. It seems that Sharon, the architect of the settlements, will succeed in something even the most leftist governments have been unable to do. Reflect that proponents of Sharon's blueprint include Ami Ayalon, former head of both the Navy and the Shin Bet (Israel's internal security agency), Yom Tov Samia, ex-commander in Gaza, and former chief of staff of the IDF and Israeli Prime Minister Ehud Barak. Not to mention the USA, the European Union and the UN. As one Israeli scholar noted, the vote in the Knesset last week represents the end of Israel's romantic politics and the marginalisation of supporters of the Greater Land of Israel vision.

Most Likudniks admit that Begin made a mistake when he did not transfer Gaza to Egypt during Israel's pull-out from Sinai in 1982. It is worth remembering that four years ago, the same opponents of withdrawal from Gaza, accused then Prime Minister Ehud Barak of treason, defeat and capitulation. Imagine how many soldiers would have come back in body bags had Barak listened to their cries. Importantly, Sharon has stated that the extreme right will not decide the fate of the nation.

More critically, this is sheer pragmatism at work. Sharon has always been a pragmatist. The Prime Minister always viewed the settlements in the West Bank in strategic, not biblical, messianic terms. Now that the threat from the west is gone (Israel has peace with Jordan, Iraq is liberated, Syria is a weak, pariah state), Sharon understands that demographics, not territory, is the fundamental question to be tackled. Israel cannot afford to allow 7,800 people to occupy 20 per cent of the land inside 'The Fallujah of Palestine', among 1.3 million Palestinians. Indeed, many soldiers in Gaza have been killed in hit-and-run tactics similar to those the Americans face in Iraq.

Sharon understands the Israeli people. He has recognised that a Palestinian state is inevitable, that Israel cannot run the lives of millions of Palestinians against their will indefinitely, and that by 2020, on present trends, the population in Israel will be 6.4 million Jews and 8.5 million Arabs in the territories. He also knows that control over areas in the West Bank is far more vital to Israel's survival than Gaza, which has little security value.

This is the first time in 37 years that an Israeli government has decided to voluntarily dismantle settlements and give up land not for negotiation, or as part of a treaty, but solely for the welfare of its people. Now, Egypt is coming on board, with President Mubarak telling Sharon he would do all he can to implement the Gaza plan.

Sharon's change of heart is commendable. Surely a small step is better than no step at all. Addressing his critics, Sharon said that as a soldier who fought in every Israeli war he had never taken a more difficult decision. Also, speaking directly to Israel's Arab neighbours he said, 'In this long war between peoples, many civilians were killed … and tears were met with tears. I want you to know that we never wished to build our life in this homeland on your destruction. We feel pain for the innocent victims among you.'[1]

To the casual observer, Sharon is a controversial, hard-line figure. For those who know better, he may prove to be one of Israel's greatest leaders.

Farewell Pope John Paul II

April 6, 2005

Who would have thought that last Sunday, Israelis and Jews would collectively hail a pontiff as a true friend in an astounding outpouring of emotion? Who would have imagined that *Yediot Ahronont*, Israel's biggest selling daily, would call him 'The Pope of the Jews'? Yet, it is no surprise that both Jews and Muslims in the Middle East paid unanimous respect to Pope John Paul II for his dramatic and critical role as a builder of bridges between the faiths and as a champion of reconciliation. A force for justice, it is noteworthy that during his acclaimed 2000 Middle East tour, he impassionedly called for more dialogue and harmony between Jews and Muslims in the land 'where God chose to pitch his tent'.[2] To his credit, he prudently saw through the propaganda to support the aspirations of Israelis and Palestinians, tirelessly calling for a peaceful end to the Arab-Israeli conflict, and urging both sides to call on their courage to find a resolution.

Mending broken ties, John Paul II was a bold and visionary leader whose legacy represents the most important change in Catholicism in history. Laying the ground for future changes and putting in place new theological structures of belief and practice, he affirmed religious pluralism and advocated tolerance between the world's religions. Crucially, he broadened the church's parameters to look beyond just the Catholic realm, shifting from internal debates into global issues of peace and interfaith.

He led the church to rapprochement with the Jews, issuing extraordinary apologies for the Inquisition and the Crusades and stating that 'Anti-Semitism is against God'. In 1998 he released 'We Remember',[3] a much admired penitence for the Holocaust. The tears flowed when in 2000 he became the first modern pontiff to visit Israel in 36 years and pray at Jerusalem's Western Wall, Judaism's holiest site, where he slipped a note of apology into a crack in the wall, and when visiting Yad Vashem, Israel's' Holocaust memorial, he was reunited with a concentration camp survivor who recalled how as a young cleric the pontiff had saved her life. Earlier, in 1979, he knelt in prayer at the Auschwitz death camp, and in 1986 he impressed as the first pope to visit the Great Synagogue of Rome. In his book *Crossing the Threshold of Hope*[4] John Paul II revealed that growing up in the heavily Jewish town in Poland during the rise of the Nazis, deeply shaped many of his views, especially his enduring friendship with Jerzy Kluger, a Jewish childhood pal.

Again and again, John Paul II used the Holocaust as a point of moral reflection, reminding us that acknowledging another person's pain is often the first step to creating real friendships. His watershed and sweeping apology for the past sins of the church, not just against the Jews, but against women and the poor exemplified his candor and spiritual strength.

The Israeli President observed that the Jewish people will remember the Pope as one who 'bravely put an end to historic injustice by officially rejecting prejudices and accusations against the Jews'. Persistently reaching out to the Jews, he was the first modern pontiff to enter a synagogue, embracing Jews by referring to them as Christians', 'elder brothers' in faith, and telling the world's Catholics that the Jewish covenant with God is irrevocable. Significantly, he emphatically cleared Jews of killing Jesus, healing a festering wound in Catholic-Jewish relations and renouncing the idea that Judaism has been replaced by Christianity – reversing thousands of years of contempt and denigration. His sponsorship of a Holocaust concert in 1984 marked the first time the Vatican commemorated the Shoah, coming a week after the Vatican established diplomatic relations with Israel. To that end, he noted that the Jews, dispersed for 2000 years, have decided to return to the land of their ancestors, and that it is their right, stunning Jews who had never heard a pope say Jews have the right to a homeland.

During his 26-year tenure he always insisted on interfaith reconciliation and brotherhood, using his frequent homilies and travels to promote dialogue between various cultures. Indeed, in 1986, he gathered a remarkable group of religious leaders in the Italian town of Assisi in a day of prayer. And in 1994, he began working on an ambitious plan for world peace that would culminate in a meeting of Muslim, Christian and Jewish religious leaders in Bethlehem, Jerusalem and at Mount Sinai at the end of the 20th century. More than anything else, he sought to find the common denominators in the various faiths, believing that this was the only way to overcome the evil and injustice bedeviling our society. He taught us that we all have a moral duty to confront and combat prejudice, and that when symbols of intolerance appear, they should be repudiated by Jews, Christians and Muslims. His notion of the 'civilisation of love', embodied in his outreach and personal appeal for heroic harmony in a time of bitter ethnic division, will be one of his gifts to the world. John Paul II's profound and long-term imprint a will make it almost impossible for any new pope to go back in time.

9/11: A frightening new world of terror and horror

September 12, 2005

A day after the fourth anniversary of September 11, 2001 it would be impossible to summarise even a tenth of the effects, repercussions and aftershocks of the attacks. In different ways, 9/11 was a rude wake-up call to anyone who thought the menace of terrorism and the threat of fanatics itching to be destroyers of the world, was off the radar screen in their country.

Four years after those planes smashed into New York's twin towers, the Pentagon and a Pennsylvanian field, a quick scan of the global environment shows we have indeed awoken to a different world.

September 11 pulled the rug out from under our essential beliefs about how the world works. It opened our eyes to the universal nightmare of destructive radicalism and reminded us that we are living in the age of super-terrorism.

As an *India Today* editorial pointed out, terror does not require an entry pass or a city guide to choose the venue. It has acquired an anytime, anywhere banality.

We live in a kind of a horror film where death can strike and erupt out of the corner of the screen. Erica Jong has written that the disaster raped Americans' innocence and let them know how vulnerable they really were.

For us it was Bali.

This year's London bombings and the fourth anniversary of 9/11 should jolt many Australians into wondering about their own security and to ask how vulnerable we are. In the backwash of global terrorism, Australians living in transit-oriented cities such as Melbourne and Sydney may need to get used to random checks on trams, trains and buses by police officers, or get used to walking through metal detectors or become accustomed to sniffer dogs.

We will all need to become more vigilant.

In New York, the ads on trains read: 'If you see something, say something.'[5]

In coming to grips with the twin challenges of terrorism and radical extremist Islam, the Australian Government has already started to make decisions on the tough question of how far civil liberties should be sacrificed for security.

The Government has realised the advent of the kamikaze requires fresh thinking. Frighteningly, it seems terrorists don't appear to have any problem recruiting home-grown suicide bombers to spread a bloody trail of human destruction in the service of their fanatical goals.

As terrorism expert Roland Jacquard explained: 'Most militant groups are forming on their own initiative and aren't going to wait for the fatwas permitting attacks on civilians. They figure the previous ones are all they need. It's a free for all.'[6]

Some radical propaganda videos are now even shot or subtitled in English so those who don't speak Arabic can understand them. And there's plenty of evidence that terrorist cells are interested in acquiring small amounts of biological, chemical or radiological weaponry. Just imagine if the London bombs carried Anthrax or Sarin.

Bali, Jakarta, Morocco, Turkey, Saudi Arabia, Egypt, Casablanca, Karachi, Tunis, Grozny, Nadterechny and Sringar, India, the Philippines, Jordan, Nairobi, Riyadh and Madrid have shown that terrorism flings its disciples across borders.

Even opponents of the Iraq War must surely realise by now that the coalition in Iraq deserves backing in its support of anti-terrorist democratic governments in the Middle East and in its creating of a catalyst for similar transformations elsewhere.

Nazism vanished as a threat once it was significantly defeated, and fighting it did not strengthen it. The argument that the US's participation in transforming Iraq from a brutal dictatorship to struggling democracy has somehow unleashed a terrorist breeding virus ignores the fact that 9/11 was conceived and executed before the operations in Afghanistan and Iraq.

Terrorism is a tactic that must never produce concrete awards.

And yet, there are difficulties. Philosopher Lee Harris has noted that the West plays by a stringent set of rules while permitting terrorists to play without rules. We restrain ourselves in accordance with the standards of civilised conduct.[7]

The overriding message of September 11 is that equivocation in the face of evil invites another assault, just as appeasement in the 1930s led to the subjugation of all of Europe. Australia and Britain will not accede to the terrorists' demands to pull out of Iraq because Prime Ministers Howard and Blair know that it's a slippery slope once foreign policy decisions of democracies are made by young men and women bent on murder.

Tom Delay, majority leader of the US House of Representatives has emphasised that, 'Terrorism will not go away by itself. It's up to people and nations of good will to stand up to it wherever it attacks. Evil cannot be negotiated away; it must be fought on every front and with every resource at our disposal.'[8]

Goodbye Simon Wiesenthal

September 25, 2005

Nazi hunter Simon Wiesenthal, who died this week in his sleep aged 96, was one of history's true heroes.

Despite suffering unspeakable barbarities first-hand, he was never motivated by a thirst for revenge, outliving Hitler and most of his henchmen, and defying the fate the Nazis had destined for him.

We must never forget, he said, that what happened to the Jews could happen to any minority. In addition to the six million Jewish victims, he always included the five million non-Jews who also perished.

He often said that when history looks back, he wanted people to know that the Nazis were not able to slaughter millions and get away with it.

Opposed to the death penalty, he argued against collective guilt, believing that we are all responsible for our actions as individuals.

His dogged campaigning led to the creation of today's international war crimes tribunals. An inmate of twelve concentration camps who lost 89 of his family members in the genocide (he often despaired that he did not have a single photograph of his mother), he drew attention to the need to bring the murderers to justice at a time when the world had lost interest.

Born in 1908 in Buczacz, now part of the Western Ukraine, he narrowly escaped a series of brushes with death. Liberated by US forces from the Mauthausen camp in Austria in 1945, he was able, using his photographic memory, to provide the American War Crimes Unit with a list of 91 Nazi tormentors.

He established the Jewish Historic Documentation Centre and gathered evidence that led to the prosecution of 1100 archfiends.

In 1947 he blocked an application by the wife of Adolf Eichmann to declare her husband dead, and was credited with partly helping the Israelis capture in Argentina the foremost planner of the final solution.

Among his other celebrated catches were Karl Silberbauer, the police inspector who arrested teenage diarist Anne Frank in Amsterdam.

Asked about the reasons for his extraordinary crusade, he replied: 'When we come to the other world and meet the millions of Jews who died in the camps and they ask us, "What have you done?" there will be many answers. I will say, "I didn't forget you".'[9]

Wiesenthal's noble purpose was that no Nazi, however old, be allowed to die quietly, wanting to ensure that the murderers of tomorrow – who may not yet be born – know they will have no peace.

Rabin: Israel's peaceful warrior

November 3, 2005

This week, a sombre Israeli nation will pause to observe the tenth anniversary of Yitzhak Rabin's murder.

The November 4, 1995 assassination of Israel's first native-born prime minister at the hands of a Jewish fanatic remains a blood-spattered defining moment, a trauma which sent tremors through the Jewish heartland.

The ex-general turned warrior for peace died from three bullets fired by Yigal Amir, a 25-year-old law student, now serving a life sentence, who claimed he was acting on orders from God to put a stop to land concessions to the Palestinians.

Rabin's death gave birth to unprecedented soul searching and to the 'candle generation', the jeans-clad, young people lighting candles in memory of the courageous man who gave them hope. In the aftermath, Israel was dotted by a sea of *'Shalom Haver'* (goodbye friend) bumper stickers memorialising the famous closing words uttered by US President Bill Clinton upon hearing of his peace-partner's death.

The Rabin killing released forces bubbling under the surface, exposing the deep rift between Israel's secular and orthodox, Right and Left. For the first time, violence became a political tool and the notions of legitimate dissent, tolerance and common purpose that saw Israel through various wars took a back seat to incitement.

Like the Kennedy shooting in the US, Israelis and Jews still ask: 'Where were you when Rabin was shot?' I can still remember my grief, shock and disbelief, amplified when I visited the sunlit pine groves of Mount Herzl cemetery where Rabin is buried.

And like President Lincoln, Rabin became a larger-than-life symbol because, like the slain American leader, he emerged as an emblem pointing towards a positive orientation in society at a time of struggle for national destiny.

Rabin spent his last hours at the largest peace rally held in Israel. The shy prime minister joined in the collective singing of a peace song. A bloodstained copy of the lyrics was found in his pockets. His wife, the late Leah Rabin, would later remark that he never looked happier.

So admired was Rabin on the world stage that his funeral was attended by representatives from 72 countries, including Egypt's President Hosni Mubarak, who chose this event as the occasion of his first visit to Israel, and the late King Hussein of Jordan, who bade farewell to his 'friend and brother'.[10]

It is noteworthy that Rabin's legacy goes beyond the 1993 Oslo Accords (an agreement to reach peace between Israelis and Palestinians in faith-building stages) and rises above partisan politics because he was involved in many of Israel's heroic chapters. Rabin freed 200 people from a British detention camp in 1945; he played a historic role as Israel's chief of staff in the 1967 Six-Day War; he served with distinction as ambassador to the US; he approved the spectacular 1976 Entebbe raid to rescue Israeli hostages; and he signed a peace treaty with Jordan in 1994.

The White House handshake with Arafat on September 13, 1993, under the beaming gaze of Clinton, that initiated the Palestinian-Israeli peace process, was recognised by a Nobel Peace Prize, shared with Israeli Foreign Minister Shimon Peres and Palestinian Chairman Yasser Arafat.

After affixing his signature to the accords, Rabin said to the Palestinians, 'We have no hatred towards you, we do not wish for revenge.'[11] Later, he declared to the US Congress, 'I, serial number 30743, Major General Yitzhak Rabin, am a soldier in the army of peace'.[12] Even Rabin's opponents have acknowledged that he was a visionary, a patriot who did what he genuinely thought was best for the people he loved so dearly.

Rabin showed that peace was at the core of all Israeli values. Crucially, he was the first to talk of political accommodation with the Palestinians, and the first to decide that the tiny land had to be split between two peoples, opening the door to a course that remains unaltered as Sharon's dramatic disengagement from Gaza vividly illustrates.

Rabin paid with his life trying to bring peace, but took a giant step trying, in his own words, to put an end to 'blood and tears'.

Truth given the flick in
Steven Spielberg's *Munich*

February 1, 2006

Steven Spielberg's film *Munich* is a deeply flawed work, a sermonising, propagandist film that takes liberties with the truth and fails on numerous levels.

Inspired by real events, it is based on the discredited book *Vengeance*, by George Jonas.[13]

This book draws on the accounts of Yuval Raviv, who claimed to be a Mossad assassin but only worked as an airport gate guard.

Spielberg was offered a chance to speak with key people such as General Zvi Zamir, former head of Mossad, as well as Mike Harari, who supervised the hit-teams.

But he declined, insisting on overlaying his post-September 11 attitudes regarding American retaliation onto the script. Additionally, co-writer Tony Kushner has stated that the founding of the state of Israel was a mistake and a moral calamity.

While the Israeli agents are presented as vengeful, vicious and aberrant, and the slain athletes are merely cameo figures, the Palestinian murderers are invested with humanity.

One terrorist is shown reciting poetry, another being generous, and another playing with his daughter – before being felled. They are never shown committing any atrocity or plotting the Munich barbarity, or clamouring for the destruction of Israel. Spielberg allows one Palestinian terrorist to eloquently make the case that the Israelis stole their land and that the Holocaust was at the core of Zionism. When the terrorist talks about a homeland, he is not referring to the West Bank or Gaza but to the whole of pre-1967 Israel.

By contrast, the Israeli argument for a homeland is warped. The mother of the central hero, Avner, sounds amoral when she says: 'We had to take Israel because no one would give it to us. Whatever it took, whatever it takes, we have a place on Earth at last.'

But this is not how Israel became the Jewish state and such ignorance is inexcusable. The leader of the Israeli hit-team Avner says that Israel should have arrested the terrorists as they did Adolf Eichmann. But Israel could not have arrested the Nazi criminal.

Israeli agents were forced to kidnap him because several nations, including European countries, refused to extradite Nazis.

It is significant that the three terrorists who survived the Munich massacre were quickly let go after the German Government concocted a phony hijacking to release the killers.

In making *Munich*, Spielberg has stated that a response to a response does not really solve anything. That begs the question as to what the terrorists were supposedly responding to when they murdered the eleven unarmed athletes. Spielberg gives no answer. Prime Minister Golda Meir is given a line about every civilisation needing to compromise its values. This in spite of Meir never saying that.

In the Israeli Parliament a week after the massacre, Meir explained that Israel had to defend itself by fighting for survival.

Nowhere in the film is there historical background or context. Decades of conflict are reduced to clichés.

Munich fails to mention that Israel suffered a series of attacks before the Munich massacre. There was the bombing of a Swissair jet flying to Israel, grenades thrown at an Israeli airport killing 27 people, hijacked planes and shelling of civilian targets.

Two weeks after Munich, Israel's cultural attaché in London was assassinated. But after watching Spielberg's *Munich*, moviegoers might think that Israel acted precipitously after being fuelled by a need for revenge.

The film blurs the lines between the murder of innocents and the bringing of killers to justice. It begins when Spielberg interposes the photos of the Israeli athletes with those of the terrorists responsible. In one insulting scene, a disillusioned Avner flashes back to the massacre while making love to his wife. He reaches orgasm as the tied athletes are slaughtered.

One of the messages buried in the film is that the Zionist enterprise is morally bankrupt. Avner, played by Melbourne actor Eric Bana, suffers a crisis of conscience, questioning his role and finally rejecting not only Israel's actions, but Israel itself. But this scenario is refuted by *Time* magazine's Jerusalem reporter, Aaron Klein, who interviewed more than 50 Israeli operatives. Klein has said that none had misgivings about the Munich mission, or any other mission they had carried out.[14]

The image of the World Trade Centre at the end of *Munich* seems to suggest that Israel's counter-terrorism policy in the 1970s led to the September 11 atrocities in 2001.

Munich is a fiction, with no obligation or links to historical accuracy. For the true story, see the Oscar-winning documentary, *One Day in September.*

Ariel Sharon still casts a giant shadow

April 3, 2006

As Ariel Sharon lay in a coma in a hospital bed, still casting a giant shadow over Israel's elections, his country's political boundaries were historically realigned and redrawn.

Kadima, the centrist party he formed, received an emphatic endorsement of its plan to separate six million Israelis from nearly four million Palestinians by 2010.

Although receiving fewer seats amid the lowest turnout of voters in any Israeli election, the results endorsed a movement founded only five months ago. Sharon split from Likud in a manoeuvre known as the 'big bang' and Kadima emerged overnight as Israel's dominant political force.

Kadima's leader and acting Prime Minister, Ehud Olmert, is determined to complete Sharon's unfinished program, which began with the disengagement from Gaza last year. Olmert, a determined and pragmatic bureaucrat, said in his victory speech that he was ready for new peace talks with the Palestinians.

But they would be talks that would require Israel to make painful compromises. Courageously, he admitted that the Zionist vision of a Jewish homeland, within biblical territory that included the West Bank, was over. In the face of reality and circumstances, Olmert said, 'We are ready to compromise, to give up parts of the beloved Land of Israel and evacuate, with great pain, Jews living there so as to prepare the conditions that will allow the Palestinians to fulfil their dream.'[15]

Olmert has indicated that he is willing to relinquish some Arab neighbourhoods in East Jerusalem but will maintain Israeli control of sites holy to Jews and Muslims in the Old City.

The Hamas-led Palestinian Government, sworn in on the same day that Israelis cast their ballots, has little time to meet international demands.

There is not much time, either, in which to recognise Israel and implement the Road Map peace proposal, which requires, among other things, a renunciation of violence on the way to a two-state Israel-Palestine outcome.[16]

Otherwise, Olmert promised, Israel would take its fate into its own hands. 'We will act even without an agreement,' he said. 'We shall not wait forever.'[17]

At heart, this is divorce, Middle-Eastern-style, that reflects the wishes of the majority of Israelis. Olmert broke with tradition by providing voters during the campaign with a timetable and the extent of the proposed pull-out. Such clarity transformed the elections into a referendum on the withdrawal model.

Kadima's coalition partners are likely to be the Left-wing and dovish Labor; Meretz; the pensioners' party; and the ultra-Orthodox Shas. In the years to come, they are likely to act unilaterally to determine Israel's permanent borders, after consulting and gaining the backing of the US and other international players.

Kadima won majority rule because of its policy of not wishing to perpetuate control over the Palestinian people. It would do this by proactively getting out of the territories and setting the country's ultimate borders by 2010.

This struck a chord with an Israeli populace fatigued and weary after 39 years of conflict and more than five years of suicide attacks. It is also a populace acutely aware that Hamas, which still calls for Israel's destruction and is regarded by the US and the European Union as a terrorist organisation, might not prove a viable negotiating partner.

This go-it-alone consolidation or convergence approach would mean annexing the larger West Bank settlement blocs. These are where most of the 253,000 settlers live. It will also call for the traumatic uprooting of close to 60,000 Jewish settlers from other smaller areas and their resettlement on the Israeli side of the security barrier. This fence is to be completed next year and will become the new final border between Israel and a future Palestinian state.

The aim is to preserve Israel's demographic character as a Jewish state and to only hold on to about 10 per cent of the territories.

A sweeping pullback, no doubt, but it presents a breathtaking opportunity to defuse and perhaps resolve a 50-year conflict. Some commentators expected the Israeli people to stagger back to the right following the election of Hamas and the collapse of the hawkish Likud party, which now has only twelve seats compared with

Kadima's 29 seats. Instead, the election result symbolises the seismic shift in Israeli politics towards the centre. Likud is now headed by former Prime Minister Benjamin Netanyahu, who bitterly opposed the Sharon-Olmert agenda of territorial concessions.

The Israeli people have placed their trust in a politically mature and realistic leader who will not permit Hamas to dictate terms. The international community and the Australian Government should applaud this sound choice.

Jonathan Pollard's two long decades behind bars

June 22, 2006

Jonathan Pollard, prisoner 09185-016: now here's a name you don't hear very often.

Yet, in 2006 (this month marks 20 years since Pollard pleaded guilty) the continued drumming for his release has been amplified amid a swirl of developments.

In his 21st year of incarceration, after spending seven years in solitary confinement, Pollard's cause célèbre has come into the foreground. Only last week the Israeli Supreme Court rejected a suit by Pollard asking that the Israeli government request his release from prison, deeming the matter diplomatic. Still, the lawyer representing Pollard, Darshan-Leitner, stated, 'we asked that Israel confront the US ... and ask for his immediate release from prison'.[18]

Earlier, the court refused to recognise him as a 'Prisoner of Zion' or to block the appointment of his former handler in the Mossad Rafael Eitan as Minister of Pensioner's Affairs. Another appeal to the US Supreme Court in March 2006 to give Pollard access to records that could bolster his case for presidential clemency was declined.

There are scores of unanswered questions, contradictions, mysteries and intrigues concerning this saga that may never be resolved. The main question is why Pollard has been in prison for so long with no end in sight.

Astoundingly, as time recedes, the crusade for Pollard has grown. IDF soldiers and chaplains have been issued with an IDF prayer for Pollard; in 2004 the Israeli Parliament gave its approval to recognise the creation of a forest to be named *Pollard Freedom Forest* and recently 77 Knesset members signed a petition calling on President Bush to pardon Pollard.

On Jerusalem Day, Pollard's prepared remarks contained the following:

> My brothers and sisters! I have been slowly bleeding to death before your very eyes ... I cry out from the depths of my soul, won't you seek the welfare of your captives.[19]

And in 2004, Pollard whispered to a *Yediot Ahronot* reporter, 'Don't leave me in the *bor* (pit); get me out of here'.[20]

For those who are too young to remember, Pollard, a civilian analyst with the US Navy, was sentenced in 1987 to life imprisonment after fully cooperating with authorities and admitting to passing military documents to Israel – relating in the main to Syrian, Iraqi, Libyan and Iranian nuclear, chemical, and biological warfare capabilities – being developed for use against Israel. At that time, the US was obligated to share information with Israel under the 1983 Israel-USA Intelligence Exchange Agreement, but failed to do.

So, should Pollard be released? There are those who wish he rot in prison. But a deeper looks reveals that this is not an open and shut case. Many feel that a sense of proportion and mercy must prevail. Several legal scholars (the President of the American Bar Association for instance) maintain that the punishment is so out of proportion that by now elements of compassion and humanitarian considerations (Archbishop of San Francisco) should come into play. Journalist Sarah Honig claims that it's absurd that Zacarias Moussaoui, who could have prevented the deaths of 3000 on 9/11, is to do the same time as Pollard.

Eli Wiesel believes that Pollard has suffered enough and that justice has been served, stressing that Pollard admitted the error of his ways, regrets his actions and has impressed him with his feelings of remorse. Wiesel also contends that Pollard was a victim of immaturity, misplaced idealism and of various intelligence agencies.

Federal judge Stephen Williams, the lone dissenter in one of Pollard's appeals, stated that Pollard's plight 'was a gross miscarriage of justice'. Investigative reports show that initially the US government promised to refrain from asking the court to impose a life sentence, but that a last-minute damage assessment document prepared by KGB mole Aldrich Ames blaming Pollard for the crimes he himself committed, sealed Pollard's fate.

Former New Yorl Mayor Rudi Giuliani has observed that the life sentence is far too long compared with sentences in similar cases, while former CIA Director James Woolsey noted, 'Israel is a friend. I think we ought to look at it.'[21] A comparison with others who have spied for allied nations shows that Pollard's life sentence is far longer, and even when juxtaposed with those who spied for enemy nations, Pollard is the only person in US history to receive a life sentence for one count of passing classified information to an ally.

The spectrum of voices advocating his release is extraordinary: four past prime ministers of Israel, President Katsav (Pollard is a national consensus issue), Netanyahu ('I signed the Wye Plantation Accords with the clear understanding that Pollard would be released'[22]), Yitzhak Rabin, Ariel Sharon, Yossi Sarid, former Prisoners of Zion, Senator Arlen Specter ('sentence is excessive'[23]), Senator Weiner, Alan Dershowitz, the Canadian Jewish Congress, the American Jewish Congress, the European Congress, the European Parliament, the Simon Wiesenthal Centre, the World Jewish Congress, and the World Zionist Congress.

Now, Pollard's legal appeals have run their course; only President Bush can pardon him.

Is this the time for clemency? I wonder how Australian Jewry feels.

Jimmy Carter's book *Palestine: Peace Not Apartheid* is distortion, not truth

December 15, 2006

I'm often seized by the ungovernable sense that pro-Israel activists are just not cutting through and face a Sisyphean task. Yes, no matter how many letters are written to the papers, how many emails with sensible articles are circulated, no matter how many advocacy workshops are held, no matter how many representations are made, the Israeli narrative is getting very little traction.

Consider, Israel is doing poorly in the court of public opinion. More and more people are convinced that Israel is a colonial aggressor and embrace its delegitimisation, cultivated by the persistent rewriting of history.

This startling moment of clarity resurfaced when I finished reading Jimmy Carter's one-sided polemic *Palestine*: *Peace Not Apartheid*.[24] The harsh indictment of Israel is a brilliant case-study of how intelligent people swallow, hook, line and sinker, the anti-Israel pie and its attendant cache of myths, distortions and untruths. The reprehensibly titled bestseller has already led to the resignation of Professor Kenneth Stein from the Carter Institute. Stein stated that the work is full of 'factual errors, copied materials not cited, superficialities, glaring omissions and simply invented segments'.

I trawled through the book searching for anything resembling objective, honest analysis, to no avail. Soon, the documentary *Jimmy Carter Man of Plains* produced by Jonathan Demme (*Silence of the Lambs)* will be available for mass consumption, trumpeting the line that apartheid Israel is to blame for the troubles and ill-will in the volatile region.[25]

Carter doesn't let facts get in the way. He uses the misleading subject of race to characterise the conflict between the two nations and to suggest Israel is subjugating and dehumanising the Palestinians. He joins those who absurdly equate Israel with South Africa and its former racist regime and see Israel as the root of all evil. The title immediately creates an analogy with South Africa, even though Carter admits, in the book's final pages, that what is going on in Israel is not racism but the acquisition of land.

According to Carter, Israel's persecution of the Palestinians is one of the worst examples of human deprivation he knows. Not Darfur, Zimbabwe, Burma, Cuba, Chechnya, Tibet or North Korea. He conveniently forgets to tell his readers that Israel has, on several occasions, traded land for peace, only to see the end of Kassam rockets, havoc in the streets, and the Second Lebanon War. He neglects to explain that Israel has clung to the territories for security and survival reasons, rather than for some expansionist motives. That this Nobel Peace Prize laureate, who brokered peace between Israel and Egypt, can now claim that violent Israel is the main obstacle for peace, that it executes Palestinians prisoners, while Arab leaders have been craving compromise only to be rebuffed, should set off the alarm bells.

Carter erroneously contends that Security Council Resolution 242 requires Israel to withdraw to the 1949 armistice line. He overlooks the recalcitrant Palestinian and Arab negotiators, laying the blame for the failure of the peace talks at the feet of Israeli officials. He writes that the PLO 'never advocated annihilation of Israel' and that historically the Palestinians have supported a two-state solution and Israel rejected it. Outrageously, he misunderstands the ramifications of the Arab right of return. Simplistically, he buys into the fabrication that it is the Palestinian issue which is the reason for strife in the Middle East, and that once it is solved, even the Iraq problem will go away. Even Rabin is depicted as a cruel and manipulative. Dealing with the 2000 Camp David talks, Carter wholeheartedly accepts the Arafat version, sidelining Barak's generous offer. He trivialises the blaze of terrorist attacks (which he labels 'acts of violence') that were ordered by Arafat.

For Carter, the Security Fence is an 'imprisonment wall', which Israel plans to extend along the Jordan River, not a barrier to stem the terrible human toll of attacks. The Road Map has failed because Israel has been using it as a delaying tactic. Appallingly, Carter accuses 'powerful political, economic and religious forces' in the US for America's 'submissive' Israeli policies.[26] Not surprisingly, he castigates Israel for destroying the nuclear Iraqi reactor in 1981.

Too many will buy Carter's version. To address the anti-Israel bias, there needs to be an overall strategy that beats the drum of truth, that energetically debunks the lies and creatively disseminates the facts in order to repair Israel's tarnished image.

Death of the Kibbutz?

January 10, 2007

Check out your telly nostalgia and romanticism at the door.

The kibbutz, that symbol of pioneering, communal spirit is no more. These are its last days.

As a report recently noted, within the next two years only 20 of 250 kibbutzim will remain, 'clinging to the vestiges of their past'.

Nearly 100 years after Degania, when the first kibbutz was founded, a large number of these communal farms are being undone by commercialisation. Indeed, the socialist dream seems to be nearing an end. In a significant move, the Israeli government has ceased its provision of free land and subsidised water to kibbutzim.

I have a warm spot for the kibbutz. As a kid, it represented a kind of Garden of Eden in a pastoral settings, an idyllic experiment of Zionism-Socialism that, in the words of philosopher Martin Buber, did not fail.

I spent several summers at Kibbutz Givat Brenner, savouring the glorified principles of egalitarianism and redemption of the land.

I loved the collective Friday night meals, the openly welcoming atmosphere, the haystacks, chugging tractors, the scent of livestock and ploughs and milking cows in the dairy.

I knew exactly what author Amos Oz meant when he remarked of the kibbutz, 'It is the least bad place I have ever seen. And the most daring effort.'[27]

The egalitarian way of life that shone as a symbol of Israel attracted young idealistic travellers and volunteers from Europe, the US and Australia.

In the 1960s and 1970s the kibbutz way of life dovetailed perfectly with the tie-dyed peace and love philosophy many young westerners were living, or pretending to live. Jew or not, there was something groovy about being equal to everybody else, being judged only by your willingness to work, being fed well and getting free cigarettes at the end of the week. It didn't even matter that the work week was six days long. There were no bills to pay, no food to buy and the weather was wonderful. You paid for everything with the sweat from your brow.

And so my heart sank when I read the sad news that Kibbutz Givat Brenner had come to an end.

Depressing, but the precedent was set a few years ago when Kibbutz Mishmar David decided, without much convincing, to vote itself out of existence in order to become an ordinary Israeli community.

Contentiously, the once farming enterprise will be transformed into the site of 350 new villas that will be sold on the open market. Debts of more than 70 million shekels are seen as the cause for the demise, but this is just the tip of the iceberg. There's a further, deeper reason: in a consumerist society that idolises individualistic impulses and materialistic yearnings, sooner or later all kibbutzim are headed down the same road.

In today's shrinking kibbutzim what is emphasised is the private. One of the few to vote against the disbanding of the Kibbutz Mishmar David was Mike Skyte, 47, deputy manager of the printing press, who left Leeds 24 years ago. He remarked that 'the early Zionist intellectuals had advocated that the Jews try to become like other nations rather than be different. But the kibbutzniks dared to be different.'[28]

Bottom line: the majority of kibbutzim have long ago ceased being a kibbutz in all but name, beginning to resemble grassy country clubs. What you have now, as one scholar noted, is an urban neighbourhood in the countryside.

Let's face it, grand utopian ideals such as sharing are not only doomed, they just don't work. The writing has been on the wall since the hyperinflationary crunch of the 1980s. Drifting into economic ruin because of mismanagement and reduced subsidies, plus an inability to keep its younger generation (the median age on the kibbutz is 53), many kibbutzim made the decision to abandon the Marxist lifestyle that had been their bedrock and embrace good old market capitalism.

Even with the changes, very few kibbutzim are financially solvent. Many are facing a descent into the oblivion. About 110,000 people still dwell on Israel's kibbutzim, down from the zenith of 125,000 in 1990.

The troubling part is that there are now North American youth movement graduates who 25 years ago gambled their future on this life and who find themselves unemployed, without a pension and unable to send their children to university. And yet, while they only constitute 2 per cent of Israel's population, kibbutzniks make up over 40 per cent of the personnel in the elite air force units and a fifth of the army's officers – proving they are still a prime engine in Israel's military structure.

What would Zionist pioneer Aharon David Gordon say of the profound crisis? Certainly, if there is one individual who can claim credit for providing shimmering inspiration to those early kibbutzniks it is A. D. Gordon who left Russia in 1901, at age 48, to work as a farm labourer in Palestine. Gordon strove to cure what he viewed as an ailing entrepreneurial instinct in Jewish life using the honour and dignity of labour. Gordon noted, '... the first thing that opens my heart to a life I have not known before, is labour. Not labour to make a living, not work as a deed of charity, but work for life itself.'[29]

According to Gordon, the only effective revolutions were the ones that occurred within the soul of man, and such revolutions were attainable only through physical endeavour. He felt strongly that a return to the land would cause many to traverse a journey that would lead them to rediscover religion, and the Jew to revive his Judaism. No doubt, his underlying philosophy sustained the movement for many decades.

The truth is that the kibbutzim had no choice. Put simply, the disintegration of the kibbutz is a case study in how difficult it is to light the spark of ideology among generation X. I recently read that anyone who decides to remain in a kibbutz is made to feel like a sucker. In fact, it is near impossible to find anyone under 30 willing to settle on a kibbutz in order to stem the mass exodus that has seriously depleted the ranks (an ongoing joke is that the kibbutzim risk becoming 'old-age homes').

Gone is the credo 'from each according to his ability, to each according to his needs', replaced by 'Greed is good'. Privatisation was in full swing: the dining halls, a hallmark of kibbutz life, were closed or charged members for their food; chicken coops were rented to small businesses. Unbelievably, differential wages were introduced (where each member was paid according to the value of his work) violating a fundamental principle, while at the same time kibbutzniks were allowed to work outside the community.

Likewise, the children's houses, a bulwark of tradition, were replaced with families sleeping together, and another taboo was shattered when outsiders were hired to work in education and management. Now, most members get a salary and pay income tax, own credit cards, mobile phones and cars, buy their own food and clothing and pay to send their children to day care. For example, in Kibbutz Gezer, city slickers renting homes outnumber actual members.

Alongside these transitions, a large proportion of kibbutzim have created a bed and breakfast cottage industry, renting guest rooms to visitors or tenants who are not members.

Who would have thought that a factory that exports para-military equipment such as riot control hardware to Zimbabwe, Angola and Uganda would one day bring in a majority of a kibbutz's earnings? Or that you would see health clubs, a McDonald's, tennis courts, four-star hotels, a hot springs park, discount bookstores, shopping centres and golf clubs on a kibbutz? The event sector providing tourist havens is the fastest generating area of the kibbutz economy. Under pressure from debt, the once utopian Kibbutz Gan Shmuel now hosts a McDonald's and other businesses.

Milton Friedman is smiling somewhere.

Is there still a role for the kibbutz after almost a century or has it outlived its usefulness? Can it dig its way out of this hole or will it become a museum? I don't know. But one thing is for sure – the kibbutz I used to know is dying and something irreplaceable has been lost.

Shimon Peres: Shalom Mr President

June 18, 2007

Despite the tag of perennial loser, Shimon Peres is the closest thing Israel has to a national elder. Israel's vice-prime minister will be the country's ninth president. The Nobel Peace Prize laureate and 83-year-old statesman could not resist throwing his hat into the ring one more time.

Although he has been prime minister three times, Peres was never elected in his own right. In an emotional victory speech after his landslide election, Peres vowed to unite the nation and to devote himself to its service. He also swore to crusade for the release of the three Israeli kidnapped soldiers – Gilad Shalit, Eldad Regev and Ehud Goldwasser.

He phoned his wife of 62 years, Sonya, to tell her: 'You married a dairy farmer and got a president.'

Surveys taken before the vote showed that 60 per cent of the Israeli public wanted Peres as president. In endorsing his deputy, Prime Minister Ehud Olmert summed up the prevailing mood: 'Peres is the man most perfectly suited for this job. His personal history and dedication to Israel has no comparison. There is no one in the entire world who has done as much as Peres for the state of Israel.'[30]

Even the right-wing Likud party, headed by Benjamin Netanyahu, voted for the left-wing politician.

But Peres will have to adjust to the largely ceremonial role of national representative. An eminent intellectual and author, the new president will work tirelessly to elevate Israel's standing in the world. Free of the customary political deal-making, he is a seasoned diplomat and will advance the cause of peace. He enjoys respect abroad, even among Israel's staunchest critics, and will work towards peace between Israel and the Arab world.

The guests at his 80th birthday celebrations included former US president Bill Clinton and former Russian president Mikhail Gorbachev. Woody Allen sent a greeting: 'From a bad Jew to a very great Jew.'

Born in Poland and raised on a kibbutz, Peres was a trusted aide and protégé of David Ben Gurion, Israel's legendary first prime minister. He was elected to the Israeli Parliament in 1959 and has held senior posts in twelve governments.

His achievements and contributions to the Jewish state are unparalleled. He is credited with building Israel's defence capabilities and with authorising the 1976 raid when Israeli commandos rescued 100 hostages at Entebbe airport in Uganda. His close partnership with the late Prime Minister Yitzhak Rabin ushered in new hopes of reconciliation with Palestinians.

When Peres assumes office next month, he will begin restoring the presidency. President Moshe Katsav chose to step down to fight impending criminal charges and his predecessor was forced to resign over a business scandal. Peres was seen as a safe pair of hands who would restore dignity to the office. During his campaign Peres said this might be his last contribution to the state.

A half-page advertisement in Israel's newspapers said: 'Say Yes to the Old Man.'

The elder statesman will be 91 if he completes his term.

The Israeli rocket man: Ilan Ramon
February 29, 2008

I still remember the jarring grief and sense of disbelief that gripped me five years ago this month, when upon reentry into the Earth's atmosphere, the space shuttle Columbia broke apart in flames over Texas, killing Colonel Ilan Ramon, Israel's first astronaut, along with six Americans.

Ilan Ramon boldly went where no Israeli had gone before. Intensely humble, he captured the public's imagination with his youthful optimism and bravery, emerging as a symbol of national pride, a reflection of an Israel that can soar to the stars. 'In Israel,' Ramon maintained, 'we have the best people with phenomenal abilities.'[31]

As journalist Avi Shavit observed, Ramon epitomised the hope of 'freeing ourselves from our gravitational destiny, of floating in some weightlessness normalcy in utter disregard of the gravity of our fate.'[32]

In a world devoid of heroes, he was a hero we could look up to.

Like an angel, transcending the familiar squabbles and brutality here, he floated in another universe, a latter-day Elijah ascending in a storm to the heavens.

More than anything else, Ramon shimmered with unwavering devotion for his beloved land and people. Indeed, Colonel Zev Raz, the commander of the 1981 mission in Iraq (at 27, Ramon was the youngest member of the F-16 squadron that bombed the Osirak nuclear reactor) recalls Ramon telling him while training at NASA that he felt at one with the Jewish nation, not only the state of Israel.

Ramon said, 'I feel I am representing all Jews and all Israelis.'[33]

What I especially admired about Ramon was that he never downplayed his Jewish roots or hid the tremendous pride he felt in his heritage. He publicly proclaimed and reaffirmed his Jewishness – the cluster of keepsakes he chose to take on his journey powerfully reflected that connectedness.

In various ways, Ramon epitomised the modern Jew – not orthodox, but unmistakably attached to his tradition. He asked for kosher food on the shuttle. He took a selection of Jewish ritual objects, including a tiny scroll of a Torah used by a thirteen-year-old boy in the Bergen Belsen concentration camp, mezuzahs, a credit-card-sized microfiche of the Bible, and an illustration called 'Moon Landing', drawn by fourteen-year-old Peter Ginz, who within the dark belly of Auschwitz imagined how the world would look from the moon. Ramon felt that his exploration fulfilled the dream of Peter, 58 years on.[34]

During his mission, he recited the *Shema* while flying over Jerusalem and celebrated the Sabbath. And when he found out that a launch was to take place on the fast day of the Jewish festival of Tisha b'Av, he spoke to the commander and arranged for its postponement.

Norman Lamm, President of Yeshiva University, praised Ramon: 'Here was a self-proclaimed secular Jew who nevertheless demonstrated marvelous respect for the Jewish tradition and sensitivity for the feelings of his observant fellow Israelis.'[35]

The underlying message was that just because one left planet earth and became a global citizen, it did not mean abandoning one's identity. Ramon drew strength and meaning from Judaism.

On another level, his inclusion was a tribute to the enduring and staunch partnership between two great democracies who share similar values. In fact, Ramon had a Star of David sewn onto his silver suit, interwoven with the Stars and Stripes, fragments of which were found in Louisiana along with his remains.

A soldier who fought in two wars, he yearned for a lasting peace, believing that the view from the stars, with no national boundaries, no religious markers and no skin colours, served as the model towards reconciliation. Three days before his death, the fallen 'rocket man' asked us to keep the earth clean and good, and to work our way for a better life for everyone on earth.

Ramon inspired us to dream even in dark times, to pursue excellence and to lead by example. Like Peter Ginz, Ramon showed us that the spirit of man can never be imprisoned by walls, and that its imagination and nobility will always triumph over evil.

The son and grandson of Holocaust survivors admitted that he carried the suffering of the Holocaust generation, and yet he was proof that despite the horror, the Jewish people were going forward.

Through his incredible achievements, Ramon was able to unify a riven nation behind him, to slice through the divisions as he sliced through the sky. I still smile when I recall his remarks when first he saw Israel from space: 'Small but beautiful.'[36]

Despite conquering the skies, Ramon remained strikingly human. Looking from above, he yearned to share the sunrise with his wife. Seeing the wonders of God's creation, his heart still beamed at his son's perfect mark in maths.

To paraphrase Thomas Campbell, Ilan Ramon will live in the hearts he left behind.

And to do so, is to never die.

Are we ready for a Jewish PM?

August 15, 2008

Suddenly, the possibility of a Jewish prime minister in several countries seems more and more likely. David Miliband, the current Foreign Secretary, is favourite to replace Gordon Brown as Labour leader and Prime Minister. Another Jewish politician, Jack Straw, the British Justice Minister, is also being mentioned as a possible successor. If that happens, it would be the second time that a Jewish person served in that position (Benjamin Disraeli was the first in 1868). The French have had two Prime Ministers in Leon Blum and Pierre Mendes-Frances, and last year elected President Sarkozy who is of Jewish heritage.

In New Zealand, where Jews comprise less than 0.2 per cent of the population, voters have elected two Jewish prime ministers (the last one more than 80 years ago) and are about to choose the third one. John Key, opposition National Party Leader, has a huge lead over Helen Clark, and while he is not ardently religious, he considers himself part of the Jewish community.

A poll taken in the Netherlands revealed that a majority would accept a woman, black or homosexual prime minister, but only half would accept a Jewish one. Amsterdam's Jewish mayor, Job Cohen, often touted as potential candidate for the top job, said that it was outrageous and incredible that 50 per cent of Dutch nationals would object to a Jewish prime minister. In Denmark last year, 25 per cent disagreed with the statement that a Jewish prime minister would be totally acceptable.

It seems that being Jewish costs votes.

When British Conservative leader Michael Howard was running against Blair in 2004, a poll conducted in the UK concluded that almost 20 per cent of Britons thought that a Jewish prime minister would be 'less acceptable' than a non-Jewish one. It did not end there, with 2005 Labour campaign posters showing Howard and Shadow chancellor Oliver Letwin, who is also Jewish, as pigs in the sky. In other posters Howard was made to look like Fagin and Shylock.

Would Australians vote for a Jewish candidate running for the job? Anti-Semitism is still an unknown quantity in Australian politics. Arguably, Jews have been accepted as full partners in Australian society with the country producing a dazzling array of Jewish luminaries in a spectrum of fields. The Jewish contribution to Australian politics has covered local, state and Federal. Sir Zelman Cowan and Sir Isaac Isaacs as Governors-General come to mind, and Michael Danby was for years tagged as the only Jewish member of Federal Parliament until Mark Dreyfus came along. But at present, Jews do not hold any ministerial positions and the prospect of a Jew occupying the Lodge seems remote if not fantastical.

If there was a Jewish candidate running, it would test the nation's religious tolerance. Would the Jewish community feel compelled to support him or her because of their history-making ticket? We know that the notion that there is some sort of 'monolithic' Jewish electorate is a myth.

Still, imagine for a moment the outpouring of collective joy, pride and sense of triumph among Jews if a Jewish prime minister became a reality. If anything, it would give Jewish mothers lots of *naches*.

Seriously though, it would shatter one of the last remaining cultural barriers in Australian politics, and would not only be a milestone for the Jewish community but would empower minority groups who wish to participate in the politics of the nation. It would demonstrate that nothing is impossible in this great land.

Australia would never be the same.

Naturally, there would be those who would question the Jewish prime minister's loyalty and the prime minister might have to bend over backwards to show that he or she was not playing favourites when it came to Israel and Jewish causes. The moment things flared up in the Middle East, the nation would closely observe the prime minister's actions and words to see if they were objective and even-handed.

The Jewish prime minister might have to consider whether to sell weapons technology or uranium to countries technically at war with Israel, whether to transfer the Australian embassy to Jerusalem, whether to meet with international leaders whose countries ban Jews from entering or whether to fund terrorism against Israel.

Other fascinating questions abound: Would a Jewish prime minister be representative of the Jewish secular experience or be more observant and showcase Judaism's ancient traditions? Would they keep the Sabbath or violate it to participate in crucial meetings and functions? Would there be a kosher kitchen in the mansion and a Succah? Would a Christmas tree stand next to a Menorah? How many compromises to their faith would they have to make so as to fulfil their governing role? Certainly, any future summit (like the 2020) would not take place on Passover.

Is Australia ready for a Jewish PM? It remains to be seen, but somebody ought to try.

Roseanne Barr's attention-seeking behaviour
August 14, 2009

By now it's clear that when it comes to the Holocaust nothing is off-limits. It seems that there is no aspect or symbol of the Shoah that is not subject to perverse abuse and cheap trivialisation. And this trend is hitting new lows.

In order to grab attention and resurrect her forgotten career, comedienne Roseanne Barr has done a photo-spread titled 'That Oven Feeling' for *Heeb* Magazine's German issue, in which she's dressed as a domesticated version of Hitler.[37] *Heeb*, established with backing from Spielberg and CEO of Warner Music Group Edgar Bronfman, is described as a satirical Jewish cultural magazine.

Wearing the Fuhrer's moustache, with her hair pulled back to imitate Hitler's parted cut, she is shown holding a tray of burned gingerbread 'Jew cookies'. In another picture, wearing an armband with a large swastika, she takes out the 'burnt Jew cookies' ready to take a bite. Apparently, Barr believed she was channeling Hitler's soul![38]

According to the magazine's reporter, Barr was having fun and nailed 'the Fuhrer's facial expressions with twisted glee'. He writes that she 'got off' dressing like a Nazi.

Barr, who is Jewish and who wrote on her blog that Hitler killed her entire family, claimed that she was combating anti-Semitism, only meant to make fun of Hitler and that she is 'sick of being mis-understood'. Last year in the midst of 'Operation Cast Lead' she labeled Israel a 'Nazi State'.[39]

And believe it or not, *Heeb*'s publisher Josh Neumann insisted that the photos were done for satirical, not for shock value. He mocked those who dared challenge the immoral photos: 'I want to cry from remorse, but I'm afraid the ensuing suds would cake the lenses of my glasses.'[40]

So, burning and eating Jewish people is somewhat funny to Roseanne and the folks at *Heeb*, ah?

In tune with the mocking tone, Barr saved a Polaroid of her Hitler depiction in a sandwich bag so she could give it to her thir-teen-year-old son. 'Maybe this will make my kid like me,' she noted.

Just because Barr is Jewish doesn't give her the right to re-trau-matise survivors and stamp on their feelings. Barr and *Heeb* should have known that the horrors of the Holocaust must be approached with respect and sensitivity and that there is nothing funny about Hitler and the millions of Jews who were cremated in the ovens.

More broadly, what worries me is that Hitler and the Holo-caust are becoming increasingly associated with laughter and are no longer an oxymoron. Holocaust memory has softened, and the results are everywhere. Just watch Seinfeld's Nazi soup episode, *Curb Your Enthusiasm*'s 'The Survivor' episode, *Borat* and *Bruno* and of course, *The Producers*.

What's worse, people are not appalled, but enjoy such objection-able, tasteless rubbish and are able to laugh without guilt about the inconceivable crimes against humanity and about those who perpe-trated them.

There is nothing beyond the pale or too vulgar for today's shock-less society. Afflicted with historical amnesia, moral parameters have so shifted to the point where nobody bothers to question whether a dancing Hitler is crass and offensive. Instead, everyone is having too much fun and getting their ticket's worth. They don't understand that treating the Holocaust as a comedy is an outrage.

Why we cry for Gilead Shalit

October 30, 2009

Anyone watching the two and a half minute video of 21-year-old Gilad Shalit,[41] the Israeli soldier abducted and held captive by Hamas for 1222 days, must have shed a tear. The image of the young man, alone, helpless, scared, with a forced smile (doctors have speculated that Shalit was given sedatives) pleading for his life and telling his family that he loves them was heartbreaking. And all parents know, deep in their hearts, that they would trade the world to save their child.

The Shalit case has placed Israel in an agonising existential dilemma – what should the government to do when it knows that the ransom demanded by Hamas (1000 Palestinian and Israeli-Arab and East Jerusalem prisoners) includes freeing hundreds of terrorists with blood on their hands who are likely to kill again?

Shalit's father, Noam, who has appealed to Israeli PM Ehud Olmert's 'moral duty' to save a soldier sent to serve on behalf of the state, has the backing of public opinion in Israel, which sees Shalit's release as a sacred duty.

Journalist Ben Caspit states that 63 per cent of Hamas prisoners and 67 per cent of Islamic Jihad prisoners that were released in hostage exchanges, returned to the ranks of their groups and carried out or attempted to carry out terrorist attacks in Israel.

The Israeli organisation *Gam Ani* (Me Too) includes on its website pictures of eighteen Israeli citizens, out of 180, that were killed in terrorist attacks so as to show that there are:

> real people with a smile and a face that will pay with their lives for this deal. The murder of each one of them could have been prevented if the terrorists were not freed in the past in exchange for a few soldiers or the bodies of dead soldiers. Do we really want to add more pictures to this terrible collection?

Nahum Barnea, a prominent Israeli commentator, maintains that, 'The unwritten contract between a State and its troops says that the soldier pledges to risk his life for it, and that the State pledges not to risk his life in vain and do everything possible to free him from captivity.'[42]

In various demonstrations by groups set up to advocate for Shalit's release, signs held up read, 'Don't let Gilad become another Ron Arad', a reference to the Israeli officer who has been missing, presumed dead, for the last 23 years.

The families of the victims of terror have come out in opposition to a prisoner swap, especially after Yael Zeevi, the widow of assassinated politician Rehavham 'Gandhi' Zeevi stated that she would be willing for her husband's killers to be swapped for Shalit, stressing that her husband saw the *mitzvah* or commandments of redeeming prisoners as paramount. Chair of the Victims of Terror, Ze'ev Rap, whose fifteen-year-old daughter Helena was murdered, reacted angrily, 'The memory of our beloved cries for revenge from the ground', while Stanley Boim and Efraim Kastiel, who lost a son and a daughter, expressed similar sentiments. Yet, Dorit Ben Dor, whose daughter was killed by terrorists said, 'Shalit is still alive so we must take him back, alive, to his parents. I think now Shalit is my son, I hope they will not give up.' Yitzhak Ovitz, who serves in the same unit and tank that Shalit served in, has written to Ehud Barak stating that if he falls captive, he does not want to be released as part of an exchange deal. Ovitz said that he cannot see an entire state on its knees begging for Shalit's release.

There are reports that the IDF knows where Shalit is held, that the building where he is held has been booby-trapped with explosives and that his guards have been instructed to immediately shoot him if a rescue raid is staged. The government has ruled this option out since it does not want another Nachshon Waxman, the Israeli soldier who was killed in 1994 during a military rescue attempt.

Some commentators argue that any deal would only strengthen Hamas in the upcoming elections; that a swap would embolden future terrorists with the knowledge that even if they are caught they will be released eventually; that a deal would encourage the kidnapping of Israeli soldiers; that the government must declare that from now onwards all negotiations are off and that if Shalit is harmed Hamas leaders will be targeted and tough sanctions will be imposed on the Palestinians; that agreeing to Hamas's delaying tactics and blackmail has humiliated Israel and embarrassed a proud nation; that turning the case of a captured soldier into a national priority invites failure, as the Ron Arad experience demonstrates; and that Shalit, as a soldier, knew the risks of being killed (like his two fellow soldiers) in battle or taken by the enemy.

There aren't any easy choices. And there are no easy answers.

John Safran's silly antics

November 26, 2009

By now, many have watched the antics of John Safran's deliberately provocative *Race Relations*.[43] Supposedly, Safran's show is about the shock-comedian's exploration of deeply personal attitudes and obsessions about race and intermarriage.

Yet, in essence, *Race Relations* is about Safran's search for a way to escape and erase his Jewishness. It's as if being a Jew has ruined his life and left him emotionally and psychologically scarred. So, he attempts a circumcision reversal, participates in an African death ritual to purge himself of the past, wants to create 'Jellystinian', a new Jewish-Arab baby, by donating sperm to a Palestinian sperm bank, and in the ultimate obliteration of his Jewish identity is nailed to a wooden cross in a crucifixion ritual in Manila.

And then he uses the murder of millions as material for cheap gags.

Sixty-one years ago this month the Nazis unleashed a two-day spree that came to be known as Kristallnacht. Six years later, Anne Frank died from typhus at Bergen Belsen. Her testimony has become a symbol for the senselessness of bigotry and as a plea for universal tolerance.

That is, unless you're Safran. I squirmed in my seat as Safran claimed that he was 'brainwashed, played like a two-dollar chump-machine' by the Jewish community because it has used the Holocaust to make him feel guilty about dating non-Jewish women.

That's right, the enormity of the Holocaust has been reduced to a manipulative tool by the Jewish community to induce in Safran a fear of intimacy with non-Jewish girls.

In order to 'get rid of this bullshit' he convinces Katherine Hicks, in his words, a 'blonde-haired, Aryan' to make out with him in Anne Frank's attic so he can break free of that fear. As visitors walk around the Anne Frank Museum in Amsterdam taking in the images and information, Safran and Hicks wait for their opportunity to passionately kiss.

A friend told me he nearly died laughing watching Safran. Well, I said, millions actually did.

Had Frank survived the Holocaust, she would have been 80 this year. I'm sure she would not have had a chuckle at Safran's tasteless skit.

Safran's exploitative approach drains the Holocaust of its tragic context (the death camps, the starvation, the shootings, the gassings, the burning of bodies, the mounds of hair, shoes and glasses) at a time when one in twenty British kids think Hitler was a football coach, and one in six believe Auschwitz is a theme park.

Safran's carnival approach to the Holocaust continued last week when he mock-gassed Holocaust Denier David Irving.

Wanting to prove that he is not a self-hating Jew, Safran decides to employ 'old school Simon Wiesenthal Nazi hunting' tactics to fight anti-Semitism and 'take out' Irving. While eating a sausage he notices the BBQ's gas bottle, and hey presto, his lame scheme is hatched. Safran not only distorts Wiesenthal's message of justice, not revenge, but given that Safran's grandmother lost her family in the Holocaust, should have known better.

Prior to 'luring his prey' for the interview, Safran 'rigged' the radio studio by inserting a pipe through the ventilation system so as to convert the room into a 'gas chamber'. Taking a pause from their chat, Safran walks out, jams the door with a broom and, opening a gas bottle, screams at Irving through the glass, 'You're locked in a room and it's filling with gas and if you try and tell anyone, I am going to deny it.' Irving was visibly amused by the stunt.

The ABC may have figured that any publicity is good publicity and will draw a large viewing audience. But the inclusion of these two hurtful pranks reveals a lamentable shirking of managerial responsibility and a staggering absence of prudent thinking. I wonder: why didn't anyone sit down with Safran and explain to him that this was in terrible taste, that mining humour from the Holocaust and that belittling the deaths of millions for cheap, silly laughs is unacceptable?

What a comedian does is up to him, but when the ABC, and our tax dollars, fund such a show, the question should be asked – is this the role of a public broadcaster?

Comedy does not bring with it unlimited licence. There will be those who will say that since Safran is Jewish, this makes it all right.

But this is no justification. The insult does not become sanitised or acceptable just because it is made by a Jew.

When the Holocaust is used to attract ratings, it is not just a failure of the imagination. It is a sign that in this age of moral trespass, nothing has remained sacred.

Did Michael Jackson hate Jews?

January 13, 2010

The Michael Jackson soap opera keeps bubbling along with reports that his doctor Conrad Murray will soon be charged with involuntary manslaughter for the pop star's death. And in less two weeks, *This Is It*, the film showcasing his pre-concert rehearsals that has become the top grossing music-documentary of all times, will be released on DVD, reaching millions of additional teenage viewers.

One song performed by Jackson in the movie is 'They Don't Care about Us', a 1995 release that features the racially notorious lyrics, '*Jew me, sue me, everybody do me/ Kick me, kike me, don't you black or white me.*' It reminded me of the hubbub that flared then and the ongoing controversy whether Jackson was an anti-Semite.

The self-proclaimed King of Pop immediately denied the accusations, telling Diane Sawyer of ABC News that the song is a cry against bigotry and that:

> It's not anti-Semitic because I'm not a racist. I could never be a racist. I love all races. My accountants and lawyers are Jewish. My three best friends are Jewish: David Geffen, Jeffrey Katzenberg and Steven Spielberg. These are friends of mine. They're all Jewish. How does this make sense?[44]

Yet, even close friends such as Steven Spielberg publicly stated they were not happy about Jackson using such a hurtful slur and found the track offensive. In fact, Spielberg was so angry at Jackson that he refused to join him at an apologetic press conference that the singer planned to do at the Simon Wiesenthal Center in Los Angeles.

Consider this: in a song that has 'They' in its title, clearly indicating a group rather than an individual, and is supposedly about all kinds of prejudices, the fact that Jews are the only group that is singled out casts doubt on Jackson's denial that he was pointedly critical of Jews. In response to the barrage of criticism, Jackson apologised for using the anti-Semitic slang and recorded a new, reworded version. However, the insensitive lyrics were reinstated for the video release, even though Jackson gave his assurances that the song would not appear again with those offending words.

Moreover, the apology wasn't enough for Dawn Steel, former president of Columbia Pictures who wrote in the *LA Times*: 'Oh, please, Michael! Why does your apology feel so facile, so much a part of a strategy to clean up your image? I for one don't buy it. The images and words and sounds you create don't just go away. They are indelibly etched into our consciousness, the damage is done. Your public relations problem might go away, but how can I forgive you for teaching my child the word *kike* ... You are an adult. You must act like one. Stop blaming everyone else. Stop seeing yourself as a victim who has been misunderstood.'[45]

In various ways, the claim by Jackson that he was unaware that these lyrics would have such a distressing impact was a defence that many found hard to believe. Patrick Mcdonald of *The Seattle Times* observed: 'It makes you wonder: Is there no one in the Jackson camp who confronts him when he does something stupid? He may have lived a sheltered life, but there really is no excuse for using terms like 'Jew me' and 'kike' in a pop song, unless you make it clear you are denouncing such terms, and do so in an artful way.'[46]

This was not Jackson's last brush with allegations of anti-Semitism. In 2005, telephone answer machine messages left by the singer to his former adviser Dieter Wiesener were aired on American TV, in which Jackson blames the Jews for his financial woes and declares 'They suck. They're like leeches ... I'm so tired of it ... they start out the most popular person in the world, make a lot of money, big house, cars and everything. End up penniless. It is conspiracy. The Jews do it on purpose.'

Jackson never publicly responded to the revelations, though his attorney at that time, Brian Oxman, did not dispute that Jackson left the 'leech' message'. Jackson's former spiritual confidant Rabbi Shmuley Boteach was disgusted by the comments and issued a statement that said, 'I watched in sadness the tragic and catastrophic decline of Michael Jackson since disowning him more than four years ago. But even I never believed that he would fall so low and become a racist, bigoted anti-Semite. I pray that Michael finally seeks out the serious spiritual and psychological help he needs to rediscover the inspiration he once brought millions.'[47] At the same time, Jackson's Israeli fan club told the press in 2005 that they did not believe the tapes reflected the true nature of Jackson's beliefs.

Interestingly, these scandals did not prevent the Jewish Museum in Vienna from displaying a life-size photograph of Jackson in a 2009 exhibition titled 'Typical! – Cliches of Jews and Others' – examining the use and abuse of ethnic stereotypes in popular culture. Jackson's 2002 image was used to show how the performer, through his surgical transformation, demolished stereotypes and literally cut himself off from the restrictions of physical definition.

And the Jewish connection does not end here. A continuing mystery is whether his two children, Prince Michael and Paris, are indeed Jewish? Given that their mother Susan Rowe, who was married to Jackson, is Jewish, according to Jewish law, the twelve- and eleven-year-olds are Jews. In 2005, Debbie Rowe did in fact disclose that she and the children were Jewish, releasing that information because she was concerned Jackson was embracing the teaching of The Nation of Islam.

And the saga continues ...

Oliver Stone and Holocaust denial
January 18, 2010

Miep Gies, the sole surviving member of the group who helped protect Anne Frank and her family from the Nazis by providing them with food and other necessities while they hid in a concealed apartment, died last week aged 100.

Gies, who found Anne's diary, gave it to Anne's father Otto after he returned from Auschwitz. Throughout her life, Gies became an ambassador for the Holocaust, travelling extensively and actively campaigning against Holocaust denial.

I wonder what Gies would have made of Oliver Stone, who in promoting his ten-hour documentary *Secret History of America* for Showtime said a few days ago:

> Stalin, Hitler, Mao, McCarthy – these people have been vilified pretty thoroughly by history, we can't judge people as only 'bad' or 'good'. Hitler was an easy scapegoat and it's been used cheaply. Hitler is the product of a series of actions. It's cause and effect. People in America don't know the connection between WWI and WWII ... Go into the funding of the Nazi party. How many American corporations were involved, from GM through IBM. Hitler is just a man who could have easily been assassinated ... I've been able to walk in Stalin's and Hitler's shoes, to understand their point of view. We're going to educate our minds and liberalise them and broaden them. We want to move beyond opinions ... You cannot approach history unless you have empathy for the person you may hate.[48]

Stone, who admires despots Fidel Castro and Hugo Chavez, hopes that schools will use his 'documentary' in their teaching curriculum.

So let us understand: the director of films such as *Wall Street* and *Platoon* wants to empathise with Hitler, and thinks the mass murderer was an easy scapegoat who needs to be put in context? As *The Guardian* put it: 'The implication that Stone is seeking to put forward a good side of the German dictator hitherto not seen by Americans is, even by Stone's own accomplished record of stirring up stinks, pretty radical'.[49]

When you have killed millions, as Hitler did, you are going to be judged as bad and be vilified. To take a bloodthirsty dictator such as Hitler and to suggest that somehow he is the victim of political or psychological factors or that some dark forces were pulling his strings behind the scenes is obscene. And yes, we can and should judge people by their horrific actions, and yes, there are good and bad people in this world.

It would seem that like his fictional film *JFK*, Stone, who must fancy himself as a serious historian, has used his cinematic talents to produce another revisionist work that fits neatly with his ideological worldview and seeks to humanise Hitler and turn history on its head. This kind of trendy, moral relativism and trivialisation not only diminishes the significance of the Holocaust but makes it easier for Holocaust denial to take root in the public arena.

A case in point was the BBC's lamentable decision in October 2009 to put Holocaust denier and leader of the British National Party, Nick Griffin, on its popular talk show *Question Time* with more than eight millions viewers tuning in. Griffin was even chosen to attend the Copenhagen summit on climate change as part of the EU Parliament's delegation.

Of course, it didn't help that last year Pope Benedict lifted the 20-year-old excommunication of Richard Williamson, an ultra-traditionalist bishop who also happens to be a public Holocaust denier.

Benedict, who admitted he was part of the Hitler Youth (though the Vatican first denied then acknowledged the fact) and served in the German army during WWII, also angered many when in a 2006 address at the Auschwitz death camp he appeared to absolve or limit the complicity of the German people in the Nazi atrocities. The pope ascribed responsibility for the systematic program of extermination to a 'ring of criminals' that ascended to power 'with the result that our people was used and abused as an instrument of their thirst for destruction and power'.[50]

The passage of time and the death of eye-witnesses is an inevitable aid to Holocaust deniers. Also, the internet has provided Holocaust deniers with a powerful new weapon in disseminating material worldwide, with sites such as Facebook and YouTube serving as fertile grounds.

I, for one, do not share Oliver Stone's desire to walk in Hitler's shoes.

Chelsea Clinton and Mark Mezvinsky: The demise of the Jewish people?

February 4, 2010

Boy meets girl. They fall in love. She is a Methodist. He is a Jew. She is the only child of a former US president and the current Secretary of State. He's the son of two former Congress representatives.

Chelsea Clinton, 29, and Marc Mezvinsky, 31, announced their engagement recently. They told friends that they are looking forward to this June when they will marry.

Bill Clinton praised his future son-in-law as a 'great human being'. Hilary said she was very excited, and gushed, 'It has been extraordinary ... to see how happy my daughter is and to have such a wonderful young man that will become my son-in-law.'

Former New York mayor Ed Koch, who is Jewish, advised Chelsea to learn a few Chinese dishes. Koch, who reckons all Jewish men like Chinese foods, joked that Chelsea might be a better cook than Jewish women, saying 'My mother burned everything she ever made'.

Chelsea has attended Yom Kippur services with her groom-to-be. But there is no indication she intends to convert to Judaism, unlike Ivanka Trump, daughter of real-estate mogul Donald Trump, who underwent an orthodox conversion to marry Jared Kushner, supposedly at Jared's request. As part of the process, Ivanka, also known by her Hebrew name Yael, would have been immersed in the *mikveh*, the ritual bath required of women wanting to convert.

So should Chelsea take the dip? How will Bill and Hilary feel about it? Should any woman, or man for that matter, convert to the religion of their partner?

If Chelsea does not convert, children born to the couple will not be considered Jewish according to traditional Jewish law. Still, the reform movement will accept that child as Jewish if he or she are brought up in a Jewish household as a Jew.

Celebrity conversions to Judaism have become trendy. I hear that Leonardo Di Caprio is strongly thinking about becoming Jewish so he can marry Israeli model Bar Rafaeli. It has been reported that Lindsay Lohan is on her way because of the love of her life, Samantha Ronson. Isla Fisher converted to Judaism before her marriage to Sacha Baron Cohen. And let's not forget Marilyn Monroe Miller who converted when she married playwright Arthur Miller.

Some are saying that conversion to Judaism has become a matter of convenience. Here's a joke one columnist offered: 'For appearance's sake, Daddy tells Christopher jnr, that if he wants to marry his daughter Princess, he must become a Jew. What's a Jew? Christopher asks. Like me, answers Daddy.'

For a small minority, the news of the impending nuptials is another sign of the decay of the Jewish people, a loss of Jewish continuity.

Several commentators have argued that if Marc cares about his heritage, and if he wants his children to be Jewish, he should encourage Chelsea to convert. In the US, where the intermarriage rate has reached more than 50 per cent, research has shown that 90 per cent of the children of mixed marriages themselves marry non-Jews. Here, in Australia, the figures of intermarriage are in the mid-20 per cent, crawling towards the 30s.

In *The Vanishing American Jew*, Alan Dershowitz predicts that if present trends continue, diaspora Jewry may virtually vanish by the third quarter of the 21st century.[51]

A 2006 American study concluded that intermarriage 'does indeed constitute the greatest single threat to Jewish continuity today'.[52] Demographers are predicting that zero growth and high disaffiliation from Jewish life could cut the number of Jews significantly in the next two decades. Nevertheless, reports of the Jewish people's demise are premature.

Intermarriage has left its mark on popular discourse. *The O.C.*, a popular American TV series, featured a Jewish public defender married to a wealthy non-Jewish developer. Their son dealt with his mixed religious heritage by promoting the family's adoption of Chrismukkah. On the show, Chrismukkah was described as 'eight days of presents followed by one day of many presents'.

Now, Chrismukkah has been listed in *Time* as one of the buzz words of 2006 and has been added to the respected *Chambers* dictionary. There are even books: *Chrismukkah! The Merry Mish-Mash Holiday Cookbook* and *Chrismukkah: The Official Guide to the World's*

Best-Loved Holiday. A line of Chrismukkah products such as the 'yarmuclaus' (yarmulke/Santa hat combo) are now available.

Gradually, Judaism is perceived as folk culture – bagels, *Seinfeld*. Even in Australia, a few are celebrating Chrismukkah. There is even a Hanukkah bush, a sort of a Christmas tree for Jews.

Films and TV have openly dealt with the theme of inter-dating and intermarriage, depicting Jews blending smoothly into such situations. Examples: *When Harry Met Sally, White Palace, Prime, The Nanny, Northern Exposure, Mad About You, Friends, Will and Grace, Dharma and Greg, Thirtysomething, LA Law*, to name but a few. For the characters on these programs, being Jewish is marginal. They find emotional and spiritual meaning elsewhere.

Sometimes, things get ugly. There were rumours that Jean Sarkozy, son of the French President and a Catholic, was planning to convert to Judaism before marrying his childhood sweetheart, Jessica Sebaoun. After the engagement, French cartoonist Maurice Sinet wrote an article saying Jean 'has just said he intends to convert to Judaism before marrying his fiancée, who is Jewish, and the heiress to the founders of Darty. He'll go far, that kid.'[53] The link Sine was drawing between Jews and money, conversion and social success, was hard to miss.

I have heard intermarried couples assert that we should learn to appreciate all cultural traditions, not be immediately bound by the faith of our parents since one's religious background is not one of voluntary choice but an accident of birth. A Melbourne Jewish man whose wife is Catholic explained to me that his parents-in-law vehemently oppose their daughter converting or raising their children as Jews as it is outside their faith and culture.

Whatever you think, let us all wish Chelsea and Marc a *mazel tov*.

Mel Gibson's Jewish problem

February 2, 2010

After a long absence Mel Gibson stars in a new film. Last week, he was interviewed by Sam Rubin, a reporter for KTLA TV in Los Angeles.

After a brief exchange, Rubin, who is Jewish, remarked: 'Some people will welcome you back, and other people will say he should never come back.' When Gibson asked why, Rubin reminded him of the barrage of anti-Semitic slurs he made when arrested for drunk driving in 2006. According to the officer's report, Gibson said: 'F—ing Jews – Jews are responsible for all the wars in the world.' Gibson then asked the officer if he was Jewish.

Gibson later apologised for his hate-filled rant, saying: 'I acted like a person completely out of control when I was arrested and said things that I do not believe to be true and which are despicable. I am deeply ashamed of everything I said.'[54]

Gibson insisted that he is not bigot, adding: 'There is no excuse, nor should there be any tolerance, for anyone who thinks or expresses any kind of anti-Semitic remark. I want to apologise specifically to everyone in the Jewish community for the vitriolic and harmful words that I said to a law enforcement officer the night I was arrested on a DUI charge.'[55]

Gibson seemed to be genuinely sorry and remorseful. Yet four years later, Gibson apparently denied saying those hurtful things. Leaning forward he told Sam Rubin: 'The remarks that were attributed to me? That I didn't necessarily make. OK.'[56]

Gibson then must have picked up that Rubin was Jewish. In an allusion to Rubin's Jewishness, Gibson told him, 'I gather you have a dog in this fight. Do you have a dog in this fight? Or you're being impartial?' The implication was clear.

Gibson's 2006 outburst amplified people's anger about what they saw as anti-Semitic overtones in his 2004 blockbuster *The Passion of the Christ*. Others were disappointed that he failed to disassociate himself strongly enough from remarks by his father denying the Holocaust.

The Passion of the Christ script that Gibson co-authored is based on the visions and ravings of a 19th century German Catholic nun, Anne Catherine Emmerich. Emmerich's work is riddled with anti-Jewish tones and has very little scriptural or historical legs to stand on.

Gibson should have listened to those who told him of the inflammatory potential of the film. For centuries, the performance of Passion plays in Europe led to vicious attacks and pogroms against Jews.

The Passion of the Christ depicts the brutal tyrant Pontius Pilate as a sympathetic, humane character while making the Jewish priests bloodthirsty sadists who are the main instigators of Jesus' death. When an interfaith group of scholars condemned an early script for blaming the Jews for the crucifixion, Gibson paid no heed to their concerns.

When Gibson was asked to appear on screen at the end of the film and clearly state that Jewish people are not to blame for the death of Jesus, reflecting the Vatican II pronouncement, he said no. When he was told that *The Passion of the Christ* threatens to undo decades of interfaith dialogue he was not moved. Yes, he removed the subtitles from a scene in which a Jewish mob says, 'His blood be on us and on our children' but left the offensive quotation in the film.

Gibson said he had no wish to offend Jews, but added, 'Anybody who transgresses has to look at their own part or look at their own culpability'. What culpability, Mel?

Gibson's father has said that the Jews of Europe 'simply got up and left' and were all over the Bronx, Brooklyn and Sydney;[57] that the Holocaust was mostly fiction because the Nazis never had enough petrol to burn six million Jews; that the genocide was fabricated by 'financiers' seeking to facilitate the movement of Jews to Palestine; that Holocaust museums are a 'gimmick to collect money', and that the concentration camps were just 'work camps'.

He has further claimed that the Jews are taking over the Catholic Church, are after one world religion and one world government and that former Federal Reserve chairman Alan Greenspan should be lynched.

Sadly, Gibson fudged an opportunity to forcefully refute his father's views when he was questioned about the Holocaust. After stating that he had friends with numbers on their arms, he noted, 'Yes of course. Atrocities happened. War is horrible. The Second World War killed tens of millions of people. Some of them were Jews in concentration camps. Many people lost their lives.'[58] Gibson minimised the mass murder, depicting it as another aspect of the overall toll of the Second World War rather than the industrial, systematic extermination campaign that it was.

Gibson told American broadcaster Diane Sawyer: 'My dad taught me faith and I believe what he taught me. The man never lied to me in his life.' And: 'He's my father. Gotta leave it alone.'[59]

Well, Gibson did not have to leave it alone. He could and should have unequivocally rejected his father's views. He should publicly disavow Holocaust denial. Sons can love their fathers but still admit they are wrong. Arnold Schwarzenegger reacted to the revelation of his father's past by asking the Simon Wiesenthal Centre to examine whether his father committed atrocities, and publicly denounced right-wing Austrian politician Joerg Heider. The California Governor also visited Yad Vashem, Israel's National Holocaust Museum and laid a wreath.[60]

In his post-interview monologue, Rubin questioned whether Gibson was ever honestly sorry for the anti-Semitic remarks he made in 2006, especially since he now contests the comments for which he sought forgiveness. There will be many asking the same question.

Jews and Christian Zionists:
A marriage made in heaven?

March 4, 2010

Question: Who said the following: 'Israel has no better friends in the world than Christian Zionists. This is a friendship of the heart, a friendship of common roots, and a friendship of common civilisation.'[61] It wasn't a pastor at a local church. It was Prime Minister Bibi Netanyahu speaking at a conference of American evangelicals in Jerusalem in April 2008.

In a 2008 poll taken in the US, more than 80 per cent of Christians stated that they had a 'moral and biblical' obligation to love, pray and support Israel, while 62 per cent of evangelicals said that Jerusalem should remain Israel's undivided capital.

I recall witnessing the waves of love when 400 Christians, representing more than ten organisations, gathered two years ago in Melbourne for a Stand with Israel evening. The affection for Israel was palpable. Shorn of Christian signs such as the cross, the event featured Israeli dancing and songs, banners, waving of the Israeli flag, a pep-rally eruption of cheers and standing ovations for Israel, and speeches praising and praying for the Jewish people. Particularly striking was an apology offered by an elderly German woman to the Jewish people for the evil perpetrated by the Nazis and another apology by a pastor for anti-Semitism.

Such words of contrition are not often heard.

Baffling? Only to those who don't understand a controversial end-time theology that began in 19th century Britain and which divides history into eras (dispensations). According to this theology, Israel's creation and the 1967 war were galvanising signs that God's hand moves in history and the clock of prophecy had started up again. Driven by a literal interpretation that prophesies Israel's establishment as a prelude to the second coming of Jesus, tens of millions are now convinced they are living in the final days as described in the Book of Revelation. They are often called Christian Zionists.

This intense passion was given a boost with the publication of Hal Lindsey's 1970s blockbuster book *The Late Great Planet*[62] and continues today with Tim LaHaye's prophetic *Left Behind Series*[63] that has sold 70 million copies.

A review of the recently released documentary *Waiting for Armageddon*[64] explains the four stages: 1) The Rapture, when, in a microsecond, all true believers, living and dead, will be transported into the clouds with Jesus. 2) The Tribulation, during which untold horrendous catastrophes, ecological and man-made, will rain down upon those haplessly left behind. 3) Armageddon, when Christ will return with a sword to judge the sinners and defeat the Antichrist, who will then be placed in a bottomless pit for 1000 years. 4) The Millennium, encompassing the 1000-year reign of heaven on earth reserved for Christ and his followers (along with 144,000 converted Jews).

Standing with Israel guarantees evangelicals that they will be on God's side when the Battle of Armageddon occurs in Megiddo, Israel. This occurs after the Antichrist is released from his imprisonment, recruits the armies of Gog and Magog and attacks the New Jerusalem. In the final battle, it should be noted, most Jews are wiped out and the rest embrace Christ after he defeats the Antichrist and throws him into the Lake of Fire or Gehena. Jews who don't accept Jesus are condemned to eternal damnation, while Christians ascend to heaven.

Gershom Goremberg, author of the book *The End of Days*, is unsure about the evangelicals' affection. He explains the evangelical attitudes towards Jews as: 'We love you and want you to give up what is most basic to your identity.'[65]

Historical examples of Christian Zionists include William Blackstone, author of *Jesus is Coming*, who organised a petition for restoring Palestine to the chosen people, Lord Balfour and his 1917 declaration promising a homeland for the Jewish in Palestine and President Harry S. Truman and his support for US recognition of Israel despite the objections of the American State Department.

Indeed, an increasing number emphasise that Christian Zionism is based on the biblical promise that God will bless those who bless the Jews, and curse those who curse the Jews. For many, at a time when Israel faces a nuclear threat from Iran and global anti-Semitism is on the rise, biblical motives count for little.

To properly understand the level of evangelical devotion to Israel, one only has to mention the International Fellowship of Christians and Jews,[66] which has raised $US250,000,000 (A$277,000,000) for various projects in Israel. The Joshua Fund,[67] an evangelical organisation, aims to marshal more than $100 million to fund projects for health, immigrant integration, education and victims of terrorism in Israel.

Yet, there are those who feel a discomfort with this backing. Tel-evangelist Pat Robertson, a leading Christian Zionist, said at the time of Ariel Sharon's stroke that Sharon was being punished for withdrawing from Gaza and 'dividing God's land'.

Jerry Falwell, regarded as the father of the movement in the US, described the Antichrist as being Jewish. John Hagee, John McCain's pastor, who organises an annual Night to Honour Israel and heads Christians United for Israel, wrote in his 1996 book that the assassination of Yitzak Rabin 'launched biblical prophecy onto the fast track' and has made several offensive remarks about Jews.[68]

An Israeli journalist noted that this extending of a hand in friendship is offered in good faith and that the 'ancient tribal instinct to slap that hand away' is an unwise one. Christians United For Israel executive director David Brog, who last year arranged for 34 Christian students to take part in the March of the Living in Poland's Nazi camps, claims that Christian Zionists are the heirs of the righteous gentiles. His book *Standing with Israel: Why Christians Support the Jewish State*[69] is fascinating read.

Jews as pawns in a Christian prophecy leading the way to the end-of-days battle? Only if you believe it.

Fifteen years after the assassination:
Yitzhak Rabin's failed Oslo legacy

November 5, 2010

Today marks the fifteenth anniversary of the Rabin assassination. Many will reflect on his legacy, especially his signing of the 1993 Oslo Accords.

Even the most starry-eyed optimists now admit that the Oslo Accords were an unmitigated disaster and were doomed from the start. Making a deal with a terrorist and a despot like Arafat meant that he was given a free hand to continue his decades-long campaign of indiscriminate murder in order to achieve his goal of a Palestine over all of Israel.

Oslo was based on the pie-in-the-sky belief that if only Israel offered more and more unilateral concessions, the Palestinian Authority would make peace.

It's hard to understand Rabin's misplaced confidence in Arafat.

In fact, Rabin saved Arafat from oblivion. After supporting Saddam Hussein's vicious occupation of Kuwait Arafat had few backers. Then the Oslo accords brought him and his henchmen from exile in Tunis to a hero's welcome in Gaza. The Accords furnished him with control of the West Bank and Gaza as well as billions of dollars in aid. And did I mention a Nobel Peace Prize?

In return, Arafat created an armed camp in the territories and protected Hamas and Islamic Jihad. Following Oslo, Israel was treated to a full-scale suicide bombing campaign that killed more than a thousand of its citizens. During the Oslo years, every pronouncement of hate, incitement and glorification of violence by Arafat was ignored.

Reflect, only after Oslo did terror escalate.

For Arafat, Oslo was always a tactic, never a goal. A golden opportunity to continue the next stage in his perpetual war against Israel, he now had territory (granted to him on a silver platter) closer to Israeli cities than ever before. Oslo was a modern-day Trojan horse.

Editor of *Al-Quds Al Arabi* newspaper, Abd Al-Bari Atwan, recalls Arafat telling him, just before he returned to Gaza in 1993, that 'The day will come when you will see thousands of Jews fleeing

Palestine ... The Oslo Accords will bring this about.'[70] When Palestinian commentator Yunis Udeh told Arafat that Oslo meant the end of the Palestinian cause, Arafat replied, 'I am hammering the first nail in the Zionist coffin'. When asked how, Arafat said, 'I will go to Gaza, I will go to Palestine'.[71]

Following Oslo, Fatah enshrined a rule of terror that violated Palestinians' basic human rights, and crushed any opposition through kidnapping and summary execution. Arafat did everything possible to prevent the establishment of a Palestinian state.

Israeli Prime Minister Ehud Barak's flawed logic led him in 2000 to offer Arafat 100 per cent of Gaza, 95 per cent of the West Bank and sections of East Jerusalem for a future Palestinian capital. Arafat walked out on that deal and unleashed a savage war that claimed the lives of 1000 Israelis.

Arafat figured that the Israeli public would yield to this kind of blackmail and pressure its leaders to make additional concessions.

Earlier in 2000, Barak withdrew Israeli troops from South Lebanon's security zone. That gesture became a nightmare as Hezbollah built up a massive arsenal of rockets. The second Lebanon War followed six years later.

Israeli Prime Minister Ariel Sharon did not learn the lessons of Oslo or of South Lebanon. His disengagement plan repeated the failed experiment of turning land over to terrorists. It enabled Hamas to take over Gaza and create an Islamist, Iranian-allied terror camp that has fired more than 10,000 rockets into Israel. When the Palestinians elected Hamas, they voted for war over statehood and peaceful coexistence.

Three seasoned army generals – three huge mistakes. Not learning the lesson of the past, Israeli Prime Minister Ehud Olmert, beholden to the land for peace formula, no matter what, offered Chairman of the Palestinian Liberation Organisation Mahmoud Abbas in 2008 an independent Palestinian state. Abbas was not interested, and still insists on the right of return, which would see millions of Palestinians come into Israel – not into their own country of Palestine.

Two months ago, when Hamas killed four Israeli civilians near Hebron, thousands celebrated on the streets of Gaza, carrying flag-waving children on their shoulders.

And earlier this year, the Palestinian Authority named a public square and a children's summer camp to honour a terrorist who murdered 37 Israelis, and staged a hero's funeral to Amin Al-Hindi, who played an organising role in the Munich Olympics massacre. Abbas and Salam Fayyad, Prime Minister of the Palestinian Authority, attended the funeral.[72]

In September this year, Um Yousuf Abu Hamid was presented by the PA's Minister for Prisoners' Affairs with the Shield of Resoluteness. She was praised since, 'The Palestinian mother is a central partner in the struggle, by virtue of what she has given and continues to give. It is she who gave birth to the fighters, and she deserves that we bow to her in salute and in honour.'[73] Abu Hamid's four sons are in Israeli jails serving eighteen life sentences for carrying out terrorist attacks.

The Fatah charter still supports 'armed military struggle' against Israel,[74] and Abbas still oversees incitement. In July 2010 he told Palestinian TV that if the Arab states were to wage a war against Israel, the Palestinians, though not fighting alongside them, would support it.

Seventeen years after Oslo, most Israelis, as opposed to Kadima leader Tzipi Livni, are not in the mood for additional risk-taking. They know that the West Bank as a terrorist haven will threaten Israel's survival. They can imagine what would happen the moment Israeli forces leave.

It's time to face up to the truth that rejectionism has been a hallmark of successive Palestinian leaders. As such, it's up to Palestinian society to democratise and institute law and order; it must dismantle and arrest the terrorist gangs, dislodge Hamas, renounce violence, recognise Israel's right to exist and agree to a demilitarised state.

Only then, will it give peace a chance.

David Landau: 'Israel wants to be raped'

December 2, 2011

David Landau, former editor-in-chief of the Israeli daily *Haaretz*, has the habit of spewing extreme, offensive utterances. In 2007, he told then Secretary of State Condoleezza Rice that Israel wanted to be raped by the USA into submission.[75] And last year, he called for a boycott of Israel's Parliament.

Now, on a speaking tour in Sydney and Melbourne for *The New Israel Fund*, he got on his high horse and called on Australia's Jewish community to 'stop slavishly following the Israeli government line'.[76] As usual, Landau missed the mark and got it wrong.

Uninformed, and indulging in moral posturing and self-righteousness, Landau reduced the Australian Jewish community to simplistic stereotyping, as if we are all identical twins. Landau condescendingly paints Australian Jews as a kind of submissive Pavlovian zombies who all sing the same tune and blindly stand by the actions of the Israeli government.

Pluralistic in their beliefs, Australian Jews are regularly critical of Israeli government decisions and are unafraid to vigorously air their views. Anyone scanning the newspaper columns and the letters section in the *Australian Jewish News*, or Australian blogs, or attending community forums, would know that members of the Australian Jewish community are certainly not slavish, and are far from uniform about a host of issues.

Surprise, surprise – the Australian Jewish community acknowledges that Israel is not a perfect society and it has no problem highlighting its faults.

Again and again, Australian Jews have taken different positions and challenged policies and decisions by the Israeli governments on: the 1993 Oslo Accords, Ehud Barak's 2000 Camp David offer, Ariel Sharon's 2005 Gaza Disengagement, the 2006 Second Lebanon War, Ehud Olmert's 2008 offer to the Palestinians, Operation Cast Lead, Netanyahu's freeze on settlement building. The list goes on.

Australian Jews and their umbrella institutions welcome a lively and robust debate on Israeli society and politics in which young and old passionately bring their attitudes to the fore, warts and all. The

Jewish diaspora is an independent actor, and does not rubber stamp the decisions of the Israeli sovereign as Landau patronisingly argue. Presidents of key Australian Jewish organisations, both secular and religious, feel comfortable putting their own perspective on policies by the Israeli government in a forceful and vocal manner.

Landau also claims that Israel's leadership wants diaspora communities to 'engage in propaganda'.

Really?

I would challenge Landau to cite one example in which Israeli Prime Minister Binyamin Netanyahu has demanded any Diaspora community to propagandise on behalf of the Israeli government. In fact, the heated exchanges and inter-communal clashes about a wide array of Israel-related issues amply demonstrate that the Australian Jewish community, and its leaders, will exercise assertive decision-making regarding the political agenda of the Israeli government, and are unafraid of promoting their own views. 'We have an opinion and the right to express it, no matter what the Israeli Prime Minister believes' is the prevailing mood.

Landau urges Australia's Jews to 'stand up and say it's in Israel's interests to have a two-state solution'.

Frankly, we don't need Landau to tell us this. If Landau had a modicum of insight about the Australian Jewish community, he would realise that 99 per cent accept and advocate for a negotiated peace that will result in Israel and Palestine coexisting side by side. This has been the default position for many years.

Anyone following the pulse of the contemporary Australian Jewish landscape would not be surprised by the diversity and multiplicity of viewpoints. There is a plethora of Jewish sectors and voices, part of a living, breathing, incredibly multivalent and complicated community where the dynamic between unity and diversity is a defining element. Consider that in 2007, Jews, including members of Parliament, judges and unionists declared: 'We endorse free speech and diversity within the Jewish community ... Australian Jewry is a "broad church" and most communal roof bodies include a wide range of opinions.'[77]

One hopes that on his next visit Landau will do better.

The victims of the Munich Olympics deserve a minute of our time

June 4, 2012

It was a simple and small request from the Israeli government.

Devote one minute of silence during the opening ceremony of this year's London Olympics to honour the memory of the eleven Israeli athletes, coaches and officials who were murdered in cold blood by Palestinian terrorists at the 1972 Munich games.

Such a ceremony makes sense.

First, London will mark the 40th anniversary of this terrible event.

Second, the International Olympic Committee has repeatedly turned down similar requests and could now make amends for its lack of moral rectitude in ignoring this atrocity.

No big statements, no fancy declarations, no mention of politics. Just silence. An acknowledgment that honours and memorialises eleven sportspeople who came to compete, and returned in body bags.

Remembering deceased Olympic athletes during the Olympic Games is not unprecedented. Two years ago, at the Winter Games in Vancouver, a moment of a silence was held during the opening ceremony for Georgian luger Nodar Kumaritashvili, who died several days earlier in a training accident.

And in the 2002 Salt Lake City Winter Olympics, members of the US team were allowed to walk into the stadium with a flag recovered from the rubble of the World Trade Centre. Yet, earlier this month, the plea for the Munich tribute was rejected by IOC president Jacques Rogge.

And what lame, indefensible excuse did the IOC come up with for not recognising the darkest hour in the history of the games? Here it is: The IOC has already paid tribute to the memory of the athletes, and a minute's silence would politicise the games. In plain talk, the IOC doesn't want to risk alienating countries that don't like Israel, or cause any dictatorships to walk out and boycott the games.

But don't be so shocked.

In terms of the history of the Olympic Committee, this is business as usual. In 1972, following the massacre, IOC head Avery Brundage at first said that the Games were too important to be delayed by the tragedy. If it was up to him, the rest of the day's events would not have even been cancelled. He ultimately backed down.

So, instead of closing them down, the Munich Olympics were suspended for a day and a memorial service was held. And then the show went on as if nothing had happened.

Today, there are scores of youngsters who have no idea about the Munich tragedy and about the victims whose lives were brutally cut short. They should be reminded, and London is the perfect opportunity to both educate the world again and to stand together against terrorism.

John Coates, the president of the Australian Olympic Committee, as well as members of our parliaments, should throw their weight behind the campaign to reverse this decision.

They can take their lead from US House Representative Ileana Ros-Lehtinen, who said: 'Such a gesture would be a small tribute to the memory of the families of those brave Olympians, who deserve much more than that. But it would do even more than that: it would do credit to the Olympic Games, the IOC, and all Olympians. It would reaffirm Olympic values of honour, harmony, and fraternity, the very values that violent extremists horrifically repudiated by butchering the Israeli Olympians.'[78]

The Israeli Deputy Foreign Minister, Danny Ayalon, wrote to Rogge: 'This rejection told us as Israelis that this tragedy is yours alone and not a tragedy within the family of nations. This is a very disappointing approach and we hope that this decision will be overturned, so the international community as one can remember, reflect and learn the appropriate lesson from this dark stain on Olympic history.'[79]

Resolution 663, introduced to the US Congress by Eliot Engel and Nita Lowey, calls on the IOC to provide a minute of silence. It reads in part: 'The Munich eleven were part of the Olympic family, and IOC's rejection thus far of a minute of silence is unacceptable. We intend to put the US Congress on record that those who died deserve to be remembered in a respectful manner to mark this anniversary.'[80]

It is heartbreaking that things have got to such a stage that Ankie Spitzer, widow of slain Israeli fencing coach Andrei Spitzer, has said that she would now be content with 30 seconds of silence.

A moving documentary, *20 Million Minutes*, to be released next year, makes the point that since the Munich savagery, there have been 20 million minutes.

The IOC should be ashamed that it refuses to find just one.

Taking on Leunig

12 December 2012

Yesterday in Melbourne's *The Age* Michael Leunig defended his cartoon 'First they came for the Palestinians',[81] previously published in that newspaper, and attacked those who supported Israel and who found his work objectionable.

Leunig's cartoon takes the noble words of anti-Nazi cleric Martin Niemoller decrying the passivity of bystanders in the face of Nazi evil, and substitutes the Nazis referred to in the original poem with Israelis: 'First they came for the Palestinians and I did not speak out'.

Leunig obscenely equates the actions of Israel in Gaza to those of the Nazis and asserts the people who were once the objects of Hitler's extermination and their descendants are now committing genocide against the Palestinians and are thus the present world's Nazis.

I wonder if Leunig paused to consider how a survivor of the Holocaust would react when they came upon his cartoon.

Understandably shocked, they would ask, 'How is it possible for anyone to compare the organised, industrial murder of six million Jews in gas chambers, in death camps, in ghettos and in open fields to what is happening in Gaza?' And, 'Why would any person liken Israel's protection of its citizens from rockets to the genocidal and bestial liquidation of the Jews?'

Equating Israeli policies to those of the Nazis has been identified as anti-Semitic by the EU, the US State Department, the Organisation for Security and Cooperation in Europe and the European Monitoring Centre on Racism and Xenophobia, since it calls for Israel's destruction.

Yesterday, Leunig reiterated some of the themes of his cartoon. Amazed that anyone would think comparing Israeli policy to Nazi behaviour is anti-Semitic, Leunig calls Israel's military policy 'excessively homicidal' in his piece.[82]

Equally worrisome, Leunig implies that Israel is already in the process of becoming Nazi-like, saying 'all nations that throw their military weight around, occupying neighbouring lands and treating the residents with callous and humiliating disregard are already sliding towards the dark possibilities in human nature'.

Anyone with the vaguest knowledge of the Holocaust will know that by any measure comparing Israel to Nazi Germany is a kind of deliberate amnesia of the monstrous policies of the Nazis that minimises their genocidal extent and intent, and instead maligns Israel.

Consider how Leunig describes the way the Palestinians have been treated by 'homicidal' Israel and see if you can hear the disturbing echoes Leunig is pushing: 'The Palestinians have been massively robbed and abused, and are engaged in a desperate struggle for survival and liberation.'

I wonder: did Leunig's 'duty and conscience' compel him to sound the alarm all those years while thousands of rockets systematically fell on Israelis, attacks that Israeli author and peace activist Amos Oz called 'a war crime and a crime against humanity'? Did Leunig ever express the 'unspoken grief' of Israeli families who lost loved ones to terrorism?

Did he liken the actions of state genocides, brutal executions and large-scale massacres of civilians in Rwanda, Darfur, Congo, Nigeria, Syria, Myanmar, Somalia and Ethiopia to those of the Nazis? Did he call Hamas, Hezbollah or Iran's President Mahmoud Ahmadinejad 'excessively homicidal' for wanting to wipe Israel off the map? Or is this epitaph reserved only for Israel?

Why does Leunig absolve Palestinians of all responsibility for their situation and ignore their behaviour against Israel? Criticism of Israeli policies is entirely acceptable and Leunig is entitled to his views. But such cartoons not only poison public debate, they close it. After all, how do you discuss the conflict with someone who compares Israelis to Nazis?

In his opinion piece this week, Leunig labels his critics in the Jewish community as 'aggressive Israel supporters', 'cynical', 'bullying', 'lazy', 'false accusers' and 'boys who cry wolf' who are engrossed in 'obsessive and vapid denunciation'. He accuses anyone who dares to see anti-Semitic tones in his cartoon as frauds who 'are not really upset by any "anti-Semitism" in my cartoons (there is none) but by the possible impact of a cartoon on the doubters'.

Can you imagine any other community described in such an

offensive way in an Australian newspaper?

In his cartoon, Leunig also descends into parroting another anti-Jewish screed, that of the nefarious, all-powerful Jewish lobby that is lurking behind the scenes, ready to pounce and stifle critics of Israel. He writes that he and many others are silent about the Palestinians because they would be subjected to 'hateful mail, doors closing, hostility, fear and spiteful condemnation'.

This all-powerful cabal of elders did not prove omnipotent enough to prevent Leunig from publishing his cartoon and yesterday's piece.

In Leunig's world there is no lobby group or publicity machine for the Palestinians. Conspiratorial stereotypes about a predatory Jewish lobby that intimidates Palestinian supporters into silence have no place in any newspaper.

The B'nai B'rith Anti-Defamation Commission, a human rights organisation, felt that it could not tolerate such inexcusable expression.

It asked *The Age* for an opportunity to provide a balancing response to Leunig's cartoon after it was directly attacked in another opinion piece that saw nothing troubling about Leunig's cartoon and instead accused the Jewish community of thoughtlessness and bitterness.

The Anti-Defamation Commission was told that *The Age* would not publish its objections because its claims about the cartoon were unreasonable. So Leunig's 'First they came for the Palestinians' is OK while offering a counterpoint is unreasonable. Leunig accused the Jewish community of closing doors.

That is exactly what *The Age* did.

It's a strange world.

An open letter to Adam Goodes

May 31, 2013

Dear Adam,

At the outset, I want to say how much I admire the strong and courageous stance you took last Friday. Racism is an affront to every human being and should never be ignored.

Your actions have reopened an important debate about the damage biased language causes. It's gratifying that so many have registered their distaste for this disturbing occurrence, declaring their zero-tolerance to racism, on and off the field.

Sadly, racism remains a pervasive menace and a blight on our community.

I agree with you that blame must not be ascribed to Julia Surowka. The demeaning words she employed sprang from a place of ignorance, rather than malice.

You rightly stated that, 'Unfortunately it's what she hears and the environment that she's grown up in has made her think that it's OK to call people names'. No one is born a bigot. Prejudice is a learned trait.

We in the Jewish community are accustomed to such racial taunts and vilification. The history of anti-Semitism teaches us that no society is immune to hate.

Only last month, a Jewish soccer player reported being spat on and racially abused for being Jewish. Apparently, supporters spewed such anti-Jewish slurs as 'f—ing Jew', and 'go back to Germany'.[83]

As a sportsperson and role model, you now have the opportunity to engage and inspire young people by your anti-racism message, reaching hearts in a way that politicians will never reach.

Just last month, the UN observed the International Day for the Elimination of Racial Discrimination with the 2013 theme being: 'Racism and Sport'.[84]

It recognises that sport can play a positive role in countering bigotry and is a vehicle of social cohesion, enabling people of different ethnic, cultural and religious backgrounds to reach excellence beyond the narrow parameters of their origins.

You are already doing your part, but I'm sure you'll agree that parents are equal partners in this fight and must take the initiative. I have been told that parents feel uncomfortable discussing issues of racial abuse because they know that the questions their children will ask will be painful and embarrassing for them to address.

Perhaps, but apathy and indifference are not options. When children use offensive language, it needs to lead to a deep and meaningful conversation. Not to punishment.

Parents have to walk the talk by setting an example of what it means to be a tolerant person. For example, they can show their children websites, books, music, films and art that describe other countries' religion, culture and history. Above all, parents must all be mindful of their own behaviour and think about what they say in front of others, especially their children.

Young people should be taught that demeaning words and vicious stereotypes are often the beginning of harassment and physical violence. They should learn about the Holocaust and about the genocides in Cambodia, Bosnia, Rwanda and Darfur so that they understand the dangers of words that dehumanise others.

Together with parents, schools and sporting clubs are important allies in fostering compassion, understanding and acceptance of minorities. Players and coaches must send the message that hateful words are not cool and that racial sledging denies not only the victim but also the perpetrator of their worth and value.

Each one of us has a duty to make the evil and horror of racism a thing of the past. As I write this letter, someone, somewhere, somehow, is suffering abuse because of their race, skin colour or religion. Often, with deadly consequences.

Like you, we must respond every time we hear a slur, regardless of whether it was used in a joking or a serious manner. We should not brush it aside as just silly, unintentional talk. We must muster the nerve to tell a father, a sister or a grandfather that what they've just said was vicious and unacceptable.

I am hopeful that Julia Surowka will teach her children to value all people. After all, that is the best way to raise decent, moral and tolerant adults.

Yours in friendship and solidarity,
Dvir Abramovich

Lessons from Israel's 9/11

October 4, 2013

The Yom Kippur War of 1973 was a threshold moment, a watershed in Israeli history.

Surprised by the massive invasion of Egyptian and Syrian forces, Israel staved off the destruction of the Jewish state. It paid a heavy price though, with the loss of 2,569 of its best men and women.

In a way, the Yom Kippur War was to Israel what 9/11 was to the United States, a stealth attack by a determined enemy, hell-bent on destruction, whose menace should have been plainly obvious.

Of course, the circumstances and motives for the assault were very different. Still, the Israelis, just like the Americans, underestimated how hatred fuelled by fanaticism can result in such havoc.

The salutary lesson of the Yom Kippur War is that Israel always needs to be alert and on guard. A small country, with big problems, it lives in a bad neighbourhood where states use poison gas on their own people and seek nuclear weapons.

So many articles marking this occasion are underwritten by a sense of shame and guilt that one is tempted to forget that Israel's heroic warriors repelled the invading forces and were only kilometres away from the Syrian and Egyptian capitals.

This mindset of total self-blame chimes with much of the prevailing discourse about Israel today. In a speech addressing those who lost relatives in the Yom Kippur War, former Israeli Prime Minister Barak rightly noted that 'states much larger than ours and supposedly much stronger, collapsed within weeks under surprise attack'.[85]

I share Barak's sentiments. We need to remember and celebrate the magnitude of Israel's achievement and stunning reversal of fortune.

That the Israeli army was able to turn the tide and bring the war to an end after nineteen days is a monumental triumph that should be taught to every student learning about this remarkable chapter.

One commentator maintains that the Yom Kippur War was the IDF's greatest victory, and one of the most spectacular in the annals of military history.

This does not mean we sideline the mistakes made or the traumatic loss of life. But we do need to acknowledge that the IDF mobilised within a day, that squadrons and battalions were dispatched to critical locations where the war was eventually won, and that the political and military leadership functioned, under unbelievable pressure, in a responsible, resourceful and cool-headed manner.

Tellingly, the Arab states understood that prevailing over Israel in the battlefield was now out of reach. President Sadat of Egypt recognised the harsh reality that he now needed to negotiate a peaceful resolution to the conflict.

A true two state-solution will only be achieved when the Palestinian people and the Arab states, like Sadat, accept that Israel is not a passing phenomenon, but an unmovable entity in the Middle East. Diplomacy is the only route.

The Palestinian leadership has continuously rejected all generous offers tabled by successive Israeli prime ministers. Yet it is Israel that is constantly pressured to capitulate to the irrational demands of the international community. Referring to the Yom Kippur War, former Israeli Prime Minister Ehud Barak has observed that Israel can only rely on itself during turbulent times and in matters of its own survival.

In 1973, Golda Meir was told by the Nixon administration not to mobilise Israel's reserves, or to shoot first. Meir felt obligated to obey the American administration's admonition, rather than follow the doctrine of a pre-emptive strike that was so effective during the 1967 War.

Twenty years later, Rabin, wanting to curry favour with President Clinton, trusted Arafat to abandon his terrorist ways and honour the Oslo Accords.

Israeli leaders should take a leaf out Menachem Begin's playbook.

When on November 9, 1977, Sadat told his parliament that he was ready 'to go to the ends of the world in search of peace … and ready to go to the Knesset', Begin did not do political somersaults, but made sure Sadat knew that Israel would not be bending over backwards to give in to any territorial demands. Begin said, 'Israel categorically and absolutely rejects conditions named by President Sadat',[86] namely total withdrawal to the June 1967 lines.

Yes, Begin withdrew from the Sinai Peninsula.

But he steadfastly held on to his convictions that Israel would never again return to a territorial position that could jeopardise its survival. For him, peace did not mean that everything was negotiable.

Sadat later remarked that Begin, in contrast to Rabin, was a strong leader. The message: Peace can only be made by a strong Israel, with strong leaders who stick to their guns.

The failure of the Oslo Accords and the Gaza Disengagement is a case study in the costs of wishful thinking. It is a warning about the desperate quest for an end to the conflict, no matter the risks, and about the dangers of bending over backwards for a paper peace that will never bring security.

I think Begin would agree.

Vale Ariel Sharon

January 17, 2014

I grew up learning stories about General Ariel Sharon's bigger-than-life exploits on the battlefield, defending his beloved and cherished Israel from its enemies.

I always knew that he was part of that mythical group that shaped the nation I was part of. When they referred to him as the bulldozer, I took it to mean that he just got things done, no matter what, no matter the odds. The Israeli way. Totally. Heroic. Charismatic. Aggressive. Tough. Complex. A farmer. A Zionist. A politician. A warrior.

As kids, we read with reverence how at age fourteen he served with the Haganah, and how aged 20 he led a platoon during the War of Independence. And how he was badly wounded in the Battle of Latrun.

Most of us could only dream of being as brave and as fearless. A larger-than-life icon, he occupied our thoughts and imagination.

At school, we were captivated by his incredible and stunning feats of bravery as a tank commander in the Six Day War, or how he again put on his soldier's uniform to command thousands of soldiers and cross the Suez Canal, essentially turning the tide in the Yom Kippur War.

The famous image of 'Arik', with a blood-soaked bandage wrapped around his head, is still etched in our collective memory. Sharon's iron-willed tenacity and resolve in ploughing on regardless of the hurdles was always evident. And always admirable.

Like the astute military strategist he was, he took us all by surprise with his change of heart about territorial concessions and withdrawal. I was stunned when he spoke of an Israeli occupation, or when he embraced the two-state solution, or when he implemented the unilateral disengagement from Gaza.

Despite the constant up-and-downs, and setback after setback, he never gave up. Consider, the Likud's central committee rejected his endorsement of a two-state solution; a party referendum voted down his Gaza plan; and the Likud convention refused his idea of bringing Labor into his governing coalition.

But he triumphed. As usual. He established Kadima and demonstrated a breathtaking ability to walk a tightrope and win. Traversing a treacherous terrain like Nixon, who had to contend with China, he is counting on the backing of most Israelis who during the election campaigns shouted 'Arik, King of Israel', to push through his historic plan.

Those who voted for him felt like former President of Israel Ezer Weizman, who said, 'In war, I'd follow him through fire and flood.'[87]

Far from being the poster boy of the often naïve peaceniks, Sharon was risking it all in the battle of a lifetime, out of a sober realisation that Israel could not hold on to all the land it captured in 1967. The architect of settlement growth succeeded in something even the most leftist of Israeli governments had been unable to do.

More critically, the evacuation was not the act of an old man mellowing. It was utter pragmatism by a master pragmatist.

Sharon always viewed the settlements in strategic, not Biblical terms. He understood that demographics, not territory, is the fundamental question to be tackled. Israel could not afford to allow 7,800 people to occupy 20 per cent of the land inside 'The Fallujah of Palestine', among 1.3 million Palestinians.

With Sharon at the helm, the Israeli government took the risky decision to end its presence in the Gaza Strip and pull out the settlers who had been there for decades. This unilateral action offered a genuine opportunity for progress towards a peace, a gesture that, lamentably, was not taken up by the Palestinian leadership. Addressing his critics, Sharon said that as a soldier who had fought in every Israeli war he had never taken a more difficult decision.

Addressing the Israeli nation, he said:

> I know what this decision means to thousands of Jews who have lived for many years in Gaza, who built homes and planted trees and flowers, who had sons and daughters who never knew another home, I sent them there. I was a partner to this enterprise ... I am well aware of their pain, their anger and their despair.[88]

Yes, the disengagement plan did not turn out as Sharon had planned. Hamas made sure of that, choosing terrorism instead of peace. But Sharon's vision of a two-state solution, with Israelis and

Palestinians living side-by-side, will prevail. One day.

Journalist Uri Dan knew Ariel Sharon for more than 50 years. He wrote several books about his friend and confidante. He rightly stated that Sharon was 'fundamentally a man of peace'.[89]

And if you think this was hyperbole, reflect that in 2005 *The Economist* magazine labeled Sharon 'Israel's unlikely dove' and called on the international community to 'swallow its natural skepticism about Mr Sharon's motives, and – in this internal fight at least – do what it can to help him prevail'.[90]

To the casual and uninformed observer, Sharon was simply a hard-liner. For those who knew better, he proved to be one of Israel's greatest leaders.

He will be sorely missed.

An open letter to Mike Carlton

August 8, 2014

Mike,

I hope you don't find my response to your article[91] abusive, pornographic or threatening violence. I also don't intend calling you a Nazi, a Holocaust denier or an anti-Semite, as you pre-emptively predicted would happen, though I think that your op-ed peddles anti-Semitic themes.

But more about this later.

I'm also not calling for your resignation, though I can't speak for the cabal of the 'Elders of Zion' who may use their global tentacles of power to orchestrate your sacking. That was a joke.

I am, nevertheless, hurt that you would consider the Australian Jewish community to be so intimidating and vengeful that they would threaten to physically assault you simply because you expressed an opinion, albeit delusional and misguided.

Incidentally, do you know many journalists who have been threatened with violence by Australian Jews? But at least you did not say that some of your best friends are Jewish.

Anyway, back to your piece.

I believe that the media is a hotbed of persistent Israel-bashing and anti-Semitism. The bias is incremental. Story after story, day by day, week by week, until a distorted and warped picture of Israel seeps deep into the collective consciousness.

In old times, the Jew was demonised as the embodiment of evil. Today, Israel, the 'Jew amongst nations' to borrow from Alan Dershowitz, is vilified in the same way.

In your selective, skewed article, you accuse 'brutal' Israel of indiscriminate killing, of going against civilised behaviour, of genocide, of ethnic cleansing, of having one goal – killing Arabs.

I get it, this ploy. Israel, victimised by terror, is conducting a war of extermination against all Arab people, not just the Palestinians. This is an update of the old libel of the Jews as cruel and heartless, with an alleged lust for blood, as evidence by their killing of Jesus and Christian children.

Worse, you attribute these 'atrocities' to the Jewish people everywhere, who, according to you, have not learned the lessons of the Holocaust. In your imaginary world, Jews, who lost six million to the most thorough and industrialised genocide in the history of mankind, now stand accused of the same crime, having become the modern Nazis, viciously tormenting the Arabs.

What's more, your entire article is told from the perspective of the Palestinians. There is no context, background or acknowledgment that Israelis have been robbed of a normal life by Hamas for more than a decade.

In an article of 1054 words, you spent 28 words on Hamas, concentrating instead on the supposed 'evils' of Israel's retaliation which you describe as 'monstrous'.

You systematically look away from the fact that Hamas openly calls for the annihilation of Israel (I think genocidal is the word a journalist would use); has been conducting a relentless, unremitting campaign of murderous terror against Israel; that it executes Palestinians who oppose it; that it has used children as human shields and that 160 children have died after they were forced to dig tunnels into Israel that were to be used to murder and kidnap civilians; that it glorifies homicidal bombings; that it forces its own people to remain in combat zones; that it has violated successive ceasefires; that its stockpile of rockets and launchers is being warehoused in UNRWA schools and in living rooms; and that its leadership sits under the Shifa Hospital in Gaza City. The list goes on.

No mention that the IDF has, in the words of Colonel Richard Kemp, developed the 'most comprehensive and sophisticated measures to minimise civilian casualties during attacks against legitimate military targets',[92] and even warns Gaza residents of planned operations, furnishing them with maps dotted with safe zones. No mention of the Gaza disengagement and the multiple offers of a just peace Israel has made in the last 20 years.

Tellingly, you fail to reflect on the trauma Israeli children are enduring, having to grow up under the shower of constant rocket fire and having to run into bomb shelters several times a day. And why do you pass over in silence the suffering and deaths of Israelis?

A Martian visiting earth would conclude from your essay that Israel is the worst human rights transgressor in the world.

I wonder: why are you so obsessed with indicting Israel, so swift in peddling baseless accusations that blow Israel's actions out of all sensible proportions, and so eager to exculpate Hamas? Why do you paint the Jewish state as evil incarnate, as an implacably warmongering, pariah state that must be isolated?

You also seem to claim that Israel is descending into fascism. Do you mean like Hitler's Germany and Mussolini's Italy? Are you serious? And since when is Gideon Levy, a radical journalist on the far-left fringe, a credible authority? You quote Hanan Ashrawi, a PLO official. Why didn't you quote an Israeli official? Sorry, I forgot. That would be too even-handed.

If your attack is representative of Fairfax media, where it might be chic to target and single out Israel for calumny, I wonder what is said privately amongst your colleagues.

My turn for a quote. Amos Oz:

> What would you do if your neighbour across the street sits down on the balcony, puts his little boy on his lap and starts shooting machine gun fire into your nursery?[93]

Criticism of the policies of the Israeli government is fine. But your grotesque smear and stigmatisation of Israel, and the Jewish community, was rank and rotten. It could not go unchecked.

Notes

1   Laura King. 'Lawmakers Begin Heated Pre-Vote Debate on Gaza'. *LA Times*, October 26, 2004.

2   http://www.vatican.va/holy_father/john_paul_ii/travels/documents/hf_jp-ii_spe_20000321_israel-arrival_en.html

3   http://www.vatican.va/roman_curia/pontifical_councils/chrstuni/documents/rc_pc_chrstuni_doc_16031998_shoah_en.html

4   Pope Paul John II. *Crossing the Threshold of Hope*. New York: Knopf, 1994.

5   http://www.dhs.gov/if-you-see-something-say-something

6   https://www.dur.ac.uk/resources/psru/briefings/archive/Brief44.pdf

7   Daniel Pipes. 'Is the west too civilised?' *CNSnews.com*, July 22, 2003.

8   http://www.jerusalemsummit.org/eng/razdel.php?article_id=70&id=16

9   http://www.wiesenthal.com/site/pp.asp?c=lsKWLbPJLnF&b=4441293#.VAlmyvmSy_g

10 http://www.mfa.gov.il/mfa/mfa-archive/1995/pages/rabin%20funeral-%20eulogy%20by%20king%20hussein.aspx

11 http://www.mfa.gov.il/mfa/foreignpolicy/peace/mfadocuments/pages/remarks%20by%20pm%20yitzhak%20rabin%20at%20signing%20of%20dop%20-%2013.aspx

12 Rebecca Kaplan Boroson. 'Remembering Rabin, 'a soldier in the army of peace' *Jewish Standard*, November 6, 2008.

13 George Jonas. *Vengeance : the true story of an Israeli counter-terrorist team. New York : Simon and Schuster,* 1984.

14 Aaron J. Klein. *Striking Back: The 1972 Munich Olympics Massacre and Israel's Deadly Response.* New York: Random House, 2005.

15 Tim Butcher. 'Victory puts Olmert at centre of Israeli politics,' *Telegraph*, march 29, 2006,

16 http://www.un.org/news/dh/mideast/roadmap122002.pdf

17 Ehud Olmert. 'Victory speech by Ehud Olmert after elections to the 17th Knesset' March 28, 2006.

18 Hillel Fendel. 'Supreme Court turns down Pollard again.' *Israelnation-*

alnews.com 6 September, 2006.

19 http://www.jonathanpollard.org/2006/052506.htm

20 Shimon Shiffer. 'Jonathan Pollard: Take me out of the bor'. *Yediot Ahronot*. April 5, 2004.

21 http://edition.cnn.com/TRANSCRIPTS/1206/13/sitroom.02.html

22 http://www.jpost.com/Diplomacy-and-Politics/US-rejected-Netan-yahus-request-to-free-Pollard-ahead-of-negotiations-with-Palestin-ians-320716

23 http://www.jonathanpollard.org/1994/051994.htm

24 Jimmy Carter. *Palestine: Peace Not Apartheid*. New York: Simon Schuster, 2006.

25 http://www.participantmedia.com/pm-films/jimmy-carter-man-from-plains/

26 Abraham Cooper and Harold Brackman. 'Carter veers from path of peace into fantasy' *The Sun-Sentinel*, December 19, 2006.

27 Amos Oz. *Under this Blazing Light*. Cambridge: University of Cambridge: 1979.

28 Ewen MacAskill. 'Pioneering dream ends as Kibbutz goes private' *The Guardian*, 6 May, 2014.

29 http://www.jconnect.org/Portals/0/Content/Israel%20and%20You/Hak'hel/5%20Longing%20for%20Zion%20-%20additional%20read-ings.pdf

30 http://www.jpost.com/Israel/Olmert-endorses-Peres-for-president

31 Tova Lazaroff. 'Ramon memorialized in moving ceremony' *Jerusalem Post*, February 11, 2003.

32 James Bennet. 'Loss of the Shuttle: Israel; After Sending an Experiment and a Hero Into Space, Israeli Students Grieve'. *New York Times*, February 3, 2003.

33 http://www.ramonfoundation.org.il/ilan-ramon-2

34 http://www.yadvashem.org/yv/en/pressroom/pressreleases/pr_details.asp?cid=534

35 Eric J. Greenberg. 'A Death in the Family' *The Jewish Week*, February 7, 2003.

36 Herb Keinon. 'Astronaut lifted nation's spirit' *Jerusalem Post*, January 22, 2003.

37 http://heebmagazine.com/that-oven-feelin-2/1229

38 http://gawker.com/5326677/roseanne-barr-channels-her-reincar-nated-soul-in-hitler-photo-spread

39 http://www.jpost.com/Jewish-World/Jewish-News/Roseanne-Barr-Israel-is-a-Nazi-state

40 http://www.bittenandbound.com/2009/07/31/roseanne-barr-hitler-and-burnt-jew-cookies-in-heeb-magazine/

41 https://www.youtube.com/watch?v=rUR5HIHkYUs

42 Nahum Barnea. 'Crossing Red Lines' *Yediot Ahronot*, March 23, 2009. http://www.ynetnews.com/articles/0,7340,L-3690550,00.html

43 http://www.abc.net.au/tv/racerelations/

44 Bernard Weinraub. 'In New Lyrics, Jackson Uses Slurs' *The New York Times*, June 15, 1995.

45 Dawn Steel. 'Open Letter to Michael Jackson' *Los Angeles Times*, June 26, 1995.

46 Patrick Macdonald. 'History Lesson: Jackson's Living on Past Glories' *The Seattle Times*, June 21, 1995.

47 Jason Silberman and Daniel Sterman. 'Israeli Fans Defend Michael Jackson' *Jerusalem Post*, November 25 2005.

48 'Oliver Stone says Hitler an 'easy scapegoat' *Ynetnews.com*, January 1, 2011.

49 Ed Pilkington. 'Hitler? A scapegoat. Stalin? I can emphathise. Oliver Stone stirs up history' *The Guardian*, January 11, 2010.

50 Jeff Isarely. 'Pope's Silence Rings Loudly at Holocaust Memorial' *Time Magazine*, May 11, 2009.

51 Alan M. Dershowitz. *The Vanishing American Jew: In search of Jewish identity for the next century.* Boston: Little, Brown, 1997.

52 Naomi Zeveloff. 'Patrilineal Jews Still Find Resistance' *The Forward*, April 2, 2012.

53 Angelique Chrisafis. 'Sarkozy son's marriage to Jewish heiress clouded by anti-Semitism' *The Age*, September 12, 2008.

54 Allison Hope Weiner. 'Mel Gibson Apologizes for Tirade after Arrest' *The New York Times*, July 30, 2006.

55 http://edition.cnn.com/2006/SHOWBIZ/Movies/08/01/gibson.statement/

56 Richard Corliss. 'Edge of Darkness: Is Mel Gibson Still a Star?' *Time Magazine*, February 8, 2010.

57 Jake Tapper. 'Like father like son' *ABC News* July 31, 2006.

58 David M. Halbfinger. 'Mel Gibson Developing Holocaust Mini-Series' *The New York Times*, December 7, 2005.

59 Roger Friedman. 'Mel Gibson: 5mil to Fringe Church' *Foxnews.com*, 20 February 2004.

60 Peter Nicholas. 'Gov. Tells of Need to 'Promote Tolerance' *Los Angeles Times*, May 3, 2004.

61 'Bibi: Christian Zionists our top friends' *Jerusalem Post*, April 7, 2008

62 Hal Lindsey. *The Late Great Planet Earth*. Grand Rapids Michigan: Zondervan, 1970.

63 Tim LaHaye. *Left Behind*: a novel of the earth's last days. Wheaton III: Tyndale House Publishers, 1995.

64 https://www.youtube.com/watch?v=nNvtA_q0e20

65 David Alexander Nahmod. 'Film Review: Self-Fulfilling prophecies' *Jerusalem Post*, January 2, 2010.

66 http://www.ifcj.org/site/PageNavigator/eng/USENG_homenew

67 https://www.joshuafund.com/

68 John Hagee. *The Beginning of the End: The Assassination of Yitzhak Rabin and the coming of the Antichrist*. Nashville: Thomas Nelson: 1996.

69 David Brog. *Standing with Israel: Why Christians Support the Jewish State*. Florida: Charisma House, 2006.

70 http://www.israelnationalnews.com/Articles/Article.aspx/4465#. VAmiO_mSy_g

71 Steven Stalinsky. 'Palestinians talking peace?' *New York Sun*, November 24, 2004.

72 Rabbi Abraham Cooper. 'Three things Obama Must Do To Get Peace Talks Off Life Support,' *Foxnews.com*, September 14, 2010.

73 Aaron Klein. 'PA Minister Honors Family of Suicide Bomber,' *Jewishpress.com*, September 7, 2010.

74 http://avalon.law.yale.edu/20th_century/plocov.asp

75 'Ha'aretz editor: Israel wants to be raped' *Jerusalem Post*, December 27, 2007

76 Barney Zwartz. 'Australia's Jews urged to take a more critical line,' *The Age*, November 24, 2011.

77 http://www.smh.com.au/news/national/statement-objecting-to-campaign-by-iajv/2007/03/08/1173166891037.html?page=2

78 http://archives.republicans.foreignaffairs.house.gov/news/blog/?2444

79 http://edition.cnn.com/2012/05/18/world/meast/israel-ioc-plea/

80 http://engel.house.gov/latest-news1/reps-engel-lowey-introduce-resolution-calling-for-2012-olympics-minute-of-silence/

81 http://www.leunig.com.au/index.php/recent-cartoons/65-first-they-came

82 http://www.smh.com.au/federal-politics/society-and-culture/just-a-cartoonist-with-a-moral-duty-to-speak-20121210-2b5hi.html

83 Chris Hingston and Jared Lynch. 'Claims of racism hit VicSoccer league' *The Age*, April 16, 2013.

84 http://www.sportanddev.org/en/newsnviews/news/?5473/1/International-Day-for-the-Elimination-of-Racial-Discrimination-2013-Racism-and-Sport

85 Shmuel Rosner. 'The Victory to end all victories' *The New York Times Blogs*, September 10, 2013.

86 http://mfa.gov.il/MFA/ForeignPolicy/MFADocuments/Yearbook3/Pages/118%20Israel-s%20peace%20plan-%20article%20by%20Prime%20Minister.aspx

87 Michael Kramer. 'Israel's man of war' *New York Magazine*, 9 August, 1982.

88 Laura King. 'Lawmakers Begin Heated Pre-Vote Debate on Gaza'. *LA Times*, October 26, 2004.

89 Harriet Sherwood. 'Former Israeli PM Ariel Sharon dies after eight-year coma' *The Guardian*, 12 January 2014.

90 'Israel's unlikely dove' *The Economist*, 21 October, 2004.

91 Mike Carlton. 'Israel's rank and rotten fruit is being called fascism' *The Sydney Morning Herald*, July 26, 2014.

92 Richard Kemp. 'Gaza's Civilian Casualties: The Truth is Very Different' Gatestone Institute, August 3, 2014.

93 Philip Gourevitch. 'An Honest voice in Israel' *New Yorker*, August 2, 2014.

Acknowledgments

The essays are reproduced in their original form, though I have changed some of the headlines (now article titles).

Israel

The Australian Jewish News: Toppling Saddam Hussein was the right call; Road traps on the Road Map to Peace; The case for Israel's Fence of Life; Power people as important as peace treaties; Sharon's Disengagement from Gaza plan: A gamble that might just work; Israel: The United Nations' Punching Bag; Iran: the hour of reckoning is fast; *The Question of Zion* is a case study in anti-Zionism; President Obama and Israel; Will the Israel-bashing ever come to an end?; O Jerusalem; Facing up to a two state ticking bomb; The Israel almost no-one talks about and the one they do; Twenty years after the Oslo Accords; Playing the Blame Game; Israel under Netanyahu

The Herald Sun: A momentous Chapter: The Withdrawal from Gaza; *Paradise Now* or Propaganda Now?; Peace between Israelis and Palestinians? It's Hamas's Call; Can anything be done to stop a nuclear Iran?; The Second Lebanon War: Truth gone Missing; Last chance for The United Nations?

The Age: Slowly but surely hearts are turning; Happy 60th Birthday Israel; The Gaza Flotilla

The Sydney Morning Herald: Is it time for the UN to be scrapped?; Memo to Obama: This is not the way; *Time Magazine* and Israel Bashing

The Holocaust

The Australian Jewish News: Deny these deniers; *The Reader* is pure Holocaust revisionism; Shoah amnesia at Triple J

The Herald Sun: Why we must never forget the Holocaust; Words of hate hurt; World blind to growing horror;

The Age: Don't play with the memory of the Holocaust; The Holocaust began because words of hate went unchallenged; We must never let the Holocaust's grim lessons fade away; Blood Money: Profiting from death and suffering;

The Sydney Morning Herald: Hollywood – Please stop exploiting the Holocaust!; Stopping Genocide in the age of Lara Bingle and Tiger Woods; Keep the Nazis and their crimes out of comedy shows; Triple J Holocaust Joke Sickening

People and events

The Australian Jewish News: Ariel Sharon: Peacemaker; Jonathan Pollard's two long decades behind bars; Jimmy Carter's book *Palestine: Peace Not Apartheid* is distortion, not truth; The Israeli Rocket Man: Ilan Ramon; Are we ready for a Jewish PM?; Roseanne Barr's attention seeking behaviour; Why we cry for Gilead Shalit; John Safran's silly antics; 15 years after the assassination: Yitzhak Rabin's failed Oslo legacy; David Landau: "Israel wants to be raped"; An open Letter to Adam Goodes; Lessons from Israel's 9/11; Vale Ariel Sharon; An open letter to Mike Carlton

The Herald Sun: Farewell Pope John Paul II; 9/11: A horror film that the world needs careful watching; Rabin: Israel's Peaceful Warrior; Truth given flick in Steven Spielberg's *Munich*; Ariel Sharon still casts a giant shadow; Shimon Peres to be peacemaker

The Sunday Herald Sun: Goodbye Simon Wiesenthal

The Age: Oliver Stone and Holocaust Denial; Chelsea Clinton and Mark Mezvinsky: The Demise of the Jewish People?; Mel Gibson's Jewish Problem; Jews and Christian Zionists: A Marriage made in Heaven?; The Victims of the Munich Olympics deserve a minute of our time

The Sydney Morning Herald: Did Michael Jackson hate Jews?

On-line opinion: Death of the Kibbutz?

The Australian: Taking on Michael Leunig

Anti-Semitism

The Australian Jewish News: The best of friends: anti-Zionism and anti-Semitism; J'accuse: The academic boycott and the politics of prejudice; Uncovering the mask of anti-Zionism; *Facebook* should be a force for good, not a home for hate; Free speech is not absolute; Europe vs Israel; Universities must protect student from anti-Semitism

The Herald Sun: Coming to this country, two little girls and their ... sad songs of hate?; Fight cyber hate on the home front; Hate crimes require a special unit; Hatred such as anti-Semitism is a virus that weakens the nation

The Sydney Morning Herald: When Family Guy crossed the line into anti-Semitic caricatures; South Park and Kick a Jew Day; The myth of the Jewish Lobby; When Comedy Central became anti-Semitism central

The Conversation: Global anti-Semitism: making sure 'Never Again' is not a hollow slogan

www.ingramcontent.com/pod-product-compliance
Lightning Source LLC
Chambersburg PA
CBHW021218090426

42740CB00006B/269